Creating an Inclusive School

Our other publication by
Prof. S.K. Mangal and Prof. Shubhra Mangal

— Assessment of Learning

— Creating an Inclusive School

— Childhood and Growing up

— Learning and Teaching

— अधिगम का आकलन

— समेकित विद्यालय की स्थापना

— बाल्यकाल एवं वृद्धि-उन्मुख बालक

— अधिगम एवं शिक्षण

Creating an Inclusive School

Prof. S.K. Mangal
M.A., M.Sc., M.Ed., Ph.D. (Education)
Prof. (Mrs.) Shubhra Mangal
M.Sc., M.Ed., M.Phil. Ph.D. (Education)

SHIPRA
SHIPRA

Price: Rs. 995; US$ 37.50

ISBN: 978-93-86262-37-0

First Published in India in 2017

Creative an Inclusive School

Published by:

SHIPRA PUBLICATIONS
LG 18-19, Pankaj Central Market,
I.P. Ext., Patparganj, Delhi 110092, India
Ph.: +91 11 22235152/6152, 9650028065
Email: info@shiprapublication.com
www.shiprapublication.com

Preface

The establishment and organisation of schools following the philosophy and practice of inclusion is a prime necessity as well as a big challenge now for the system of our school education. Our country is wedded to democracy and equal rights to our all citizens. We are committed to provide free and compulsory education to our children for the success of our national campaign "Education for All". Moreover the implementation of the legislative measure in the name of 'Right to Education Act' has left no alternative before the school education system other than 'Creating Inclusive Schools' in the neighbourhood of every school going child irrespective of his/her status, abilities or disabilities. However, the mission of creating and organizing inclusive schools for realizing the objectives of inclusive education can't be fulfilled in proper way unless the teachers teaching in these schools are not fully prepared for doing the same. The best earlier opportunity for equipping the secondary school teachers for playing their appropriate role in inclusive schools is the pre-service teacher education/training programmes organized for them in the name of B.Ed. courses. With due cognizance of such necessity, the 'National Council for Teacher Education (NCTE)' has issued directives to the Universities and Teacher Education Institutes for introducing a compulsory paper in their B.Ed. Courses in the name of 'Creating and Inclusive School'. Accordingly Guru Gobind Singh Indraprastha University, New Delhi has introduced a compulsory paper in the name of 'Creating an Inclusive School' in its two year B.Ed. teacher preparation course. The present text is specifically designed to serve the requirement of this paper.

Although, as said above, the discussion in the text in mainly focused on meeting the demands of the GGS Indraprastha University, however, on account of its wide coverage and depth, it has enough potential to meet the requirements of the syllabi of other Indian universities prescribed for the paper 'Creating an Inclusive School'.

How far it will prove its worth, the judgement will surely lie with its readers. However, as authors we have the obligation to specify some of its basic features as below:

- It has been strictly written accordingly to the needs of the contents and topics included in the prescribed new syllabus.
- The style as well as language adopted for presentation is simple and easy to grasp by the average readers.
- The appropriate study questions for each chapter have been provided for helping the students in the task of proper comprehension, revision and self-evaluation added in its student edition.
- Upto date references and suggestions for further study in the matter related to each and every chapter have been given at the end of the text for serving the desired needs of students as well as teacher educators.

Hoped that the text in its present form would be able to serve the interests of those for whom it is written. We express our gratitude to all those who, in one way or the other, has helped us in this venture. Our special thanks are due to those writers and publishers who works have been utilised by us in the presentation of this text. The references given side by side and also in the end of the text, would certainly help those students and teacher-educators who intend to go deep in the subject.

Any suggestions for bringing improvement in the text will be highly appreciated and thankfully acknowledged.

With good wishes to its readers.

May, 2017

S.K. Mangal
Shubhra Mangal

Contents

1

Forms of Inclusion and Exclusion in Indian Education

What is Exclusion?

In its simple meaning what is not included in or accepted by a system may be termed as exclusion in reference to that system operating in a particular environment. Where in inclusion, we try to include or accept a thing, person or event as one of our component or belonging, in exclusion we try to exclude, deny its entry, keep it away and try to maintain distance from it. Where inclusion involves integration and cooperation among the members of an inclusive unit, and advocates equity and equality among them, exclusion breads disintegration and distrust, widens the gulf between the included and excluded and deprive the excluded from the benefits enjoyed by the members belonging to the mainstream of the system. Exclusion of any sort applied to the members of a community, citizens of a country, students of an education system proves quite detrimental not only to the development and well being of the members suffering exclusion but also causes great harm to the overall health, prosperity and development of the society and nation.

Types of Exclusion

Different societies and setups exhibit different types of exclusion to their one or the other section or segment in one aspect or the other. In general, however, we may witness the following types of exclusions visible in the fabrics of society and institutions on the global basis.

1. *Exclusion based on economic status:* In such type of exclusion, poors are denied the privileges enjoyed by the economically sound segment of the society or institution.

2. *Exclusion based on educational status:* In such type of exclusion, the uneducated and illiterates are denied many rights and privileges enjoyed by the educated segment of the society or institution.

3. *Exclusion based on social status:* In such type of exclusion the section or segment of the society accepted as low in its social status is deprived of many rights or privileges enjoyed by the higher social status segments. The exclusion in relation to caste (in our country) and colour (in USA and Europe) and gender as well as locale (All over the globe) are the good

examples of such exclusion.

4. *Exclusion based on political affiliation:* In such type of exclusion the section or segment of the society who does not follow the ideology propagated by the ruling political party or followed by a particular organization/institution is deprived the rights and privileges enjoyed by the members of that political party or followers of the ideology propagated by the political body.

5. *Exclusion based on religion or faith:* In different societies different types of religions or faiths may be followed and accepted by their members. Here the majority following a particular religion or faith may follow the policy of exclusion depriving the minority groups following other religions or faiths from many rights and privileges enjoyed by the majority.

However, in case when we try to view exclusion in reference to the inclusive setup of the schools of our secular country. We may found many of the students suffering from the following types of social exclusion in the school as well as community.

A. Exclusion with respect to gender
B. Exclusion with respect to caste
C. Exclusion with respect to locale
D. Exclusion with respect to disability
E. Exclusion with respect to socio-economic status.
F. Exclusion with respect to language.

Let us try to know about these six types of exclusion,

A. Exclusion with Respect to Gender

Our students especially the girls have to suffer in many ways on account of the brunt of exclusion faced by them in the society and school. Ours is a male dominated society and the neglect and exclusion of the girls and women from the main stream is a common practice employed everywhere in all the states of our nation. Let us see the nature and patterns of this practice to prevalent in our country in general.

1. The birth of the girl child is not welcome in the Indian society in general. In many of the states there is huge declination in the population of the females simply on account of the killing of the girl child in the womb of the mother. In case if she survives, she is deprived of many rights and privileges enjoyed by her male counterpart including right to education, right to proper feeding and nourishment, freedom for expression and outside movements, etc.

2. In case, where the girls are provided opportunity for getting admissions in the schools, they have to suffer a lot of exclusion and deprivation at the hands of prevalent practices in-the ways like below:

- They may be excluded and deprived of studying a number of academic disciplines, related to mathematics, accountancy and financing, engineering and technical subjects with the assumption that girls are not meant for studying these subjects. Similarly, they may be denied opportunities for participating in adventuring events, male dominated games such as wrestling, boxing and weightlifting. In many of the schools, they are even excluded to play any outdoor games and take part in athletic events. Swimming, shooting and mountaineering activities are also denied to them.

- The doors of many cultural and social activities are also closed to the girl students in many of the co-educational institutes. They are prohibited to perform on the open stage and express them in public in the name of preserving their feminine nature.
- The girls are also excluded and denied entry to many of the occupations and professions considered exclusively as the men dominated areas. They are not considered fit and capable of joining armed forces, fire fighting, police and patrolling services, guards and security personnel, driving of vehicles and working on ports and ships. In the case of performing duties and responsibilities in other work areas also, they are excluded and deprived of getting major responsibilities and higher status simply on account of the notion that girls/women are not fit and competent enough for such rights and privileges.

The incidence of such intolerance, discrimination and exclusion shown towards girls and women on account of belonging to female gender should be checked and the misconception arising on account of the gender differences should be rooted out for bringing out desired success in the implementation of inclusive policy in the schools and social fabrics.

B. Exclusion with Respect to Caste

In our caste ridden society the students have to suffer many types of exclusion and deprivation in the community and schools on account of belonging to a particular caste especially categorized as schedule caste or tribe at the hands of the system dominated by the upper caste people in the manner like below.

1. In the social and community setup, the children and their families have to suffer a variety of exclusion and deprivation on account of their belonging to lower castes. In many of the villages they are even denied the facilities of drinking water from the village wells, cultivating their crops in a proper way and getting benefitted from the natural products and social benefits easily available to the upper caste people. Their children are denied admission in the schools and participating in the social and cultural fabrics of the community.

2. In case these children get entry into the system of school education, they have to suffer from a number of exclusion and deprivation on account of their belonging to lower castes. They have to face the consequences of negative attitude and adverse feelings possessed by the students and staff belonging to upper castes towards them in the manner like below.

- Their peers (belonging to majority group of upper castes) do not like to give them their company, sit and work alongwith them and provide cooperation in learning and performing in a proper way. They are ridiculed and insulted and a number of social and psychological barriers are created for not allowing them to learn and progress in a proper way.
- They are denied opportunities to participate along with other children (belonging to upper castes) in one or the other co-curricular activities, project and collaborative assignment.
- They are subjected to discrimination, favouritism and prejudices in the learning and performance areas at the hands of teachers, school authorities generally belonging to upper castes.
- They may experience discrimination in getting entry into professional courses, the work areas of their interests and getting entry into the job market.

The exclusion or deprivation suffered by the children on account of belonging to the lower castes in the society and school may prove quite detrimental to their development and progress in the school as well as society. It may cause harm to their self confidence and kill their initiative for needed attempts and struggle for their adequate learning and progress. It is also causing a great harm to the stability and peace of our democratic society by germinating the seeds of the bitterness and dissatisfaction among the people and students belonging to lower castes and prohibiting them to contribute significantly in the progress and development of the country.

C. Exclusion with Respect to Locale

A serious problem is slowly arising in the various areas and states of our country where the majority community (designated as local people) is pushing towards the policy of exclusion for the people and students belonging to other region or states of the country. The Maharastrian under the flagship of Shiv Sena are claiming the Maharashtra only for Maharastrians, Gujarat for Gujraties and Haryana for Haryanvies with the plea that people inhibiting the region or state as locals have the exclusive rights and privileges for getting education and employment to them and their children. As a result, we may witness a sort of hostile attitude and negative feelings on the part of locals towards the migrant people and students working and studying in their states or regions. The consequences like below may be witnessed in the educational field and work areas on account of such exclusion.

1. The migrant students belonging to other regions or states may be denied admission in one or the other schools or professional courses.
2. They may face harassment, exclusion, isolation and discrimination at the hands of fellow students, teaching or non-teaching faculty of the school and local community in the matter of their adjustment, living and getting educational experiences.

3. Their inability to follow local dialect and norms of the local traditions, culture and civics sense may put them into trouble resulting in their maladjustment in the school and community. It gets further aggravated on account of the hostile attitude shown towards them by the local students and residents.

The things like above may result in the significant exclusion of the migrant students belonging to other region or states affecting the level of their self-confidence and will to initiate desired attempts for their proper learning and progress. It can put a quite damaging effect on their welfare and progress and prove costly to the society in terms of the loss of human capital.

D. Exclusion with Respect to Disability

From time immemorial the impairment or disability suffered by a child has been major stigma or point of consideration for getting victimised, harassed and isolated at the hands of parents and community.

In the ancient civilizations including India, there has been the history of taking them as a burden, a subject of fear and danger to the welfare of the society and fellow children. Consequently, they were subjected to various types of exclusion including murder, putting them into isolated settings like orphanages, residential institutions, mental hospitals and special schools or special classes of the integrated setup.

Not only the children but the elder ones suffering from one or the other disabilities have been a subject of major exclusion in the community surrounding including the educational institutions and work places in the manner described below.

1. The disabled are taken as worthless and unnecessary burden on the society. There is a quite negative attitude prevailing against them in the society including schools and work places resulting in their exclusion or deprivation in one way or the other.

2. There is a complete lack of disabled friendly environment in the community settings, schools and work places for the needed movement, living and working of the disabled. It has resulted in an automatic exclusion or barrier for them in terms of their participation and involvement in social, academic or professional activities. They are feeling isolated and excluded from the living and working of the mainstream of the society. In schools, disabled children have to face a number of problems, obstacles and barriers in terms of their physical movements, participation in curricular and co-curricular activities, working in the laboratory or workshops and interacting with their peers and teachers on account of the inadequacy of infrastructure, unavailability of appropriate facilities and resources, assistive and adaptive means and equipments. It has created a lot of disinterest, apathy and antagonistic feelings towards the adoption of inclusive policy among the disabled children and especially in their parents or guardians. They think sending of their children to ill equipped inclusive school a mere wastage of time

and a lot of inconvenience to their children with no reasonable outcomes. It has forced the exclusion of the children from the mainstream. They are either getting no education at all or are picking up the path of getting education in special schools.

3. Parents and Guardians of the non-disabled children are not at all in favour of the adoption of inclusive policy in the schools. They have many reservations and fear on this account. Firstly, they think that it may spoil the learning environment of the school. In the inclusive classroom much time and attention of the teacher will be diverted towards the disabled for helping them in their adjustment and learning. The pace of the learning and organization of curricular and co-curricular activities will unnecessarily be disturbed on account of adjusting the disabled in the mainstream. Secondly, they think that the presence of disabled in the classrooms or work setting will cast a negative and adverse effect on the learning and progress of their capable wards. They may pick up the undesirable behaviour and inefficient functioning of the incapable disabled peers. They have pushed the school authorities to opt for the segregated setting to the education of the disabled children in the form of special classes resulting in their exclusion from the mainstream education.

4. Attitude of the teachers and other school personnel is not favourable towards the disabled children. They think them misfit and incapable of getting education along with their non-disabled peers. Moreover, they feel feared and think themselves incompetent to meet the needs of various types of children with disability. They, thus try pick up the ways and means of the exclusion of the disabled children and get them educated at the hands of special teacher in the segregating setup of the school.

In this way disabled children may get segregation and exclusion in place of inclusion for their adjustment, education and development in the society, school and work situations. Their exclusion in such a way, however may hamper their adequate development and progress in life. Their education in special schools are not at all feasible and possible for all the disabled children differing in terms of their disabilities, capacity of their funding on the part of their parents and unability of specialized schools of varying nature suiting the requirements of the disabled children affected with a variety of disabilities. The remedy, as analysed by the scholars and practitioners lies in the adoption of inclusive policy and working for the creation of the inclusive schools worth capable of realizing the objectives of inclusive education in a proper way.

E. Exclusion with Respect to Socio-economic Status

Economic status of a family must often works as a deciding factor for its position is a particular society or community. Besides, the kind of job or powers enjoyed by the members of the family on account of their jobs — services or occupation also work as a significant factor for their socio-economic status. Social position in relation to one's caste, religion or migration may also cast its significant impact over influencing socio-economic status of a family or child in the school. One's socio-economic status then in turn may be found to work for one's inclusion or exclusion from the mainstream of the society. The families having low socio-economic status may be found to feel excluded or marginalized at the hands of their neighbours while living in an affluent society or they may be denied opportunities of social communication and participation as available to the members belonging to the society. Not only in neighbourhood or community gatherings but also in schools, their children have to suffer from one or the other types of exclusion or marginalization in the ways and manners like below.

1. They may suffer exclusion or marginalization at the hands of school authorities and teachers on account of their low socio-economic status. In this connection, they may feel harassed, neglected, scorned as well as excluded on an account of the negative attitude and apathy shown to them by the authorities and teachers. It affects their learning, adjustment and progress in a quit detrimental way.

2. Their poverty may come into their way of bearing clothes and dresses like their other peers—non victims of poverty. They may not be able to afford the canteen expenses or purchase of higher order reading and writing material aids for the projects or expenses incurred in the social trips or tours. In such cases, they have to suffer exclusion from the social group of their peers and school mates and it affect their overall adjustment and acquisition of learning experiences available in social settings.

3. Their socio economic status may come into their way of seeking friendship and harmony with their peers and school mates. They may be insulted, ridiculed or intimidated on account of their belongingness to excluded strata of the society or poverty of their parents at the hands of their privileged peers or school mates while seeking participation in curricular, co-curricular activities including games and outdoor excursion activities etc. Thus, many times such exclusion deprives them with the valuable opportunities of learning valuable lessons, social learning, social behaviour acquisition as well as academic learning and overall personality development.

4. Many times, they may themselves feel hesitation, fear and lack of confidence in carrying out communication, healthy interaction and participation with the peers belonging to mainstream on account of their socio-economic status in curricular as well as co-curricular activities and encounters. This hesitation or fear is the result of the exclusion and intimidation suffered by their families and localities at the hands of the privileged one's in the society. It gets aggravated on account of hostile feelings, negative attitude or apathy received from the teachers and school authorities and waves of exclusion and non-cooperation received through their class and school mates.

Such exclusion or marginalization suffered by the children in school on account of their socio-economic status brings a quite disastrous effects on their learning, achievement, adjustment and progress in one or the other ways. Apart from this, it may also work as a quite stimulating factor in widening the gulf between the poor and rich, haves and have-nots, lower socio-economic status and higher socio-economic status endangering the peace, harmony and development of the society.

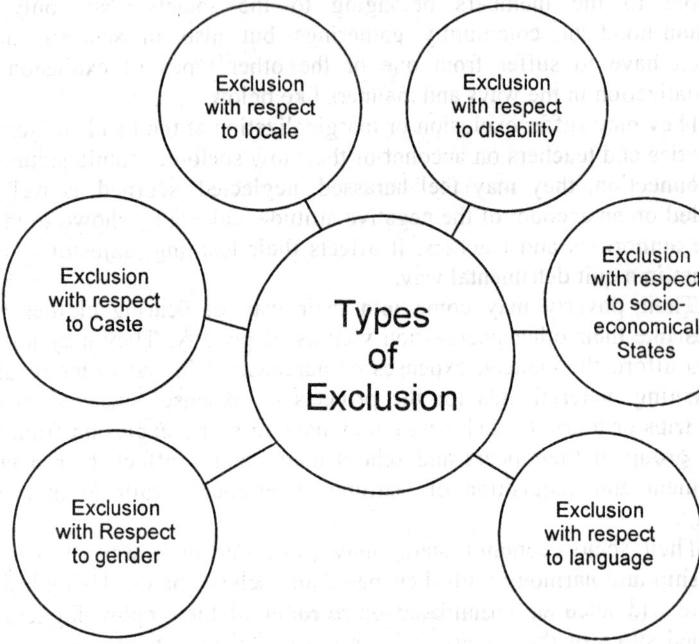

Fig. 1.1: Types of Exclusion

F. Exclusion with Respect to Language

Language is said to be a great or in fact a quite essential vehicle for carrying out the task of communication and interaction between or among the people. It is why the ability to speak and be understood, to listen and understand and to write, read and communicate in oral or written form of a well accepted mode of a particular language in a group or society is always understood as a proper sign of individual or collective progress of that group and the society. The same is also true with the social group of the school. Here what goes inside the school in terms of the communication and interaction among school authorities, teachers and students depends much on the language used for such communication and interaction. Where utilization and understanding of a common language on the part of communication in a group develops corporation and interaction among the group members creating a healthy environment for their inclusion, development and progress, the lack of such common language bond pushes the members towards lack of communications, separation and exclusion. It is much true of individual members who are unable to communicate in the common language utilized by the group in its communication and have to face exclusion or marginalization of one or the other nature on this account. The children thus belonging to families of migrants who are unable to communicate properly with their neighbours, residents of the community/society, co-workers, employers may feel a type of their exclusion from the mainstream in a variety of ways. The same is also transmitted to their children while interacting in their society or gaining learning experiences in the school. Their inability to communicate with their teachers, school authorities, peers and school mates at the time of various curricular or co-curricular encounters in the school may make them handicapped in terms of acquiring valuable learning experiences for their needed development, adjustment and progress. In fact, they may feel or experience a lot of exclusion or marginalization on account of their inability to make use of the common language of the school group is their interaction and communication with the group members.

True it is, how can students make friendship and engage in social participation with their peers and school mates when they can't make use or benefit from the conversation or communication carried out by the language of the group. The group members do not understand what is communicated by them in their native language and thus a proper link for the effective communication is hard to be established between them and the group members. It is why, they fail to be benefitted from the learning experiences provided by the teachers through their direct interaction or guidance, or can't benefit from the social learning or experiences received through the cooperative learning and group activities along with their peers. They are unable to participate in so many co-curricular activities on account of their language deficiency and experience a lot of exclusion in terms of their proper participation and it may make then feel embarrassed and cut off from the mainstream of the school. Their peers consider them outsiders and strangers in terms of involving them in their interaction and group activities and in such circumstances they themselves may be found to withdraw themselves for such interaction and participation and forced to confine themselves in their self-study, private tutoring and coaching from those who understand and communicate with them in the language they understand. It may overall hamper their proper social and emotional development, adjustment and progress according to their developmental age until proper efforts are made by them in imbibing with the proper linguistic skills of the common language utilized is the school on the part of teachers, school authorities and peers.

2

Inclusive Education: Meaning, Historical Development and Benefits

Historical Development of Inclusive Education

There was a time when children with any exceptionality (deviation from normals) lying in them were thought as a matter of great concern, fear and anxiety for the rest of normal population. Therefore for the time immemorial, the exceptional (whether genius or creative, mentally, physically or sensory disabled) were forced to suffer from isolation or segregation from the main stream of the society. As history reveals these exceptional were subjected to intimidation, harassment and isolation in a variety of ways. A number of scientists, reformers, creative and artists had to face the victimization, isolation and even death penalty at the hands of the public and authorities who considered them quite separate and away from the normals. The mentally retarded were kept in isolated wards in the hospital or residential institutions and physically disabled were seen untouchable and sin on earth. As the time changed, voices were raised and attempts were made for the rehabilitation, adjustment and education of the disabled in the integrated or inclusive setup. The journey of seeking their welfare has witnessed three types of milestones in the name of (*a*) segregation, (*b*) integration or mainstreaming, and (*c*) inclusion. Let us see what these are and how these were adopted and employed for the upkeep and welfare of the children with special needs including disabled.

Segregation and its Functionability

This approach is governed by an age old notion that exceptional children are no where the normal children. They need to be segregated and isolated from the mainstream of the society. There lies a potential danger of keeping them with the normal children. If they will be placed with the normals, they will spoil or influence the behaviour, adjustment and education of the normals in a negative way. Such attitude and feelings about exceptionals especially for the physically and mentally handicapped gave birth to have separate provision for the caring, living and education of the exceptionals in the form of separate schools and institutions. We can witness the presence of such segregation in the form of separate residential or day schools established in the country. There are schools and institutions for gifted and bright, visually handicapped (Blinds) deaf and dumb, mentally retarded, socially deviant or delinquents. The question arises how far this idea of segregation is able to provide a proper provision or option for the caring, adjustment and education of the exceptional children. Let us think over this alternative/option.

1. The children may be exceptional on one or the other ground. The categories of exceptionality thus may be quite large in number and we need to have separate provision for their adjustment and education by establishing separate institutions/schools for each category of the exceptional children. More over the proportion or percentage available in each category of the exceptional children may vary in a typical manner. We may need a large number of schools for one and a very few for the other. For taking estimate in planning and running of the institutions by taking into account the presence of exceptional children in a huge country like ours is not a joke. It is almost an impossible task for catering to the needs of all types of exceptional children by adopting the philosophy of segregation. When we are unable to provide schooling for the children belonging to each and every corner of the country in a normalized way, then how can it be thought to establish special schools for each category of the exceptional children. It makes us a point to think over their adjustment and education in the normal setup of schooling in one or the other ways.

2. In case we try to have good efforts and establish a sizable number of special schools/institutions for some challenging categories of exceptional children, then how can we guarantee to provide them the needed opportunities (equal and justified) for their adjustment and future living in the society to which they belong. Segregated setup whether provided to the gifted or creative, physically or mentally retarded, emotionally or socially deviant may not provide such experiences or learning to them as needed for adjustment and living in the society or community to which they belong. We may witness the cases of such maladjustment in the future life of the children kept and educated in the segregated setup.

3. Moreover the idea and provisions in terms of abiding with the philosophy of separation and segregation, whether through special schools or special classes actually try to breed discrimination and differentiations among the exceptional and non exceptional (*e.g.* gifted and normal and disabled or non-disabled) children of the same society, country or humanity at large. It is against the law of nature which is kind enough to propagate equal opportunities for all to grow and develop without any differentiation and discrimination. The democratic systems all over the world, are also equally wedded to the principle of providing equal opportunities to learn and grow to all its members without any sort of discrimination. Consequently our country, wedded to democracy and equality can't afford to adopt the philosophy of separation and segregation for the education and welfare of the youngsters.

Integration and its Functionability

Integration is the second option or provision that has been employed for the placement and education of the exceptional children. Actually historically as well as philosophically, integration may be understood as a concept or philosophy that has emerged as a reaction or antithesis of the philosophy of separation and segregation. It has called halt to the system of providing education to the children in segregating settings of special schools by advocating to make provision for their education in the regular schools. In this way, historically, when disabled children were primarily educated in separate special schools, integration was accepted as an approach for carrying out their successful placement into regular schools.

In this way, instead of subjecting the exceptional students to a sort of segregation by putting them in separate special schools for their education, their integration (association) with the non-disabled population of their peers was targeted to achieve through this new philosophy of integration. It can thus be safely called a proper step in putting the disabled/exceptional children into the mainstream, *i.e.* the place and opportunities of getting education and training with the population of the normal and non-disabled peers in the regular schools.

While throwing light on the meaning and nature of the term 'integration' as placement and educational provision for the exceptional or disabled children Rane (1985) writes:

> *At the level of education the integration of a disabled children into a regular classroom situation means a concurrent education with a class of non-disabled (normal) children. In such a setup there are greater opportunities for the handicapped child to mix with his non-disabled counterparts in games, sports and other activities. The aim of integrated education is to assimilate a disabled child into a group of the non-disabled and providing opportunities to make him/her as independent as possible.* (Rehman Hifzr, 2005, pp. 119-120).

In this way, what we call as 'integration' may be clearly understood as an approach or philosophy for the placement and education of the exceptional/ disabled children along with their non-disabled/normal peers in the same school setting and general education classes allowing the exceptional to drift along with the normal/non-disabled children in the same stream of educational setup, adjustment and learning opportunities.

But, what goes wrong with Integration?

Looking superficially, the philosophy and provision of integration seems to be a quite useful and workable concept for the placement and education of the exceptional or disabled children. However in true sense it does not prove so. It is good that disabled children find entry into the system of a regular schooling and thus the formalities of including them into the mainstream may also be observed? But what is the output? The school authorities may admit them into mainstream on account of one or the other factors such as compulsion to follow the right to Education Act (implying that no child, including the disabled one can't be denied admission in case they belong to the residential areas/location marked for the school). In such a way, although integration makes a disabled child to get integrated *i.e.* allowed to sit in the class and receive education along with the non-disabled peers yet it does not guarantee for the needed attention, adjustment and opportunities as needed by him in view of his exceptionality/disability. Here more often an exceptional or disabled child may get admission in a school, is allowed to receive education along with the fellow students but all what is needed for him for his adjustment and education is altogether left as his own responsibility. School and school authorities are not prepared or even not willing to take any responsibility or make any special/extra arrangement for the care, adjustment and education of the exceptional children. In this way it makes a little sense to include the child in the mainstream without making worthwhile arrangement for his proper education and needed adjustment. This approach therefore may prove more dangerous then the arrangement made on the basis of separation and segregation.

How Inclusion differs from Segregation and Integration?

Inclusion describes much more than the acceptance of children with disabilities/exceptionalities in the mainstream. Inclusive education programmes do not focus on the accommodation of these children into a general education setting, but are focused on the restructuring of schools to accept and provide for the needs of all students. In inclusive education, mainstreaming and integration are viewed as intermediary steps to the ultimate goal of teaching all students together. In inclusive program specialized instruction and support are provided to any student who is in need of support without labelling him as disabled or exceptional. In other words, no discrimination is made among the exceptional or non-exceptional children. All the children in all shades of their exceptionality/disability are welcome by making necessary arrangements and accommodations for their education in the same school and classes along with their non disabled peers.

The acceptance on the part of schools of the exceptional or disabled children may be comparably depicted as below.

Sorry, we have no provision for you. Join the special school meant for you.	You are welcome. Although we are not prepared for meeting your needs yet some how we will accommodate you, at your risk.	School welcome you with open arms. You are like other children coming to school. We will try to care for your needs along with others.
School advocating Segregation	School accepting Integration	School providing Inclusion

Inclusive Education—Meaning and Nature

In a democratic setup its citizens must necessarily be educated. Keeping this thing into consideration, a campaign in the name of education for all has been started in our country for providing opportunities to all its citizens with no discrimination at all. In arranging education for all a big difficulty has been faced that how can a worth while school education be provided to the learners with special needs (including the children suffering with one or the other type of disabilities), for providing education for these children with special needs. One alternative can be in the form of establishing special schools for them such as blind schools, deaf and dumb schools, mentally retarded schools etc. However, this alternative of providing separate provision/schools can not be a properly viable solution for the vast population of the India having so many disability figures of the prospective learners. Moreover children may differ extensively in relation to their incapacities and disabilities. In such a situation how can we establish separate schools for every type of disabilities. In case we somehow establish special schools at some selective places then would it be possible for the disabled belonging to the distant and remote places to come and attend the school by their own?

Decidedly these children should get opportunity to receive education at the nearest places possible and it should also be a quality education for them with no discrimination of any kind on account of their disabilities. Such opportunities and provisions of providing quality education to all types of children including children with special needs (non-disabled and disabled) near to their places of residence can only be possible through the adoption of the philosophy of inclusion in place of segregation.

In an inclusive setup of the school, needed specialized instruction and support are provided to any students who is in need of educational and developmental education without labelling him disabled or children with special needs or abilities. All the children in all shades of their abilities or disabilities are welcome here by making necessary arrangements and accommodation for their education in the same school and classes along with their non-disabled or normal peers.

For understanding the need, nature, meaning and concept of inclusive education in a more comprehensive way let us try to gather opinion from a few well known definitions of the term inclusive education.

Michael F. Giangreco (1997): *Inclusive education is a set of values, principles and practices that seek more effective and meaningful education for all students regardless of whether they have exceptionality labels or not.*

Advani and Chadha (2003): *Inclusive education aims to provide a favourable setting for achieving equal opportunity and full participation for all, thus bringing children with special needs well within the purview of mainstream education, it recognizes the diverse needs of the students and ensures equality education to all through appropriate curricula, teaching strategies, support services and partnership with the community and parents. In simple words, it means that all children with or without disabilities learn together,* (p. 8)

NCF (2005): *Inclusion is not confined to the disabled. It also means non-exclusion. Inclusive education, thus, is about embracing all* (p. 84).

UNESCO (2000): *Inclusive education is concerned with removing all barriers to learning, and with the participation of all learners, vulnerable to exclusion and marginalization. It is a strategic approach designed to facilitate learning success for all children.*

Uppal and Dey (2001): *Inclusive education implies synchronization of the educational needs of the normal children and the educational requirements of the children with special needs, so as to evolve a common curriculum with a view to provide education to all in regular schools itself. It is a flexible and individualized support system for children and young people with special educational needs. It provides an integral component of the overall education system and is provided in regular schools committed to an appropriate education for all.*

Stainback and Stainback (1992): Inclusive school or setup may be defined as "*a place where every one belongs, is accepted, supports and is supported by his or her peers and other members of the school community in the course of having his or her educational needs met.*" (p. 3)

M. Manivannan (2001): *Inclusive education is the implementation of the policy and process that allows all children to participate in all programmes. Policy means that disabled children should be accepted without any restrictions in all the educational programmes meant for other children. The process of inclusion denotes the ways in the system, makes itself welcoming to all. Inclusive education is nothing but making the programme for disabled children as an integral part of the general educational system rather than a system within general education.*

A close look at the cited definitions may provide the following facts about the concept and nature of inclusive education.

1. It works on the principle of inclusion, *i.e.* including all. So all students are included in this system of education in their local schools and general classes without any discrimination and consideration of their exceptionalities or non-exceptionalities/disabilities or non-disabilities.

2. Here, for the general education the neighbourhood school, (that a student would attend if he did not have exceptionality/disability) is regarded as the first placement option for any exceptional or disabled child.

3. Here exceptional/disabled children may get unique opportunities to get education with peers in the same age groups available to those without exceptionality.

4. Here in the inclusive settings children with all shades of exceptionality/disabilities/normalities get opportunities to participate in shared educational experiences while pursuing individually appropriate learning objectives with necessary teaching-learning strategies, supports and accommodations needed for making inclusion as a success for all.

5. It aims to integrate and include the education of the disabled children with the general system of education so that the education of the disabled and non-disabled may proceed side by side by fulfilling the needs and objectives of both the groups without any differentiation or discrimination.

6. It helps in putting the disabled children (redefined as children with special needs) into the mainstream of the educational system in place of separating or segregating them as happens in the case of educating them in special schools or separate classes.

7. As a policy matter inclusive education provides a right to the disabled children for being educated with the non-disabled children without any differentiation or discrimination.

8. It seeks for all-round development of the disabled children by providing opportunities and integration in terms of academic, physical, social, emotional and vocational education programmes of the schools.

9. It aims to make the disabled children learn the art of living and get adjusted to the real life situations as independently as possible by erasing their feeling of insufficiency or limitedness, or of being different and disabled.

10. Inclusive education provides placing of exceptional/disabled children as equal partners and integrating them in the mainstream schooling. It helps the children to be self-reliant and self-supporting individuals contributing in their own way to the advancement of community and prosperity of the state.

11. Special schools, if established in any country, are always few in numbers for providing accommodation to all and each variety of the exceptional children. Moreover, they are proved failures in integrating these children to the social mainstream. It is, therefore, unanimously agreed that the principle of inclusive education is the only way to realize the noble goal "education for all" as anticipated by UNESCO from all the states of the world community.

12. It tries to bring desired educational opportunities at the doorstep of the exceptional/disabled children rather than expecting from them to move and try for themselves to avail these opportunities.

13. Inclusive settings by providing opportunities to the exceptional and non-exceptional peers for coming closer to each other help in:

- helping children with exceptionalities/disabilities to establish friendship with non-disabled peers and persons in their community.
- helping to change stereotyped thinking about disabilities among normally developing children, school personnel and community.
- helping children with exceptionalities/disabilities to develop social skills which in turn will enable them to interact more effectively

with broad increasing network of acquaintances, co-workers, family members and friends as the children grow older. (Fuchs and Fuchs, 1998, pp. 204-219).

14. By all means, an inclusion education provides a foundation for the exceptional/disabled children in ways that are not possible in special education schools and classes.

In view of such nature and characteristics of inclusive education it may stand for a type of education committed to educate every child to the maximum extent possible in the school and classroom, he or she would otherwise attend. It thus requires support to move towards the child (rather than moving the child to the services) and believes that the disabled child will benefits from such integration and main streaming in comparison to placing him in some segregating setting for his overall adjustment and progress.

Philosophical and Social Basis of Inclusive Education

Philosophical Basis

With regard to the philosophical basis or root of inclusive education we may safely claim that ideas related to the philosophy of inclusion have their origin in the philosophy of humanism. Humanism as a doctrine or philosophy provides great importance to humanistic outlook and human values in dealing with human beings. It considers human being as the finest creation of the nature or God and believes in the abilities or capacities of human beings irrespective of wide diversity or differences lying among them. The evolution of the humanistic ideas and doctrine in the period of renaissance may be properly credited to say halt to the inhuman deadly treatment provided to many of the disabled children and individuals in the past. It advocated equal and fair treatment to all children, whether disabled or non-disabled with no discrimination of any kind in their brought up and education. All human beings deserve quality of life and thus need to get opportunities for developing their capacities and lead life on the principles of justice, equality and equity. The waves of reform setup in human relationships and field of education, then helped in getting rid of slavery, raising voices against discrimination and oppression, stopping cruelty to people and animals and replaced the methods of separation and integration by inclusion in the field of education and adjustment of the differently abled children. Central to the idea of accepting inclusion as the philosophy of education were thus the humanistic beliefs that each human being, including children, is quite specific and unique in himself or herself, diversity possess its own value and thus should be respected and all should get opportunity to live and develop according to their uniqueness and since all have certain specificness, they can learn from each other in so many ways.

Social Basis

The acceptance of inclusion as a basic policy of providing education to the children in the countries like ours has been necessitated on so many solid social grounds, briefed below:

- A society or country wedded to democracy, liberty, fraternity, equity and equality is bound to provide educational opportunities to all its future citizens in a fairly even way with no discrimination of any kind with an eye of providing quality education at their convenience and door steps. Inclusion provides the only best possible solution on this account.
- The living in the society needs a proper adjustment between and among the people of diverse nature, abilities and capacities. The diversities among them are bound to persist. The children should be helped in learning way of adjustment and progress while living and learning in the company of the peers having diversities and uniqueness. It can only be possible in the inclusive learning environment rather than brought up and educated in the otherwise segregated or exclusion based setup.
- Each child as a future citizen is a valuable asset to the nation. His or her capacities and uniqueness should be nurtured to the maximum for helping him or her in his total development contributing to his own as well as national welfare. The children with disabilities as well as marginalized ones should be provided with fair opportunities of quality education with no discrimination of any kind so that they may not only be saved for remaining life time burden on the society but also avail a position to feel the society proud for their contribution. The task of equipping the future citizen in this way can be well entrusted to the inclusive setup of the education.
- Society needs proper cohesion and cooperation among its citizen belonging to different segments, multiplicities and diversities. The disabled have to live with non-disabled and the marginalized ones also have their place along with the privileged. The lesson of peaceful coexistence, learning and developing in the company of each other can only be best learnt from the early childhood. Schooling is the best opportunity for the same and inclusion is the best option of serving this purpose.
- Moreover, in this age of rapid globalization, a nation has to set its pace of progress with the other nations of the globe. It has to comply with the international agreements and understandings reached on one or the other grounds. India has been signatory to all such international agreements and declarations emphasizing human rights, child rights, gender equalities, multiculturalism and right to education for all children including differently abled with no discrimination of any kind in a proper inclusive setup. Our country

is thus fulfilling its international obligations of providing compulsory quality education to its future citizens with no discrimination of any kind in an inclusive setup. The adoption of the inclusive education policy in its school education is also proven helpful to her in fulfilling its social and legal commitments and policies existing in the form of PWD Act, 1995, RTE Act, 2009, National Policy for Persons with Disabilities, 2006, etc.

Benefits or Advantages of Inclusive Education

Inclusive education provided in the school proves advantageous or beneficial to all in the manner given below.

1. *Helping in meeting the International and Global Obligation:* Adherence to inclusion policy on the part of schools may help our country to serve its international and global obligation for providing education to all children — non disabled and disabled with no discrimination of any kind. In this concern it should be well noted that India is signatory of the agreements reached among the nations of the world on this account in a World Conference on Special Needs Education held in 1994 in Spain (known as Salamanca Statement) and UN conventions on the Rights of Persons with Disabilities. 2006. The implementation of inclusion policy in the schools may help well our country to walk along the nations of the world.

2. *Helping in the implementation of national policies and constitutional provisions:* As a democratic country, India has a moral duty to arrange for the quality education to all of its citizens with no discrimination of any kind. Every citizen of the country has a right to his or her education. Government of India has therefore launched the scheme *Sarva Shikha Abhiyan* (Education for All) and brought out a legislative measure in the name of Right to Education Act (RTE Act, 2009). The implementation of the Education for All policy and RTE Act can only be possible through the implementation of inclusive policy in a proper way in the schools of our country.

3. *Helping in the establishment of an inclusive society and inclusive culture:* Where segregation in the form of special schools and special classes breeds the feelings of separation and widens the gulfs between the disabled and non-disabled, inclusion in the form of inclusive education brings them closer. They get valuable opportunities to know and understand each other and begin to cooperate and collaborate in the curricular and co-curricular activities of the school. Gradually the negative attitude developed towards disabilities and disabled children on the part of non-disabled peers gets transferred into positive and favourable one leading to the establishment of an inclusive society respecting the individualities and different abilities of each other.

4. *Helping the country in the total utilization of its human resources:* We know that a large chunk of the population of our country is affected through

one or the other types of impairments or disabilities. This segment of the society feels neglected and is forced to lag behind in terms of their education, adjustment and progress from their earlier childhood. Due to lack of learning facilities, the disabled children remain deprived with their needed education and thus may remain a burden on their parents, society and nation. Inclusive education provided to them in their neighbourhood schools can prose a best alternative and potent means for the children with disabilities to learn art and skills of their adjustment and progress in life. They can get valuable opportunities to develop and make utilization of their different abilities in a most appropriate manner contributing towards the development and progress of the society and nation. Who knows that there may be a great scientist, artist, creative and inventive mind lying among the CWSN, and nurturing of his or her abilities may prove a great asset to the nation as well as humanity at large. His or her talent can be best developed in the inclusive setup of the schools and this development in turn can prove a big asset for the progress and development of the society and nation.

5. *Proving Advantageous for all the learners of the inclusive setup (CWSN and students without special needs):* Inclusive education provided in the school may prove advantageous to the disabled as well as non-disabled population of the students getting opportunities to learn and work together in a number of ways. The position paper of the National Focus Group on Education of CWSN drafted by the team of experts in NCERT, Delhi has beautifully summarized the advantages drawn on the part of CWSN and non-CWSN in the manner given below.

Advantages for CWSN
(*i*) Spending the school day alongside classmates who do not have disabilities provides many opportunities for social interaction that would not be available in segregated settings (Sasso, Simpson & Novak. 1985).
(*ii*) CWSN have appropriate models of behaviour. They can observe and imitate socially acceptable behaviours of the students without special needs. (Brown et al. 1983. 1989a)
(*iii*) Teachers often develop higher standards of performance for CWSN (Brown et al. 1989a; Snell. 1987)
(*iv*) Both general and special educators in inclusive settings expect appropriate conduct from all students.
(*v*) CWSN are taught age appropriate functional components of academic content, which may never be part of the curriculum in segregated settings (e.g. science, social studies, etc.).
(*vi*) Attending inclusive schools increases the probability that CWSDN will continue to participate in a variety of integrated settings throughout their lives (Ryndak & Alper. 1996).

Advantages for Students without Special Needs
(*i*) Students without special education needs or disabilities have a variety of opportunities for interacting with their age peers who experience CWSN or disabled in inclusive school settings.
(*ii*) They may serve as peer tutors during instructional activities (Slavin, 1960).
(*iii*) They may play with them during recess and leisure time.
(*iv*) They may play the role of a special "buddy" during lunch, in the bus or playground.
(*v*) Children without special education needs or disabilities can learn a good deal about tolerance, individual difference, and human exceptionality.
(*vi*) They learn that CWSN have many positive characteristics and abilities.
(*vii*) Students without special education needs or disabilities have the chance to learn about many of the human service professions such as special education, speech therapy, physical therapy, recreation therapy, and vocational rehabilitation. For some, exposure to these areas may lead to career choices.
(*viii*) Inclusion offers the opportunity for students without special education needs or disabilities to learn to communicate, and deal effectively) with a wide range of individuals. This also prepares them to fully participate in a pluralistic society when they are adults (Ryndak & Alper, 1996).

Source: Position Paper of the National Focus Group on education of children with special needs, NCERT.

In this way, the provision of inclusive education in the schools of our country can prove its worth by providing advantages of various natures contributing towards the welfare and progress of all the school going children (disabled and non-disabled) along with the needed progress and development of the country.

3

Historical Perspective to Disability and Inclusion

Introduction

Children with Special Needs or Diverse Needs (CWSN or CWDN) cover a quite wide population of the school going children all over the globe. These may include the children with a wide range of diversities in terms of their possession of different or special abilities or capacities in physical, mental, social and emotional areas. Accordingly they may show their presence as gifted or creative, backward or slow learners, physically or mentally disabled, socially deviant or emotionally disturbed in an inclusive education setup. When we try to talk about the history of educational or adjustment measures taken for the look after and welfare of these children. We usually focus our discussion on the education, adjustment and welfare measures for the children with impairments or disabilities (usually named as disabled children). As we find this group as a most challenging one in terms of the satisfaction of its needs, therefore the roots of any description about the history of CWDN or CWSN lie well in the description of the history of the care and provisions made by the society and states world wide for the various types of disabilities found in the human beings.

Specifically the distance travelled in terms of the provisions of care and education of the disabled from the earliest era of human civilization to the present era of democratization and liberalization may be divided into certain distinct milestones as shown below:

1. The era of exclusion — extermination and abandonment
2. The era of acceptance as a subject of amusement and use
3. The era of legal discrimination and witchcraft
4. The era of sympathy and asylum — institutionalization
5. The era of isolated settings — special schools
6. The era of segregated settings — special classes
7. The era of inclusive settings — regular classes

Let us have a brief discussion about the facts and happenings related to the history of CWDN/disability under the above heads first on global basis and then in connection with our own country.

GLOBAL SCENARIO

The Era of Exclusion — Extermination and Abandonment

The earlier history of treating disability/exceptionality is almost dominated by the philosophy of exclusion, i.e. totally excluding and exterminating the disabled from the mainstream of the general population through a quite horrified measures like killing, mutilating, burning, exciling, abandoning or making them vanish from the scene some how or the other. Such practices were in vogue throughout the globe in almost all the ancient civilizations of the world. Let us have a look into such practices.

1. The Greeks were following the practice of infanticide, i.e. killing deformed infants by naming their such practice as exposure. Commenting on this aspect Marie Delcourt (1938), the well-known French historian writes:

> *The exposure of deformed infants means, taking them outside the settlement to an unknown location and letting them expire in a hole in the ground or drown in a course of water. If the consequence is indeed a death, the significance of exposure is not as an execution of these infants. Exposing them is only returning them to the gods. They are not killed, they are sacrificed to the gods.... Their births signal the possibility of misfortunes and are explained by the anger of these gods... If they are exposed, it is because they caused fear, they were the sign of the god's anger and they were also the reason for it.*

Apart from such rationalization of their killing of disabled children, Greeks in Athens and Sparta were also engaged in doing away with the disabled population of the children on account of their firm belief in the theory of "survival of the fittest". They treated the disabled as a useless burden on the society. Aristotle, in this connection, advocated in his work Politics "a law that no deformed child shall live". As a result, Greeks were almost following the law and custom apparently allowing parents to kill deformed children.

2. The just cited philosophy and attitude towards their disabled children, was almost followed by the Romans. Law of Twelve Tables (the ancient Roman Legal Code) dating from the fifth century B.C., about the child rearing may be cited as a solid witness in this connection.

In one of its clause it states:

> *The father with his absolute power in the family, has the right to reject a child at birth, or to kill, mutilate, excile or sell his children under three who might some way become a burden on society or to divorce a wife on any grounds.*

Following such liberty, it was a usual practice for Roman to throw many of their disabled children in to the Tiber or left them dying in the sewers than ran through the streets of ancient Rome (Winzer, 1993, p. 14).

3. Such practices of extermination and exclusion of the disabled children with the most horrified and cruel measures were also almost adopted by the Egyptians, Babolians. and other European cultures. In Carthage for example, blind children were burned on a slow fire as a sacrifice to the Sun (Bowen, 1847).

In this way, the earliest era of treating disability (any type of physical and behavioural deviance) was marked by a reaction of utter hostility towards it whether on account of the notions of the society for getting rid of the disabled by considering them as useless burden or attributing their deviation as an anger of gods on account of their own sins or an agent of some evil spirit, devil or satan who were trying to bring sorrow and unhappiness on this earth.

B. The Era of Acceptance as a Subject of Amusement and Use

Disabled children, who happened to survive these Draconian measures on one or the other accounts like undetected conditions, post-natal deformities, or humanistic tendencies (like shift in western culture with the beginning of Christian era and other humanistic faiths) grown in some societies against the brutal measures of infanticide and started in an era of accepting their existence, not as a normal human being, but as a subject of amusement and means of serving one or the other ulterior motives of the society. It got reflected in the following practices.

1. Many of the disabled children were begin to be utilized as commodities for serving as beggars, prostitutes and slaves. As revealed by many authors, many mentally retarded were usually sold as slaves, taken for beggars, or some-times deliberately maimed to add to their value as objects of charity. Similarly, blind and hearing-impaired were also utilized for such purposes, besides being pushed into prostitution (French, 1932).

2. In addition to being used for the functions mentioned before, a trend was also visible to have them a subject of amusement and entertainment. The people mostly, the rich, began to buy a disabled child for the family amusement. For example, it became a status symbol for most of the wealthy families in Rome to keep a mentally retarded person as a fool for the amusement of the household and its guests. Similarly many families and entertainment establishment like circus companies began to make use of dwarfs and other types of children with deformities and disabilities as an exhibition subjects or jesters and fools. The fashion for utilizing disabled as a source of an amusement, then went to such an extent that in Rome a special market was said to be in operation for the purchase of legless, armless, or three eyed men, giants, dwarfs, or hermaphrodites (Durant, 1944, Kanner, 1964).

3. Exploitation of the disabled children through exhibition remained quite common throughout the world for a quite long time. In 16th century at Hamburg (Germany), mentally retarded individuals were confined in a tower in the city hall, appropriately named Idiot's cage. Even as late as in 1815, parents used to take their children for Sunday outing to view the inmates of London's Bethlehem Hospital known as "Bedlom", displayed for public amusement (Safford Philip & Safford, Elizabeth. 1966).

C. The Era of Legal Discrimination and Witchcraft

1. The rise of church as a religious institution in the medieval period led to play a new tone in the treatment and attitudes towards disabilities. The Bible became a code of ethics. Disability, an everyday reality, was given a label of legal uncleanness by declaring that "*the disabled had the status of prostitutes or of woman whom menstruation made unclean. One had to be without defect in order to approach God's place of residence*". (Striker 1982/1999, p. 24). In this way, church under the doctrine of Bible tried to label disabilities as a whole as impurities, disqualifying their bearers from active participation in the cult and even went for their social isolation by declaring that *"the slow-witted, the fools, the silly, the mad, the blind, the crippled, the lame, the deaf the underage, none of these shall enter the bosom of the community, for "the holy angels dwell in its midst*" (Striker, 1982/1999. p. 25).

2. In collaboration with church, the rulers in the European society established quite discriminatory legal laws depriving the disabled people of their right of inheritance, and forbidding them to testify in a course of justice, making a deed, contract, note or will. The most powerful forces of the days, the rulers and the priests, thus almost made the disabled persons as a subject of crude humour by prohibiting them to play any role in the social life.

3. Moreover, these two forces in collision, also invented a peculiar ideology for implicating disabled in the name of witchcraft and by the end of 15th century went for declaring an open war against the witches and their associates. Not only Europe, but the world as a whole remained in the era of witchcraft for a quite long period as late as 18th century in European world and even quite late in the less developed societies. Under this ideology, people were led to believe that the illness or sufferings are due to evil spirits clouding this earth in the guise of witches (old women and widows and any person who was unusual, different, deviant or disabled). In the name of witchcraft, how many innocent women and disabled persons were accused or perished is unknown, that they were implicated seems beyond question (Bromberg, 1975).

D. The Era of Sympathy and Asylum — Institutionalization

With the advent of the second phase of the Christian era, attempts were in vogue to stop the abuse of the disabled children. Disabled children were now regarded as those poor souls who have been denied opportunities to lead a normal life on account of the annoyance of the Almighty for committing sins. They were now a subject of sympathy rather than of suspicion or amusement. As a result, Contancine-1 issued edicts forbidding infanticide, selling children into slavery and maiming them as beggars or objects of amusement. Besides this, specific measures were also initiated to assist parents who are too poor to support their children and mechanism for formal adoption. In this way, there started some efforts to provide protection and asylum for disabled children in the later part of the Christian era in the whole Europe dominated by the waves of Renaissance. In the same tone, many institutions and homes were established for the welfare and rehabilitation of the disabled people as a gesture of sympathy and asylum. Actually many of the institutional establishments across Europe, coming into existence for dealing with leprosy in past, were converted to the needs of those who were considered defective, more particularly the insane. However, the institutionalization of the mentally or physically defectives was not simply the reason of showering sympathy on them but also for the perceived need of society to protect itself against the harm that the deviant, the defective or the dependent persons might incur. However, whatever reasons might have been behind the institutionalization, it became a wide, acclaimed practice to confine the mentally ill, retarded and other defective and disabled people into a boundary wall of the institution.

As a result, a wide number of institutions, including the mental hospitals known by the term lunatic hospitals, and centres for providing asylum to other categories of disabled were seen to be coming into existence throughout the globe and asylum thus arose as a sole approved solution to the problems posed by all forms of disabilities physical or mental.

E. The Era of Segregated Settings — Special Schools

The Renaissance movement originated from Italy in 16th century and then spread throughout the western world in 17th century brought a new era of hope to the disabled population. Contrary to inhuman approach adopted in the past, this movement believed in the capacities of the disabled. The spirit of Renaissance gave birth to most of the genuine efforts in the direction of special education for the disabled population. Some of the major ideas influencing special education were thus established during the late Renaissance period.

Later on, this work was taken ahead in the mid of 18th century through the ideas propagated by an intellectual movement known as enlightenment. The main propagators of this movement like Rousseau, Condillac and especially Diderot, provided essential theoretical grounds for the action oriented work of the many pioneers in the field of special education related to various group of disabilities like hearing, visual, mentally retarded. As a major contribution of both these Renaissance and enlightenment movements now it began to be well realized that disabled persons could learn and achieve. As a result, effective procedures in term of providing special education in the segregated settings were devised all over the Europe, USA and Canada for the education and training of the diversified disabled population. The decision for establishing separate schools was taken mainly on two grounds, (*i*) The need and problems of disabled children are quite different from the normal children, they need specialized settings and special education and provision for their proper progress and adjustment. It can only be possible through establishing the specialized schools meant for each of the specific categories of the disabled, (*ii*) The segregation was also planned for keeping the non-disabled away from the negative influence of the disabled. As a result by the close of 18th century, special education was accepted as a branch of education and separate schools were established for the education and training of the diversified groups of disabled children all over the Europe including Canada and USA such as special schools for the blind, deaf, dumb and mentally retarded.

F. The Era of Integrated Settings — Special Classes

With the advent of twentieth century, there began a new era in the history of the education for CWDN/disabled in the shape of moving from the isolated settings of special schools to the integrated settings of the separate special classes within the normal/regular schools. It was the result of a new wave of humanism, coupled with the increasing demands of equality of educational opportunities to all children irrespective of their disabilities in the regular schools run by the Government or funded and supported by the public money. A few other reasons for the upsurge of the special classes within the system of regular schools may be cited as under.

- In many countries of the world, education for CWDN disabled children was accepted as an utmost responsibility on the part of state agencies. It necessitated to have either establishing a number of special schools or to make an alternative arrangement in the regular schools. However, within increasing public demand of getting the disabled enrolled in neighbourhood schools, there was no other option as to make the schools accept all types of CWSN or CWDN as their regular students.
- Schools on their part for enrolling all children, with a different special needs devised a way to create a special segregated setting within the schools in the form of separate special classes. It made them feel relaxed as most of the classroom teachers, non-disabled students and their parents were in no mood to accept the disabled children into the regular classes. In their opinion, it was quite unhealthy and disturbing to the running of normal classes and also not conducive to the disabled since specialized instructions could only be possible for the CWSN children in the specialized segregated settings.
- The evolving of certain new categories of the CWDN like children with emotional disturbance and learning disabilities also made the state authorities and public to think for the education of such children since no

special schools were available for the education of these newly disabled/defined categories of CWSN. The best alternative for their education was then preferred in the form of having their education in the special classes within the regular schools.

As a result of the reasons cited before, there started the placement of CWSN or disabled from special schools to the regular general schools right from beginning of the 20th century. By the year 1910. in many-Western countries including USA, it took the shape of permanent segregated classes for the disabled students in the regular schools (run or funded by the Government). Writing on this account Winzer (1993) submits: *The movement of disabled students from institution (special schools) to public school (regular general schools) —from isolation to segregation— may be dated from about 1910 with the promotion of permanent segregated classes in the public schools The advent of segregated classes was greeted with enthusiasm, and until the end of 1920s they seemed to meet the needs of these students (including behaviour and learning disabilities)* p. 367.

G. Era of Inclusive Settings — Regular Classes

The era of inclusive settings, i.e. educating all types of children whether exceptional or normal together in the regular classes of the mainstream schools, represents the modern era and latest development in the history of special/disability education. The beginning of this era may be traced to as back as 1970s with the evaporation of the optimism surrounding the era of integrated settings of the special classes. Many of the educationists, teachers and parents were found to air their views against the segregated classes operating within the regular schools in the manner given below:

- Segregated or special classes for the CWSN/disabled children are responsible for promoting segregation much in the same way as happens in the case of educating them in the special schools.
- Children enrolled in the special classes are not able to escape the social stigma. It becomes difficult for the disabled children or their parents to respond to the question; why the child is not attending the regular classes with other non-disabled peers?
- In special classes, the children have no role models for learning and advancing including the desired social and other adjustment behaviour needed for living a life in the community settings.
- Segregated settings of the special classes perpetuate disability culture and are not helpful in bringing desirable changes in the behaviour of non-disabled children towards their disabled peers.

Apart from such dissatisfaction with the continuation of special classes in the regular schools, a new wave of change in the name of upholding Human Rights, providing equity and equality of educational opportunities to all children, gave birth to a strong build up in favour of inclusion, i.e. the placement of exceptional/disabled children in regular classrooms without discrimination of any sort.

Internationally the drive towards inclusion was fuelled up by a number of initiatives taken world wide under the leadership of world bodies like UNO and World Bank. The special mention may be made of the following in this direction.

(*i*) Derived from the Universal declaration of Human Rights (1949) and the UN convention on the rights of the child (1989). UNESCO claimed that being included within mainstream education is a basic human right.

(*ii*) The World Conference on Education For All (EFA) held at Jomtien, Thailand, in March 1990, arrived on the fundamental principle that all should have the opportunity to learn. Children and adults with disabilities do have the right to education, and have the right to be part of the main-stream education system.

(*iii*) The UN standard rules on the equalization of opportunities for persons with disabilities (1992). emphasized that, at a minimum. students with disabilities should be afforded the same portion of ' educational resources. States should aim for the gradual integration of special education services with mainstream education.

(*iv*) The World Conference on special needs education organized by the Government of Spain in cooperation with UNESCO held in Salamanca in June 1994 adopted a framework for action on special needs education by clearly, declaring that "education policies at all levels, from the national to the local, should stipulate that a child with disability should attend the neighbourhood school, that is the school that would be attended if the child did not have a disability."

Influenced by the wave of change in their democratic setup or through the impact of the world bodies many countries of the world have come up with necessary legislative initiative in making inclusive education as a basic policy of their educational system. USA has been the first country in 1975, to come up with a legislative step for the implementation of the inclusion as a policy in all the states of USA through its Education for All Handicapped Children Act (PL 94-192) now known as "The Individuals with Disabilities Education Act (IDEA)." IDEA, through one of its major principle directs the states to follow a zero reject policy emphasizing that "all schools must educate all children with disabilities."

Other nations including India, have also taken legislative initiative for making education possible for all children including the disabled in the schools of their countries. At the World forum, "Universal Primary Education by the year 2015" has been accepted as one of the Millennium Developmental Goals by the countries of the world.

It has also been observed that it would be impossible to attain this goal without the inclusion of disabled children. The extent of the task has also been demonstrated by the fact that out of the 150 million disabled children in developing countries, only 20 per cent of them attend school as per UNESCO estimates.

Further International Work by both the World Bank and Organization for Economic Cooperation and Development (OECD) has also shown that it is far more expensive to operate dual systems of ordinary and special education than it is to operate a single inclusive system. In one of its report entitled 'inclusion education at work: Students with Disabilities in Mainstream Schools" OECD (1999) writes:

> *The rights of students with disabilities to be educated in their local mainstream school is becoming more and more accepted in most countries, and many reforms are being put in place to achieve this goal. Further, there is no reason to segregate disabled students in public education system. Instead, education systems need to be reconsidered to meet the needs of all students.*

Looking in this way we can conclude that the education and care of disabled children all over the world has surpassed many significant phases in its travelling from the era of neglect and extermination and isolated institution or special schools settings or segregated classroom settings to the present era governed by the requirements and demands of the provision of inclusive education for bringing all types of disabled or CWSN in mainstream in the true spirit of providing equal opportunities and access to all children irrespective of their disabilities or non-disabilities.

THE INDIAN SCENARIO

For a broad understanding of the status of special education in India, let us have its division into two sections — before and after gaining independence in 1947.

Pre-Independence Era

India has a very glorious past with respect to the treatment and educational opportunities provided for its disabled population. In Vedic Era, we have glaring example of 'ashtavakra' (a chronic and severe case of orthopaedic impairment) for becoming a great scholar by virtue of the educational facilities available to all irrespective of their abilities or disabilities.

The great Rishis (the sacred persons) as Gurus (teachers) were known to provide equal treatment to their pupils irrespective of their social status and exceptional or non-exceptional abilities. They were of the firm believers in the theory of Karma. Therefore, they were of the opinion to give ample opportunities to the disabled, poor and sufferers to learn the art of self actualization and doing good in the life for getting better result in the, next cycle of life. In doing so with them they also believed that, in turn, they might earn good Karma for themselves. However, the spirit of liberalism prevailed in the ancient *ashrams* quietly vanished in the later periods of Indian history and it was almost replaced by the practices adopted all over the world in the treatment and education of the disabled population.

Consequently the treatment, care and education of the disabled children in India, also passed through the phases or era of exclusion, extermination and abduction, ridicule and amusement, witchcraft, sympathy and asylum. There are instances of the disabled people being harassed, ridiculed and made a subject of amusement and entertainment. Practice of treating any deviation from the normality as a sign of the shadow or mark of an evil spirit was quite prevalent in the later periods of ancient Indian history. Mental illness/retardation was taken as some evil spirit entered in the body of the affected person and consequently was treated by the coercive methods of torturing in the name of making the evil spirit leave the body of the affected person. Witchcraft was also quite in vogue in almost all the rural and tribal belts of India. The disabled and poor people were treated as subject of sympathy, pity and asylum. In advocating humane treatment to the disabled. Lord Buddha and Mahavira. propagators of the doctrines of Buddha and Jain religions, played a major role. The rulers like Ashoka the Great, and Harsh Bardhan, who followed their preaching were earned much fame in establishing hospitals, and asylum for the disabled and destitute.

The tradition of state funding and also the charitable flow for the care and protection of the disabled continued through the medieval India during the regimes of many Muslim rulers including Mughals. During their rule, although the disabled and the poor were responsibility of the state, one of the important edicts of Islam was *Zakat*, that is, giving of alms and donations by individuals to the poor and the disabled. (Agrawal, Rita, 1994, p. 187)

Their contemporaries Maratha rulers and Peshwas like Shivaji and Ahilya Bai were also well known for their charitable acts to the disabled and poor. However what was available during this period was nothing more than the acts of caring and protection of the disabled as a matter of pity, sympathy and noble deeds of some noble persons. There is no evidence of any type of special provision for the disabled children during these eras of Indian history prior to the establishment of British rule in the country.

However, as a matter of record, the pattern of special school education followed at present in our country owes its origin to the work done by the Christian missionaries and other charitable organizations of the country. These following establishments may be mentioned specially for this purpose:

(*i*) The first school meant for the special education of the deaf was established in Bombay in 1883.

(*ii*) The first school for the blind was started at Amritsar in 1887.

(*iii*) The first school for blind and deaf was started at Mysore in 1901.

(*iv*) The first Government school "The Emerson Institute for the Blind" was started at Lahore in 1906.

(*v*) Although the facilities in the form of psycho-medical treatment were available at Ranchi from 1934, yet the first home for the mentally retarded came up at Bombay in 1941.

In this way, there were quite a sporadic and scattered efforts in the direction of education for the disabled children. In real sense, however, under the colonial rule, India had a very marginal and insignificant provisions for the education of its children, including the disabled. When India got independence in 1947, we had only 34 institutions for the deaf, 32 for the blind and three for the mentally retarded.

Post-Independence Era

After gaining independence in 1947, India tried to focus on the education of its children including the disabled. The main landmarks in the development of special provisions for the disabled children after independence may be outlined as follows:

1. In its constitution, India laid down special provisions through the article 45 stating that "free, compulsory and universal primary education should be provided to all children up to 14 years of age."

2. It tried to pay attention towards the prevention of disabilities, education and rehabilitation of disabled, by laying down specific budgetary amount in its five year plans. To meet the constitutional provision, where the task of spreading education among the non-disabled population was entrusted to the Ministry of Education (now Ministry of Human Resource Development), the Social Welfare Ministry of the Government of India was chosen as a coordinating agency for the education and rehabilitation of the disabled.

3. Education Commission (1964-66) better known as Kothari Commission, set for advising the Government on "the national pattern of education and on the general principles and policies for the development of education at all stages and in all aspects" clearly emphasized that "the constitutional directive on compulsory education to all children, includes handicapped children as well. However, very little has been done in the field so far." Since there were 115 schools for the blind, 70 schools for the deaf, 25 schools for the orthopaedic handicapped and 27 for the mentally retarded in the whole country, Education Commission felt that the existing facilities were quite in shortage and therefore suggested to experiment with integration and mainstreaming of disabled students with the non-disabled students in the ordinary schools.

4. With a view to implement the recommendations of Education. Commission, Government of India came out with its first National Policy on education in 1968. Regarding the education for disabled children this policy tried to lay down the following main provision:

> *Educational facilities for the physically and mentally handicapped children should he expanded and attempts should be made to develop integrated programmes enabling the handicapped children to study in regular schools.*

5. In an attempt for implementation of the National Policy on Education, 1968, the Integrated Education for Disabled Children (IEDC) scheme was launched in December 1974 under the erstwhile department of social welfare for admitting children with disabilities in regular schools.

6. In 1985, a well-known programme in the name of District Primary-Education Programme (DPEP) was launched. This programme worked on the very assumption that universalization of education is possible if it includes children with disabilities.

7. The emphasis on integrated education and segregated education in the form of special education were working side by side. With the encouragement from the Government incentives the major work in the direction of establishing special schools strikingly was done by the voluntary agencies throughout the country. As a result the number of schools for the deaf, blind and mentally retarded respectively rose to 180, 170 and 200 by the year 1980.

8. It gained further momentum with the declaration and implementation of the provision meant for the handicapped in the National Policy on Education (NPE) 1986. The National Policy on Education 1986, laid much emphasis on the issue of the equality of opportunities to education to all children, not only in access, but also in the condition for success. Through its Section 4.9 the policy clearly highlights the needs of the disabled children and recommended integrated education for the disabled in the following manner:

(*a*) The objective should be to integrate the physically and mentally handicapped with the general community as equal partners, to prepare them for normal growth and to enable them to face life with courage and confidence.

(*b*) Whenever it is feasible, the education of children with motor handicaps and other mild handicaps will be common with that of others.

(*c*) As far as possible, special schools with hostels will be provided at district headquarters for the severely handicapped children.

(*d*) Adequate arrangements will be made to give vocational hands to the disabled.

(*e*) Teaching programmes will be reoriented in particular for teachers of primary classes, to deal with the special difficulties of the handicapped children and

(*f*) Voluntary efforts for the education of the disabled will be encouraged in every possible manner.

For the follow up and implementation of the National Policy on Education, Plan of Action (PoA) 1992 was also formulated. Looking at the magnitude of the task involved in the care and education of about 15 million children with disabilities, the PoA came forward with a pragmatic approach by clearly emphasizing that the children with disabilities who can be educated in a general school essentially be educated in general schools only and not in special schools. PoA however, envisaged on the provision of early intervention and services for the disabled children and stated clearly that since education of the disabled in special school is quite costly it will be ensured that only children whose need cannot be met in common schools are enrolled in special schools. Once they acquire communication skills and study skills they will be integrated in common schools.

9. For the implementation of the spirit of National Policy on Education 1986 regarding mainstreaming and integration of children with disabilities, Government of India launched the Project Integrated Education for the Disabled (PIED) in 1987 for encouraging all schools in a neighbourhood to enroll children with disabilities. In this approach, a cluster usually a block of population (instead of the individual school) is taken as the project area. All the schools in the area are expected to enroll children with disabilities and training programme are also given to the teachers.

10. As a follow up of the recommendation of the National Policy on Education, 1986 Government of India took initiative for the establishment of Rehabilitation Council of India (RCI) in 1986 under the then ministry of social welfare. For equipping this body with some legal authority, Parliament of India in 1992 enacted its first piece of legislation related to special education; the Rehabilitation Council of India Act. The major purpose of this act was to mandate minimum standards of education for professionals working with individuals with disabilities including special teachers and educators. This act makes it mandatory for every special teacher to be registered by the Council and lays down that every child with disability had the right to be taught by a qualified teacher. It has also a provision of punishment for those teachers who engage in teaching children with special needs without a license.

11. A very significant landmark in the history of special/disability education of India has been the enactment of The Persons with Disabilities (Equal Opportunities, Protection of Rights and Full Participation) Act 1995. It is a quite composite act covering all aspects of education and economic rehabilitation of the disabled. This legislation stipulates that the appropriate governments and the local authorities shall ensure that every child with a disability has access to free education in an appropriate environment till he attains the age of 18 years. For this purpose, it recommends making changes in assessment and curriculum, and removing architectural barriers, to support inclusion. It also recommends providing free books and uniform to children with disabilities.

12. To provide practical shape for the practice of inclusion, there emerged an important paradigm shift in this area with the thinking that any difficulty that a child exhibited in learning was to be attributed not to a problem within the child, but to the school system. The thinking then became a corner stone of the inclusive education in District Primary

Education Programme (DPEP). Inclusive education was formally added in DPEP in 1997. It was initially introduced in the states in a small way by taking one block/cluster as a pilot project in each DPEP district. From a few hundred blocks in 1998, inclusive education was gradually implemented in more than 2000 blocks of 18 DPEP states. Ten states namely Gujarat, Haryana, Himachal Pradesh, Karnataka, Kerala, Madhya Pradesh, Maharashtra, Odisha, Tamil Nadu and Uttarakhand then up-scaled the inclusive programme to all the blocks.

13. In 1999, Government of India came up with the National Trust for welfare of persons with Autism, Cerebral Palsy, Mental Retardation and Multiple Disabilities Act. The focus of this Act has been to protect and promote the "rights of persons with autism, cerebral palsy, mental retardation and multiple disabilities on a national level".

14. In 2000, Government of India launched 'Sarva Shiksha Abhiyan', an ambitious programme seeking education for all by 2010, fully pleading that the SSA will ensure that every child with special needs, irrespective of the kind category and degree of disability, is provided education in an appropriate environment. It had a target of eight years of elementary schooling for all children including children with disabilities in the age group of 6-14 years by 2010.

15. Through its 86th Amendment of the Constitution passed in 2002 Government of India introduced a new Article 21A: Right to Education, a quite significant and major land mark in the history of education of the country. This provides "the state shall provide free and compulsory education to all children of the age of 6 to 14 years (covering children with disabilities) in such a manner as the state may, by law, determine. The 86th Amendment also modified Article 45, which now reads as "The state shall endeavour to provide early childhood care and education for all children until they complete the age of 6 years."

16. Government of India has brought, the Right to Education Bill, 2005 seeking to give the effect to the 86th Constitution Amendment. It has led to the formation of a key legislative measure in the name Right to Education, Act. 2009 enacted by Parliament of India. It aims to provide for free and compulsory education to all children of the age six to fourteen years (disabled to disabled) in the neighbourhood schools.

17. Government of India has announced in February 2006 "The National Policy for Persons with Disabilities", implementation of which has been entrusted to the Ministry of Social Justice and Empowerment, Government of India In its policy statement, it has recognized that persons with disabilities are valuable human resources for the country and seeks to create an environment that provides them equal opportunities, protection of their rights and full participation in society. By declaring education, the most effective vehicle of social and economic empowerment, it has pledged to provide free and compulsory education to all children with disabilities up

to the minimum age of 18 years by emphasizing a need for mainstreaming of the persons with disabilities in the general education system through inclusive education. It has also laid down a time limit of ensuring every child with disability an access to appropriate pre-school, primary and secondary level education by 2020 by taking care of: (*i*) making schools barrier free and accessible to all types of disability, (*ii*) making needed teaching, learning material and support services available to them.

With all such landmark development in the history of special education, India has come a long way since independence in the area of caring and education of its disabled population. A global view of such progress can easily be taken through some of the following:

- Starting from the time of independence in 1947, with quite a few special schools for children with disability, the country has now about 3,500 special schools for the various categories of disabilities spread throughout the country. The National Policy for Persons with Disabilities, 2006 has further laid down that "Ministry of Human Resource Development shall open new special schools depending upon the requirement."
- There has been a shift in the education and rehabilitation of children with disabilities from charity to right. It is no more the wish and choice of the giver to provide education, vocational training and rehabilitation, but the Right of the Children with disability. The inclusion of education as a fundamental right in the constitution and other legislative/legal provisions made for the disabled, now has made them to claim their right for education and support.
- India has now quite effective legislations for persons with disabilities like below:
    1. Rehabilitation Council of India Act, 1992 and Amendment 2000.
    2. Persons with disability (Equal Opportunities Protection of Rights and Full Participation) Act, 1995.
    3. National Trust for Welfare of Persons with Autism Cerebral palsy, Mental Retardation and Multiple Disability Act, 1999.
    4. National Policy for Persons with Disabilities, 2006.
    5. Right to Education Act, 2009.
- In addition to the legal framework and protection, India, has developed extensive infrastructure for the development of human resources as well as working as a model of special education programmes in the different areas of disabilities in the shape of the establishments of the following seven national institutes:
    1. National Institute for the Mentally Handicapped, Secunderabad (Andhra Pradesh).
    2. National Institute for the Orthopaedically Handicapped, Kolkata (West Bengal).

3. Al Yavar Jung National Institute for the Hearing Handicapped, Mumbai (Maharashtra).
4. National Institute for the Visually Handicapped, Dehradun (Uttarakhand).
5. Institute for the Physically Handicapped (New Delhi).
6. National Institute of Rehabilitation Training and Research, Cuttack (Odisha).
7. National Institute for Empowerment of Persons with Multiple Disabilities, Chennai (Tamil Nadu).

- India is a signatory to the "Declaration on the Full Participation and Equality of People with Disabilities in the Asia Pacific Region". It is also a signatory to the "Biwako Millennium Framework" for action towards an inclusive, barrier free and rights-based society. For fulfilling its pledges at the international and national levels it has made inclusion as a basic, recognized principle for providing education and rehabilitation to its disabled population.
- In this way in tune with the global call for universalization of child education like other democratic countries of the world USA, UK, France, etc. India has also preferred inclusion and mainstreaming as the ultimate placement option for the care and education of the children with disabilities. In this connection, a Comprehensive Plan for Action for children and youth with disabilities presented by the then Minister for Human Resource Development, Arjun Singh in March, 2005 has clearly advocated inclusive education by envisaging all schools "disabled friendly" by 2020. The National Policy for Persons with Disabilities, 2006 has also highlighted this need by saying that "*there is a need for mainstreaming of the persons with disabilities in the general education system through inclusive education.*" For making inclusive education as a success, it has emphasized (*i*) the development of training modules for teachers for inclusive education (*ii*) making schools barrier free and accessible for all types of disabilities (*iii*) establishing model schools of inclusive education in each state/U.T. (*iv*) identifying children with disabilities up to the age of six years and providing necessary instructions for making them join inclusive education, (*v*) taking steps for the schools not discouraging enrollment of students on account of their disability.

In conclusion, we may say that the history of CWSN/disabled education in our country has also almost passed through the same phases or eras of exclusion, institutionalization, segregation in special schools and integration before finally accepting inclusion of the all types of children with disabilities in the mainstream of general education. However, much has to be done for making inclusion a success for fulfilling the dreams of the vast army of the disabled children and youth living in the most inaccessible corners of the country. Indeed, education in its any form, setting and alternative programs needs huge finances and firm determination in terms of its planning and organizing adequate education for the different categories of the disabled children. The developing country like India, with its meagre sources is unable to attain the desired target without the active consciousness of its citizens towards disabilities and disabled education. We all need to have a quite positive attitude towards the education and rehabilitation of our brothers and sisters, or beloved young children who are trying their best in getting prepared themselves to live with us properly in any inclusive setup of education and living. Really as it is said "Disability is not a brave struggle or courage in the face of adversity... disability is an art. It's an ingenious way to live", let us stand together for helping the disabled in living their life as naturally by getting natural means of education and living as possible.

4

Disabilities: Concept, Types, Characteristics and Identification of the Educational Needs and Learning Problems

DISABILITIES — MEANING AND CONCEPT

The term disability is very much associated with the terms like impairment and handicap and that is why you must have heard quite often the terms like physical impairment, physical disability and physical handicap for addressing the deficiency, deficits and incapacity of an individual associated with his physical growth and development. Therefore, in getting acquainted with the meaning and concept of disabilities it would be quite proper to understand the underlying distinction and differences in the use of these three terms — impairment, disability and handicap. In the literature available, these terms have been widely defined and distinguished. However, let us here mention the attempts made by WHO.

In one of its publication entitled "The International Classification of Impairments, Disabilities and Handicap" WHO (1980) has defined these terms as follows:

- **Impairment** is defined as a fundamental, structural, psychological, or physiological deficit (e.g. disordered motor control in cerebral palsy).
- **Disability** is defined as the functional deficit that a person experiences as a result of impairment (e.g. spasticity interfering with walking).
- **Handicap** is defined as the disadvantage a person with disability experiences in various societal settings as a result of that disability (e.g. people who cannot walk may be denied access to particular places).

Let us try to understand these terms in a more specific way in the light of the guidelines provided by WHO.

1. Impairment in its simple meaning denotes or represents a sort of disturbance or abnormality in the structure and functioning of our body systems including psyche. In this way, it represents a certain type of loss or deficit, and deficiency at the organic or psychic level for an individual (e.g. loss of a limb, paralysis of speech, muscles or legs, disturbance in one's

vision or hearing system, disturbance and structural abnormalities in one's neurological system, brain, spinal chord, etc.)

2. The term disability is used to mean the loss of function that individual experiences because of the impairment. It limits his ability to perform certain task. For example, (*i*) vision or hearing impairment may result into one's loss or reduced function with respect to the use of his visionary or hearing system, (*ii*) orthopaedic or motor impairment may limit one's functions with regards to one's walking and other motor functioning.

3. Where impairment results into a specific type of disability, the disability in its own turn may give birth to a specific condition known as handicap. Actually a handicap stands for a disadvantage imposed on an individual on account of his disability. For example, some disturbance in the structural composition and functioning of ears may cause hearing impairment. This impairment may bring disability in terms of loss of hearing ability. Inability or incapacity in terms of hearing sounds then may turn one into aurally handicapped, i.e. experiencing problems in interacting with the environmental situations demanding hearing ability on one's part. In this way, the term handicap usually refers to environmental or functional demands placed upon an individual with a disability in a given situation. More specifically, a handicap is the effect of a disability on an individual's functioning in his environment. It may limit his social functioning or adjustment to his environment as per limits imposed upon him for doing so by his disability of one or the other kinds. As a result, a physically challenged child even after using wheel chair may feel handicapped in terms of making proper adjustment and adaptations to his self and the environment. He may find his motor disability as a major obstacle in his proper socialization. It may deny him the valuable opportunities of entering into the activities and profession of his choice, getting married and difficulty even in performing his day-do-day activities.

The previous discussion may lead us to conclude that all these three terms, impairment, disability and handicap have a perfect linear relationship (i.e. one leading to the other) in the following manner:

Impairment → Disability → Handicap

Linearity of such relationship may make us to think that it is always essential for an impairment condition to result into disability and the disabled condition to handicap. However, in practical situation it does not happen so. Let us have a few illustrations in support of such happenings.

(*i*) Visual or hearing impairment may not lead to disability. The deficits and deficiencies in one's visual and hearing ability may be overcome by the use of lenses or hearing aid. So this may not cause handicap to him while studying in his class. However, it may create obstacle in meeting some or other environmental needs, i.e. he may not participate in such activities or games in which the wearing of lenses or hearing aid may prove a major inconvenience or obstacle. Similarly, he or she may feel difficulty in getting married or even seeking employment in a society where the wearing of lenses or hearing aid is taken otherwise. In such cases, as we see individuals with disabilities are bound to experience handicaps that have nothing to do with their disabilities, but are the result of negative attitudes and inappropriate behaviour of others who needlessly put hurdles in their paths in spite of their capabilities in participating fully in school, play and other activities at job and other work situations.

(*ii*) Just as impairment may not necessarily cause disability, disability may not also necessarily lead to handicap. The fact remains with all handicaps is that these are absolutely situation-specific, i.e. a person with disability may feel handicapped in one situation but not in the other. Let us have few illustrations.

(*a*) A child sitting on a wheel chair (on account of his orthopaedic impairment and motor disabilities) in the class may not feel handicapped while listening to the lecture of his teacher and participating in class room discussion, but he may feel so while doing experiments in the science laboratory and working in a vocational course class.

(*b*) A child with an artificial limb may feel handicapped while competing against non-disabled peers at the time of playing football or cricket but may experience no handicap in the classroom.

(*c*) A blind child may experience major handicap in the situations where eye sight is most needed, i.e. travelling in an unfamiliar terrain, but he may also have advantages over sighted persons in situations where eye sight is not important, i.e. singing a song, playing on a musical instrument, etc.

However, whatever the mode may be, there exists a sound relationship between impairment, disability and handicap conditions. For the illustration of their positions in the context of person's disability and rehabilitation process, National Centre for Medical Rehabilitation Research (NCMRR), National Institute of Health, USA (1993) has developed a model, known as NCMRR Model of Disability. Let us know it in brief.

In this model of disability, (Figure 4.1) the components of disability are shown arranged around a pentagon. It emphasizes that instead of a linear or hierarchical relationship, the relationship among the components of disability is a quite complex one. The related five components in the model of disability have been explained in the following way.

(*i*) Pathophysiology is the starting and initial phase for the development of disability in an individual. It is concerned with the basic biological and psychological disturbances.

(*ii*) The second component in the name of impairment emphasizes the more generalized effects of these disturbances, e.g. brain abnormalities resulting from adverse prenatal conditions (i.e. the

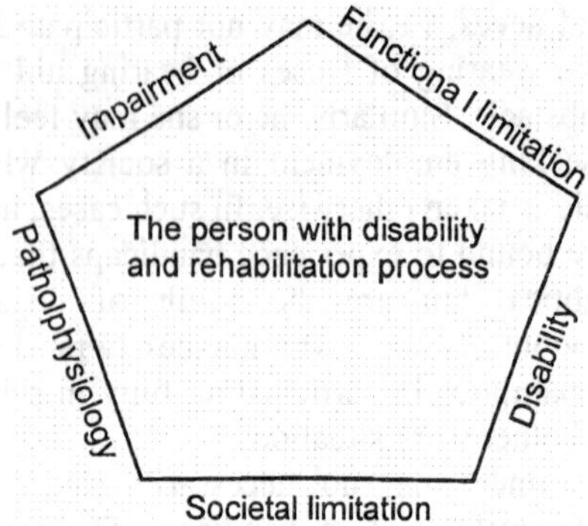

Fig. 4.1: NCMRR Model of Disability

pathophysiology) may manifest as generalized abnormalities in muscle tone and motor control (i.e. the impairment).

(*iii*) The third component in the name of functional limitation emphasizes a specific skill or set of related skills that cannot be executed and are often (but not always) a result of pre-existing impairment.

(*iv*) The fourth component in the name of disability stands for the decrement in function that a person experiences as a consequence of his or her impairments and functional limitations (e.g. dysfunctional gait is a functional limitation that may result in impaired mobility, which is the disability experienced by the person).

(*v*) Finally in the fifth component, the term handicap has been replaced in the NCMRR model by the term societal limitation emphasizing the role of the environment and society in limiting the opportunities for one's growth and development.

In this way, latest trend in the use of these terms clearly indicate to do away with the term handicap. (Since it may work as a stigma and also it is never so consistent as the term disability for it is being situation related). Now a clear-cut hypothesis that usually seems to work is:

Basic biological and psychological disturbances lead to impairment., Impairment resulting into functional limitation leads one to disability and the effects of such acquired disability are experienced through societal limitations.

In view of such conclusion and underlying relationship among the terms impairment, disability and handicap, we may now safely define the term disability in the following words.

Disability refers to the state of a person in which he faces some sort of incapacity or inability to adjust and progress well in his environment on account of one or the other serious impairment brought out by a sort of disturbance or abnormality in the structure and functioning of his body system including psyche.

CHILDREN WITH IMPAIRMENT OR DISABILITIES — CLASSIFICATION, TYPES AND CHARACTERSTICS

Impairments or disabilities suffered on the part of the children in our population may be categorized in various types depending upon the nature of their impairments and sort of inability or incapacity encountered by them in their needed adjustment, education and development. The various types of impairments or disabilities encountered by them in this concern may by generally classified as below:

1. Physical Impairments or Disabilities further classified as: (*i*) Visual impairment or disability, (*ii*) Hearing impairment or disability, (*iii*) Locomotor impairment or disability etc.
2. Mental Impairment or Disabilities such as mental retardation or disability.
3. Learning impairments or Disabilities such as Dyslexia and Dyscalculia
4. Impairments or Disabilities related to emotional disturbance.
5. Mixed type of impairments and disabilities such as multiple impairment or disability.

The presence of one or the other types of impairments or disabilities among the children may turn them quite sufficiently different from the normal or average children of their population.

In their behaviour and functioning they differ a lot with their normal peers in terms of the possession of different abilities or capacities and are thus being named as differently abled children. On account of their differing abilities, they are also characterized with the possession of different or special needs for their learning, adjustment and progress and it is why, these children are also named as children with special needs (CWSN).

These so called differently abled, disabled or children with special needs may be classified and categorized in various types depending upon the nature and type of impairments or disabilities suffered by them in their day to day functioning, learning, adjustment and progress. In this chapter we would be discussing about the characteristics, functional limitations, special educational needs and learning problems including the redressal of a few types of such children in the regular schools inclusive setup.

A. Children with Visual Impairment or Disability

CWSN or disabled children falling in this category are found to suffer from visual impairment or disability.

Visual impairment or Visual disability refers to the state of an individual in which he suffers from the impairment and defects of his eyes to such an extent as to make him feel disabled or handicapped in terms of his visual ability and perception. This handicapness or disability may represent a continuum, ranging from poor and defective vision to no perception of light at all. As a result of such of light variance the children suffering from visual disability of one or the other types are often given different names and classifications like partially sighted, children having low vision, legally blind and totally blind etc. Let us try to have a knowledge and understanding of all these terms indicative of level or degree of one's visual impairment, disability and handicapness in one aspect or the other.

(i) **Partial sightedness:** The visual disability referred to as *partial sightedness* stands for the type of disability in which individuals are found to suffer from some visual problems resulting in their partial perception of the object seen.

(ii) **Low vision Disability:** Visual disability characterized as low *vision* generally refers to a moderate to severe visual impairment, not necessarily limited to distance vision. It applies to all individuals with sight who are unable to read the newspaper at a normal viewing distance, even with the aid of eye classes or contact lenses. The persons suffering with such disability is potentially capable of using vision for executing a task with appropriate assistive device.

(iii) **Legal Blindness:** Visual disability referred to as legal blindness (as defined in Rights of Persons with Disability Bill, 2012) is the characteristic of the individuals having less than 20/200 vision in the better eye after correction or a very limited field of vision (20 degrees at its widest point). Here the visual acuity of 20/200 means that the person can see an object that is normally seen at 200 feet only at a distance of 20 feet. Limited or reduced field of vision means that the individual has tunnel vision with limited peripheral vision.

(iv) **Total Blindness:** The visual disability referred to as total blindness is the characteristic of the persons who have no vision i.e. no perception at all of the objects seen and can learn via Braille or other non-visual media.

In another way, we may classify visual impairments and disabilities as Congenial and Adventitious depending upon the nature of visual impairment (loss of vision) present at birth or occurring after birth (as a result of illness or accident).

Characteristics of Visual Impairments Visible in the Child's Behaviour

The behavioural signs like below may be well visible in the behaviour of the children in the class suffering from one or the other types of visual disabilities.

- Child often complains of eye pain, itchiness, or discomfort
- Constantly reading close to the face
- Attempts to brush away a blur
- Excessive rubbing of eyes
- Constant frowning
- Shutting or covering one eye for visual tasks
- Head-tilt or head-turn when looking at something
- Learning forward to see better
- Excessive blinking
- Undue sensitivity to light
- Excessive imitability during close work
- Stumbling or tripping over objects
- Clumsiness in reading
- Difficulty in reading letters on the blackboard
- Using finger as a line marker while reading

Source: NCERT (2014). *Including Children with Special Needs* — Primary Stage.

B. Hearing Disability

Meaning, Types and Characteristics

Hearing disability refers to the state of the individuals in which they suffer from a wide range of hearing losses (including deafness) making them disabled wholly or partially in utilizing their hearing organs for getting and exchanging information with others. Children affected by hearing disability thus include hard of hearing (benefitted with the use of hearing aids) as well as those who experience a significant loss in hearing even if they use hearing aids.

The hearing losses as such thus affect the abilities of the children to communicate with others. Since communication *i.e.*, exchange of information is the key component of any knowledge getting process and the subsequent adjustment of one's environment, the children suffering from hearing impairment are bound to suffer adversely in terms of their adjustment and educational development. The situation gets worsened depending upon the intensity and severity of the hearing losses. In terms of physiological and medical language the hearing losses are usually classified into the following four types:

1. *Conductive hearing losses* are caused by diseases or obstructions in the outer or middle ear (The condition pathways for the sound to reach the inner ear). Conductive hearing losses usually affect all frequencies of hearing evenly and do not result in severe losses. A person with a conductive hearing loss usually is able to use a hearing aid well or can be helped medically or surgically.

2. *Sensorineural hearing losses* result from damage to the delicate sensory hear cells of the inner ear or the nerves which supply it. These hearing losses can range from mild to profound. They often affect the person's ability to hear certain frequencies more than others. Thus, even with amplification to increase the sound level, a person with a sensorineural hearing loss may perceive distorted sounds, sometimes making the successful use of a hearing aid impossible.

3. *A mix hearing loss* refers to a combination of conductive and sensorineural loss and means that problem occur in both the outer or middle and the inner ear.

4. *A central hearing loss* results from damage or impairment to the nerves of nuclei of the central nervous systems, either in the pathways to the brain or in the brain itself.

Such type of classification of hearing losses and the subsequent distinction among hearing impaired is neither needed nor seems practicable in the field of education for devising ways and means of the adjustment and educational development of the hearing impaired. From this angle therefore it is more useful and practicable to classify the learning losses as slight, mild, moderate, severe or profound, depending upon how well a person can hear the intensities (loudness) of the sound, measured in units called decibels-dB or frequencies (pitch) of the sound, measured in units called hertz-Hz greatly associated with speech. Generally, only children whose hearing loss is severe or profound *i.e.,* greater than 90 decibels (dB) are considered deaf and the remaining ones suffering from slight, mild and moderate hearing losses are termed as hard of hearing.

In this way, we can attempt to classify the hearing impaired children into two broad types: (*i*) deaf, and (*ii*) hard of hearing for the clear purpose of helping them according to the degree of their disability.

Here we must be again clear in our conception that the terms deafness stands for the state or condition that prevents a child from receiving sound in all or most of its forms. In addition he may also be a dumb in case his deafness is by birth.

Consequently, he will be hardly make any profit from the sensory experiences associated with hearing even speech.

Contrarily, a child termed as hard of hearing can generally respond to auditory stimuli including speech and therefore he has the probabilities of making profits from the experiences associated with sense of hearing. Such distinction between these two types of hearing impaired thus can probe a solid base for the planning and structuring of any educational and adjustment scheme for them.

Signs of Possible Hearing Impairments in Children

The signs like below may provide necessary alarm about the presence of possible hearing impairments among the children.

- Child fails to respond to loud sounds
- Child fails to respond to soft sounds
- Child turns his head to localise (locate the direction) the sound only when it is presented on one particular side of the ear *i.e.* either left or right
- Child stops babbling after 6 to 8 months of ages
- Child shows poor or no interest in playing with noise making toys like rattle, bell, etc.
- Child when young (one and half years) fails to start using meaningful words like mummy, daddy, bye-bye etc.
- Child does not understand simple commands like 'wave bye-bye' until and unless speech is accompanied by gestures.
- Child insists on watching your face while you speak (because he/she wants to lip read).
- Child is unable to respond to your call from a distance of 5 ft. to 10 ft.

Source: NCERT (2014), *Including Children with Special Needs*—Primary Stage.

C. Mental Disability or Retardation

Meaning, Types and Characteristics

Mental retardation as a term stands for a special type of psychological disorder associated with the arrest or incomplete development of one's brain beginning usually at birth and leading to a diminution of intellectual powers relative to his chronological age. Actually retardation as a term is frequently used in the subjects Physics and Engineering as antonym to the term acceleration. Here acceleration stands for uniform increase in the velocity of a moving object and retardation for a gradual decrease.

The same sense is conveyed here in the subject Psychology through the term mental retardation. The rate of growth and development of one's intellectual powers gets diminished or arrested. It does not pick the normal speed expected from the children of that very chronological age. Certainly such affected children lag behind and become handicapped in performing expected normal intellectual behaviour. That is why, they are also named as mentally handicapped children. The other common term used for these children is mentally deficient children indicating that these children certainly suffer from a certain type of deficiency or incompleteness in terms of the expected normal intellectual development.

Let us further know about the meaning and nature of the term mental retardation or mental disability through some well-known definitions:

J.D. Page: "*Mental Deficiency or Retardation is a condition of subnormal mental development present at birth or early childhood and characterized mainly by limited intelligence and social inadequacy*". (1976, p. 354).

American Association on Mental Deficiency: "*Mental retardation refers to significantly sub-average intellectual functioning existing concurrently with deficits in adaptive behaviour and manifested during the developmental period.*" (1973, p. 326.).

British Mental Deficiency Act: "*Mental retardation is a condition of arrested or incomplete development of mind existing before the age of 18 years whether arising from inherent causes or induced by disease or injury.*" (1981, pp. 197-198).

A close analysis of the above definitions may reveal the following things about the meaning and characteristics of mental retardation or mental disability.

- Mental retardation is a condition or state of mind.
- It is not a disease or illness of the mind.
- It is related to the subnormal development of the mind or brain.
- It is also related to one's inadequate adjustment with the environment.
- The deficiency may be observed at birth or in early childhood.
- Both the inherent and external factors may cause mental retardation.

Equipped with the above meaning and characteristics of mental retardation we may now be able to evolve a definition of the term mentally retarded or mentally disabled children in the following way:

Mentally Retarded or disabled children are those children who suffer from the retarded subnormal or deficient growth and development of their brain affecting their intellectual capacities to the extent that they feel handicapped in their adaptation to the environment and thus require special care and provision for their welfare and development of their capacities.

Types of Mentally Retarded or Disabled Children

There have been many attempts to devise certain ways and means for classifying the mentally retarded into some definite types according to the degree of the seriousness of their mental deficiency or retardation. Two of such attempts based on I.Q. and adaptive behaviour are quite popular. Let us try to discuss these attempts now.

Classification based on Intelligence Tests

The concept of I.Q. and scores on intelligence tests have been found useful in labelling the individual as gifted, average (normal) or subnormal (retarded). Terman, using Stanford Binet Scale, tried to label the individual with I.Q. between 90 and 100 as normal or average and persons with I.Q. below 90 as below average or subnormal. The sub-normal were further categorized as under:

Category	*Range of I.Q.*
Idiots	below 25
Imbeciles	from 25 to 50
Morons	from 51 to 75
Border line and the dull	from 76 to 90

The individuals falling into the above categories (except a few border line cases as they have the equal chances of drifting towards subnormal and normal categories) and labelled as idiot, imbecile, moron and dull are known as mentally retarded or mentally handicapped.

But this classification based on I.Q. is quite arbitrary and we can find differences of opinion regarding the range of I.Q. and its corresponding category. But one thing is certain that all mentally retarded or mentally handicapped children possess sub-normal intellectual capacities *i.e.*, they are basically less capable of intelligent behaviour than normal children.

Diagnosis of such sub-normal intellectual capacities is not a simple task. Intelligence tests, alone do not suffice. Also latest researches in the field of sub-normality have raised doubts about the creditability of I.Q. scores. It was felt that a certain level of I.Q. score does not by itself designate an individual a mental retarded. He must also be unable to adapt to the natural and social demands of the environment. Consequently, the importance of assessment of adaptive behaviour in the identification and demarcation of the level of mental sub-normality has been realised.

Adaptive Behaviour as a Means of Classification

This criterion describes one's adaptive behaviour expected of his age and cultural group in two ways for the required assessment.

- the degree to which the individual is able to function and maintain himself independently, and
- the degree to which he meets satisfactorily the culturally imposed demands of personal and social responsibility.

Attempts have been made to devise measures for the assessment of deficiency in adaptive behaviour through Vineland Social Maturity Scale, Adaptive Behaviour Scale (AAMD) and Maxfield Buck Holz Social Maturity Scale.

The consideration of deficiency in adaptive behaviour along with the very low scores on an intelligence test resulted in the development of an altogether new classification of sub-normality. The terms moron, imbecile, or idiot are now completely avoided for determining the level of retardation. The new terminology in terms of obtained I.Q. on different tests scale is represented below:

Table 4.1: Levels of Mental Retardation

Level of Retardation	*Intelligence Quotient*	
	Stanford Binet	*Wechsler scales*
Profound	Under 20	Under 25
Severe	20-35	25-39
Moderate	36-51	40-54
Mild	52-67	55-69

In view of their typical sub-normal intelligence and deficient adaptive behaviour these categories are described below:

1. *Mild Retardation*

A majority of approximately eight-five per cent of the retarded belongs to this category. They are found to possess the following main characteristics:

- In adult life, these individuals attain intellectual levels comparable to that of the average ten years old child. Their social adjustment may be compared with that of the adolescent. Here too they lack the innovative and vigorous nature of normal adolescents.
- They show signs of delayed development early in life and learn to walk, talk, feed and toilet themselves an year later than the average. They may be identified in schools as slow learners and frequently required to repeat early grades. Speech disturbances are common among them.
- In comparison with normal individuals, the mildly retarded exhibit immature behaviour, have poor control over their impulses, lack judgement and fail to anticipate the consequence of their actions. Their sexual behaviour and adjustment, in spite of the normal sexual development and fertility, is unpredictable and leads to a variety of problems and difficulties.
- The mildly retarded individuals generally do not show any organic pathology and require little supervision.
- They are considered to be educable. With early diagnosis, parental assistance and aid of special classes, they can be expected to reach a reasonable degree of educational achievement and to make an adequate social and economic adjustment in the community.

2. *Moderate Mental Retardation*

About 10 per cent of the total mentally retarded belong to this category. Their main characteristics may be summarized as below:

- In adult life they attain intellectual level similar to that of the average six year old child.
- Physically they appear clumsy, suffer from motor in co-ordination and present an affable, dull and somewhat vacuous personality.
- As a result of their inadequate development and deficient capacities and abilities they are regarded as 'trainable' instead of being 'educable' like the mildly retarded.
- From early infancy or childhood they show signs of retardation in almost all areas of development and though they manage to speak, their rate of learning is too slow. They are unable to do any work that requires initiative, originality, abstract thinking, memory or consistent attention and cannot be expected to acquire the basic skills of reading and writing.

However, with early diagnosis, parental help and adequate training and support, most of the moderately retarded can achieve considerable independence in all spheres of life. Nevertheless, they require constant supervision and support and need institutionalization depending on their general level of adaptive behaviour.

3. *Severe Mental Retardation*

Nearly 3.5 per cent of the total retarded individuals — mostly children and adolescents belong to this category. Their main characteristics may be summarized as below:

- They never attain an intellectual level greater than that of the average four year old child.
- The mortality rate due to high susceptibility to disease is quite high among these individuals.
- They are grossly retarded in development from birth or infancy onward and show severe motor and speech retardation. Sensory defects and motor handicaps are common.
- The majority of them display relatively little interest in their surroundings and many of them never master even the necessary skills and functions like feeding and dressing themselves, or bladder and bowel control.
- The severe mental retardants are neither 'educable' nor 'trainable' and the majority of them remain dependent on others throughout their lives. They need care and supervision of others with a great need for institutionalization.
- They may profit with proper care, timely treatment and specialized training and managing their own physical well-being and doing manual labour.

4. *Profound Mental Retardation*

This group makes 1.5 per cent of the total mentally retarded population. It is characterized by the most severe symptoms of mental retardation as given below:

- The individual belonging to this category never attain in adult life — an intellectual level greater than that of the average two year old child.
- They are severely deficient both in their intellectual capacities and adaptive behaviour. The symptoms associated with them are retarded growth, physical deformities, pathology of the central nervous system, mutism, severe speech disturbances, motor in co-ordination, deafness and convulsive seizures. They are unable to protect themselves against common dangers and are unable to manage their own affairs and satisfy their physical needs.
- Their life span, as a result of their low resistance, is too short.
- Such individuals are completely dependent on others and need the care and supervision given to an infant.
- Essentially, they need to be institutionalized as their condition

deteriorates on account of the biased attitude of the parents and stressfull demands of their environment.

Locomotor Disability

Meaning and Nature

This type of disability involves locomotor disorders *i.e.* the difficulties and problems associated with locomotion — movements of the self and objects. Defining the term locomotor disability, Rights of Persons with Disabilities Bill, 2012 has remarked.

Locomotor disability refers to a person's inability to execute distinctive activities associated with movement of self and objects, resulting from affliction of musculoskeletal and/or nervous system.

Looking into this definition may clearly aware us that locomotor disability is caused

(*i*) on account of one or other types of musculoskeletal disorders or deformities (such as defects and deformity of the bones, muscles or joints or even missing or malfunctioning of certain limbs of the body) as well as

(*ii*) restrictions imposed on the movability due to some type of neurological disturbance or disorders suffered by the individual.

However, irrespective of the causes underlying the impairment the affected person experiences a lot of disability, incapacity and inconvenience in the tasks related to the movements of his body and it is why the locomotor disability is infact a physical functionability disability in its nature and consequences.

Functional Limitations Caused by Locomotor Disorders

The physiological and functional problems suffered by the affected children on account of the locomotor disorders are complex and diverse and their disabilities may be temporary, intermittent, chronic, progressive or terminal and thus may differ from individual to individual. However, in general, the following types of functional limitations may be observed in the population of the children affected with locomotor disorders.

(*i*) Poor muscle control

(*ii*) weakness and fatigue

(*iii*) difficulty in walking, talking, seeing, speaking, sensing or grasping (due to pain or weakness)

(*iv*) difficulty in reading things

(*v*) difficulty in doing complex or compound manipulations (push or turn)

(*vi*) inability to use the limbs.

(*vii*) difficulty or total inability with regard to twisting motion

(*viii*) inability in operating even well-designed products directly without assistive devices (including mobility aids like crutches, wheelchair, communication aids like single switch based artificial voice, etc.)

(*ix*) paralysis (total lack of muscular control in part or most of the body)

(*x*) interference with control like problems in accuracy of motor programming and co-ordination, uncontrolled and purposeless motion, tense and contracted muscles, etc.
(*xi*) joint movement limitation (either mechanical or due to pain)
(*xii*) difficulties and inabilities faced in motor functioning due to smallness of limbs, missing limbs or abnormal trunk size.

D. Children with Learning Impairment or Disability

CWSN or disabled children falling in this category are found to suffer from serious learning impairments, difficulties or disabilities. Now question may here arise what are these learning difficulties or disabilities. In fact learning difficulties or disabilities are nothing but a sort of handicap or helplessness that can be felt by the sufferer in terms of his or her academic performance (learning or understanding something) in the same way as experienced by a mentally disabled in terms of his mental functioning or by a physically handicapped or disabled in terms of his physical functioning. Interpreting in this way a learning disabled child suffers with the inconveniences and problems in the learning areas in the same way as experienced by a mentally handicapped in mental or cognitive areas, or by a physically handicapped in the physical and motor areas or even by a socially or emotionally handicapped in the social and emotional areas.

In the matter of defining the term learning disability the famous author S.A. Kirk (1971), has remarked as below:

> "*The term learning difficulties or disability is not meant to be used for children with minor or temporary difficulties in learning but with a severe discrepancy between ability and achievement in educational performance and such several discrepancy described as learning disabilities with significant learning problems that cannot be explained by mental retardation, sensory, impairment, emotional disturbance or lack of opportunity to learn.*"

As observed thus learning disability refers to a state or condition of a child in which he experiences a lot of obstacles and difficulties in the path of his learning. Gradually the learning problem becomes so acute as to cause severely impaired learning inefficiency in one or the other cognitive areas. It leads to a distinctive gap between one's potential and actual educational achievement which require special care, attention and remedial measures and when it happens the learner is labelled as learning disabled.

Nature and Characteristics of Learning Disabled

Researches in the fields of education and psychology have brought into notice a number of significant behavioural and personality characteristics as well as general outcomes of the nature and characteristics of the learning disabled children. Let us mention a few important ones.

1. Learning disabled children essentially suffer from serious learning problems or disorders for a number of reasons.
2. Their problems and disorders are usually manifested by significant difficulties in the acquisition and use of language (listening, speaking, reading, writing etc.), reasoning or mathematical ability or of social skills.
3. They may exhibit symptoms of hyperactivity and impulsivity.
4. Most of them may suffer from emotional problems and demonstrate signs of anxiety, moodiness or ups and downs in their behaviour.
5. Their learning disability is not apparent in the physical appearance or not demonstrable through then I.Q. Scores. They may have robust body, good vision, sound ears, and normal intelligence.
6. They essentially suffer from severely impaired learning inefficiency, or a handicap, which is just as real as crippled leg.
7. All of them essentially exhibit a significant educational discrepancy *i.e.* a wide gap between then learning potential and actual educational achievement.
8. Some of them may demonstrate equivocal neurological signs and EEG irregularities.
9. They may exhibit disorders of memory, thinking, attention general coordination, perception and motor functioning, etc.
10. The main problem for all these children lies in their observable deficiency in learning and mastering academic tasks. They are handicapped in learning and acquisition in the same way as physically and mentally handicapped are, in physical and mental performance.
11. They usually exhibit the following learning characteristics responsible for their learning impairment (*i*) lack of motivation, (*ii*) inattention, (*iii*) inability to generalize, and (*iv*) lack of adequate ability in problem solving, information processing and thinking skills, etc.
12. Their learning impairment is so severe that they essentially require special attention, care and remedial programmes for the rectification of their learning problems and disabilities.

Types of Learning Disabilities

Learning disabilities in view of their nature and characteristics may be referred to such disabilities and incapacities of the learners that may make them handicapped or face a lot of difficulties in learning one or the other things related to some specific areas of their learning. It is also be noted clearly here that the difficulties, inabilities and incapacities associated with the term learning disabilities are specifically and predominantly cognitive in nature rather than conative or affective as experienced in the case of physically disabled or emotionally disturbed children. Such learning difficulties may make the task of learning a quite difficult and challenging for a suffering child.

In such a sense, it is quite customary to classify or view learning disabilities of the learners (students in the classroom situations) in their two district forms popularly known as

(*i*) Dyslexia (difficulty in language learning)
(*ii*) Dyscalculia (difficulty in mathematics learning)

Most of the children who are designated as learning disabled are found to suffer from these two types of learning disabilities. Children suffering from these disabilities needs to be looked after well for their adequate adjustment and education in the ongoing school setup. What are these learning disabilities and how the children suffering from such disabilities may be helped in terms of the needed adjustment and quality education, should thus be properly known by the teachers entrusted with the task of educating them. In the pages to follow, thus we would be focussing our attention on the different issues and aspects of these two types of learning disabilities.

DYSLEXIA

Meaning and Definition

Etymologically, the word dyslexia is composed to dys and lexia. 'Dys' stands for a type of disorder or disturbance and the Greek word lexia originated from Lexis stands for 'pertaining to word'. In this sense the word "dyslexia" in its word meaning stands for a type of disorder or disturbance related to word or language written or spoken (Webster's seventh New Collegiate Dictionary, 1969: 259).

In this way, Dyslexia may represent a particular type of learning difficulty or disability that may create a big problem for a developing child in making use of the words or language in his study or day to day communication and adjustment.

In its broader aspect, Dyslexia causes difficulty in the acquisition of necessary language skills pertaining to reading, writing, listening and speaking of a language on the part of a developing child. Taking note of such outcomes of the disorder Dyslexia, World Federation of Neurologists has termed dyslexia as *"a disorder in children who, despite conventional classroom experience, fail to attain the language skills of reading, writing and spelling commensurate with their intellectual abilities."*

Classification and Types of Dyslexia

- *Visual Dyslexia:* It is characterized by number and letter reversals (writing 9 for 7, *p* for *q* or vice versa) and the inability to write symbols in the correct sequence.
- *Auditory Dyslexia:* Here one experiences difficulty in comprehending the sounds of letters or sentences on account of perceiving them jumbled or not heard correctly.

- *Dysgraphic or Kinaesthetic Dyslexia:* It is concerned with the difficulty faced by the child in holding and controlling a pen or pencil and thus causing his disability in terms of writing something on the paper and board.

DYSCALCULIA

Meaning and Definition

The word "dyscalculia" having its origin in Greek and Latin stands for "*counting or calculating badly*" as its prefix "dys" meaning "*badly*" has been derived from Greek and "calculia" derived from the latin means "*to count, calculate or compute*". In this way etymologically, the term dyscalculia stands for a state or condition that adversely affects one's ability to perform calculation or computation in mathematics. Dyscalculia is, therefore, fundamentally different from dyslexia. Whereas in dyslexia, a learner is found to experience difficulty and disability in dealing with words, in dyscalculia he faces similar difficulty and disability relating to numbers. Elaborating this concept, The Department for Education and Skills, United Kingdom (1999) defines dyscalculia as:

> "*A condition that affects the ability to acquire arithmetical skills. Dyscalculia learners may have difficulty understanding simple number concepts, lack an intuitive grasp of numbers and have problems learning number facts and procedures. Even if they produce a correct answer or use a correct method, they may do so mechanically and without confidence.*"

However, the further researches in the field of dyscalculia have suggested that there may be several subsets of mathematical difficulties other than the number based difficulties that may be experienced by the dyscalculia learners. These may include procedural and sequencing difficulties, problem solving, understanding basic concepts in the areas other than arithmetic like algebra, geometry, trigonometry and statistics. In this way, dyscalculia may prove a great handicap and obstacle to the dyscalculia learners not only in terms of numeracy and calculations in arithmetic but also in learning essentials pertaining to all aspects and areas belonging to the subject mathematics. It is responsible for creating disinterest, fear and phobia towards mathematics, instilling in them a feeling of utter helplessness, lack of confidence and raising their level of anxiety for engaging in any mathematical learning or performing a task involving mathematical abilities.

As a result of such adverse impact and ill influences conveyed through the term dyscalculia, it can be properly defined as a particular type of learning disability that is responsible for adversely affecting one's learning and performance in the subject mathematics demonstrable through the early symptoms like below.

- inability to write numerals and mathematical symbols correctly
- difficulty in recalling the meaning of the symbols

- difficulty in counting and performing mathematical calculations and computation work.
- difficulty in placing basic facts into long term memory and remembering and accessing information.
- difficulty in carrying out basic arithmetical operations *e.g.* addition, subtraction, multiplication and division.
- difficulty in following the proper steps and reasoning for the solution of mathematical problems, particularly the word problems.
- difficulty in acquiring proper understanding of the basic mathematical concepts like place value, directed numbers, directions and dimensions, decimals, fractions and percentages, measuring units and time sense etc.

SPECIAL NEEDS OF CHILDREN WITH DISABILITIES

The disabilities of the children according to their nature and different types are deeply associated in one way or the other with the need of the satisfaction of some of their special needs. These needs felt on the part of the children with disabilities, in general, may be categorized as below.

1. Need for the awareness of one's disability/disabilities

What is different or special about a disabled child should come out, as early as possible. He is different, it should be known to others and he himself be get acquainted with his disability in a quite clear terms. In other words, disabled children need an early detection, diagnosis, assessment and classification of their disabilities. Any delay in meeting out such need of the disabled children may invite a number of complications and problems for them in their adjustment to the self and environment. As a result they may be mistakenly identified, misunderstood and their deviant behaviour on account of disability may be taken as deliberately problematic and indisciplinary. For example, a child who is hard of hearing, his inability of rightly responding to a question of the teacher (on account of his inability to hear) may be taken otherwise by the teacher. Therefore, the prime necessity and a major need of a disabled child lies in the demand that his disability, its nature, cause and degree should be clearly identified, assessed, classified and labeled for helping him and others in the subsequent task of providing needed special service to him.

2. Need for coping with one's disability

The disabled children need to be helped in the process of coping with their disability. The disabled children who deviate negatively may feel the need and necessity of overcoming their deficiencies or may need assistance and help for minimizing or eliminating the negative effects of their impairments or disabilities. For example, a child not able to read and write properly on account of his visual disability may feel a strong need of being helped through medical, physical or educational measures to become able to read and write properly. The same may be true with the children suffering from other disabilities like learning disabilities, hearing impairments, mental retardation, emotional disturbances, etc. These children may certainly require the measure and means either to get rid of these deficiencies or try to learn the ways and means of coping with them for seeking harmony with the self and the environment.

3. Need for being accepted with their disability

The disabled children are quite different from others. It is an admitted fact that the differences or deviations from the norms on the negative side are seldom taken easily by others. The disability therefore, is bound to invite so many resistance and negative reactions from the peers, teachers and even from the parents. It is why, there lies an essential need for the disabled children for being accepted by others in their true perspectives of deficits, and deficiencies related to growth and development of their personality attributes.

4. Need for getting appropriate education

Disabled children are in great requirement of some appropriate educational measures for helping them in meeting out their exceptionalities and to cope with their deficits or extraordinary abilities. It is therefore essential for having an appropriate way to organize adequate special education services for the disabled children.

5. Need for being independent in life functioning

Disabled children on account of their disabilities demand some special measures for meeting out the needs of their being independent and self supportive in carrying out their one or the other life functioning activities. It equally applies to all the disabled children who suffer from one or the other deficits, deficiencies and disabilities in terms of their seeing, listening, sitting, walking, learning or functioning in their daily lives or world of work. All types of disabled children need to learn the art of living for functioning properly in their day to day social and emotional life, as well as earning their livelihood and becoming economically self sufficient members of their community and the country.

6. Need for the satisfaction of special learning capacities

Disabled children deviate too much from their non-disabled peers with regard to their capacities, nature and requirements of learning. Disabled children make up a huge group of children like learning disabled, mentally retarded, sensory, communicationally and emotionally deficient who may have difficulty learning in one way or the other. The redressal of such specific needs of these diversified groups of disabled children thus may become an urgent necessity of any programme and provision for chalking out special measures for them.

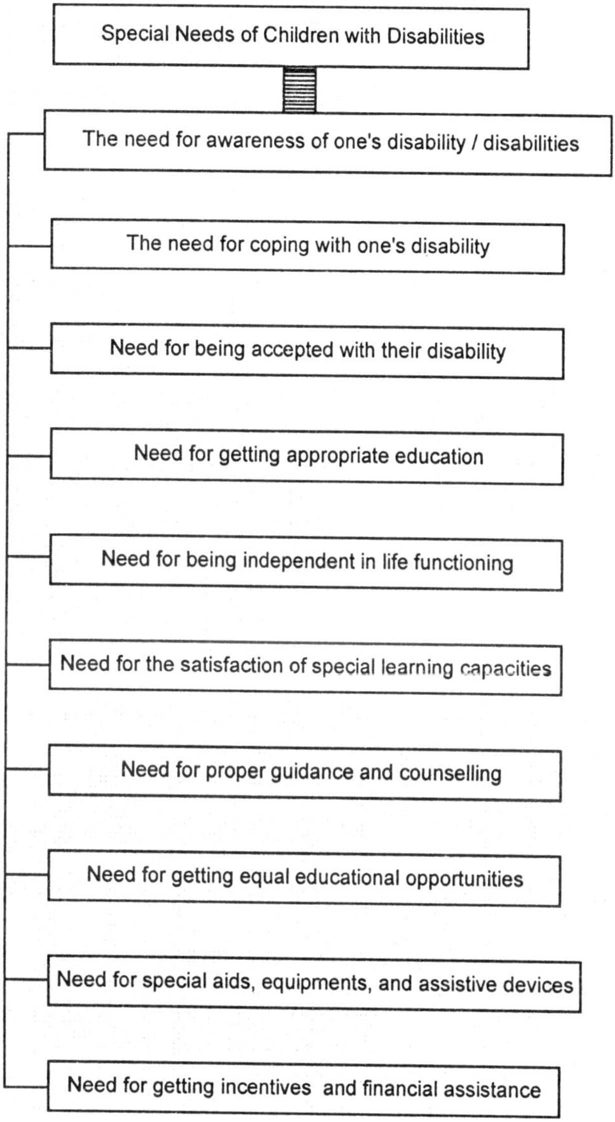

Fig. 4.2: Special Needs of Children with Disabilities

7. Need for proper guidance and counselling

Disabled children needs timely and proper guidance and counselling for dealing with the situation and consequences resulted through their disabilities. They may become victim of so many social, emotional, physical, mental and moral problem on account of their extreme deviations from the normal course and pattern of life. The visually or aurally impaired thus may be guided to make use of assistive devices for being capable of using their residual sense of sight or hearing. An emotionally disturbed child may be advised to take control of his emotions and channelize his emotional energy in some other useful ways.

8. Need for getting equal educational opportunities

Disabled children need, equal educational opportunities for their adequate, adjustment and progress in their life irrespective of their disabilities deficiencies or limitations with respect to one or the other abilities. In their life, they have to remain along with the non-disabled human beings, therefore, they must have their education along with their non-disabled peers in the normal schools in the integrated settings with some minor adjustments for their proper education and adjustment.

9. Need for special aids, equipments and assistive devices

Disabled children need special assistance for meeting out their learning developmental and adjustment needs. They, therefore, always feel the need of being helped through some or other special learning material, aids, and equipments, assistive technology and devices in the course of their being brought up and receiving education. It helps them in meeting out their special needs, overcoming their deficiencies and getting due gains from the regular and special education programmes. For example, the hearing impaired may need hearing aids, speech trainer and visual materials etc., the learning disabled may need alternate learning material, blind children may require Braille system and the children with low vision may need magnifiers and large print materials while the orthopedic impaired may require crutches and other supporting material.

10. Need for getting incentives and financial assistance

The disabled children require incentives and financial assistance for coping up with their disabilities, needs and problem. In many cases, the deficits and deficiencies are too much inproportionate for their parents and family in terms of spending money on the physical treatment, medical expenses and purchasing of assistive devices. In such cases help from the NGO and other community sources as well as from the government agencies is needed for meeting the special requirements of the disabled. Moreover, there is requirement of providing due incentives and financial assistance in terms of scholarships, free learning material, free conveyance, free day meal etc. for sustaining the enrolment of the disabled children in the special schools or regular schools.

SPECIAL EDUCATIONAL NEEDS AND LEARNING PROBLEMS OF THE DIFFERENT TYPES OF DISABLED CHILDREN AND THEIR REDRESSAL

Upto so far above we have discussed about the common needs of all types of disabled children in relation of their adjustment and education. However the nature of the special needs felt by the disabled, differs in reference to their learning in an inclusive setup. It varies according to the nature of the impairments and disabilities suffered by them in their living and learning environments. Let us try to look into the nature of their special needs in this respect.

A. Hearing Impaired or Disabled

The special needs felt by the hearing impaired vary according to the degree of the severity of their hearing impairment. In fact in this way, it seems to be an individual phenomenon. However, in practical sense, we can analyze it on two fronts *i.e.* taking cognizance of the learning needs felt for the adjustment and education on the part of (*a*) deaf children and (*b*) hard of hearing.

The Special Learning Needs of the Deaf Children and their Redressal

Deaf children are totally unable to have oral communication. The use of oral means *i.e.* the use of sense of hearing in their learning and training of any kind does not bear any fruit. Moreover they may experience a lot of difficulty in their adjustment, and living in their social environment and inclusive setup of the school. Their problems becomes more acute when their learning impairment is accompanied with dumbness. In such cases, they even can't call others for their security and help at the time of danger and difficulties. It is why in an inclusive setup there arises urgent need of teaching and training them in one or the other types of life saving skills, ways and means of adjustment and methods and modes of learning in the manner outlined below.

1. Visual communication modes such as sign language, finger spelling and cued speech (as you must have seen in the news broadcast on the television for hearing impaired) should be adopted for communication with the deaf children. These children should be made to learn and communicate in these communication mode for their needed adjustment and education.

2. A great pain should be taken for the language development of these children with the help of training received in visual communication as well as utilisation of other senses (sense of sight, smell, touch and taste). The special provision is therefore made in their curriculum for making them to learn vocabulary, grammar, word order, idiomatic expressions, and other aspects of verbal communication.

3. Their curricular and co-curricular experiences should be so organised as to impart them all the necessary education for the adjustment and education with the help of the utilisation of all other senses besides the hearing. They may thus be allowed and encouraged to see, touch, taste, smell and work out the things and experiences by themselves for gaining the desired learning experiences.

4. The deaf children are seen to be specifically endowed with the increased abilities and capacities in terms of their power of sight, smelling,

touching, tasting and physically as well as mentally working capacity etc. as a matter of compensation for their disability in hearing. Therefore, special provisions in the form of curricular and co-curricular experiences should always be made to the deaf children for developing their inner abilities to make them good artists, cartoonist, writers, fashion designers, architects, scientists, and craftsmen, etc.

5. Vocational training and education is also made a compulsory part of their curricular programmes in these schools for making them able to learn the means of their livelihood and becoming self reliant in the future life.

6. The developed means of ICT and computer based technology should also be utilized for meeting the learning and adjustment needs of the deaf and dumb children. The facilities regarding text telephone (enabling persons to type phone messages over the telephone), having e-mail messages and web text material should be well utilized for meeting the learning and adjustment needs of these children.

The Special Learning Needs of the Hard of Hearing and their Redressal

The special needs of the hard of learning (those who can benefit from their residual sense of learning) are quite different than those of their deaf and dumb peers. The measures like below may prove quite helpful in meeting their adjustment and learning needs.

1. The first and foremost task in the education and adjustment of the hard of hearing is to help them to acquire specific bearable hearing aid (selected according to the degree of hearing loss) and make them habitual in its proper use and handling. The early bearing of such hearing aid may prove quite advantageous, to some of the hearing impaired as it may bring desirable improvement in their hearing functioning.

2. Care should be taken in their brought up and schooling as not to make them feel small or inferior on account of their hearing impairment. They should never be ridiculed, made a matter of amusement or sympathy or ignored and hated. Contrarily, they should always be treated in a normal way like other normal children for helping them not to become unnecessarily conscious of their disability.

3. Teachers and audiologists both should try to work together to teach the child to use his or her residual hearing to the maximum extent possible for the task of adjustment and educational progress.

4. These children as well as the parents and teachers should be trained in the utilization of proper means of communication in the task of adjustment and education of these children. The oral or manual means of communication or a combination of the two can be utilised with these children. Oral communication includes speech, reading and the use of residual hearing. Manual communication involves signs and finger spelling. Total communication as a method of instruction may thus by a combination of the oral method plus signs and finger spelling,

5. The hard of hearing may be trained and made habitual to listen the sound of low intensity and frequency (by keeping the hearing aids at the time of training) with the help of the services of audio-aids like radio, tape recorder, VCR, television and computer assisted multimedia presentation etc.

6. The use of television, video recording and computer assisted multi-media presentation as well as the sincere efforts of the teachers, parents and instructors may help the hard of hearing not only to get the desired learning experiences and instructional material like the normal children but also to make them trained in making maximum use of their residual hearing in close combination with the learning of the art of lips reading and language of the body movements, gestures and postures.

7. The hard of hearing usually remains backward in terms of proper language development specifically in the areas related to communication of speech. The specific efforts should need to be made for the proper development of the languages. For example some of them are unable to maintain a proper language level of the loudness or pitch of their voice in their communication. It happens because on account of their hearing impairment they have no idea about the proper level of the loudness or pitch in a communication at a given situation or time. Here they should be helped and trained for communicating properly with the proper intonation, intensity and frequency, pronunciation etc. specifically with the use of modern aids and equipments.

8. In the case of hearing impairments of psychogenic origin, the services of qualified therapists; counsellors and psychologists may be taken for providing necessary assistance to the affected children for getting rid of the maladaptive behaviour and symptoms of hearing impairment.

9. Help of the one or the other suitable special educational services and measures like below may also be taken for helping the hearing impaired in their proper adjustment and educational development.

(*i*) favourable seating in the class and other learning situations (front bench and near to the teacher).

(*ii*) taking regular help of blackboard writing, sketching, charts, maps and other visual presentation along with the oral communication.

(*iii*) using captioned films/videos etc. in the instructional process.

(*iv*) regular speech, language and auditory training from a specialist services of an interpreter for those students who use manual communication.

(*v*) use of amplification systems.

(*vi*) assistance of a note-maker, who takes note for the hearing impaired, so that the impaired child can be fully benefited from instruction.

(*vii*) training facilities for the parents, teachers and peers in alternative communication methods such as sign language, speech reading, body language, etc.

(*viii*) appropriate counselling and therapeutic measures for the proper adjustment of the hearing impaired to the socio-psychological environment.

(*ix*) use of the modern helpful devices available to hearing impaired like text telephones, computer assisted or managed instructions and multi-media presentation etc.

B. Visually Impaired and Disabled

The special needs felt for their adjustment and education in the case of usually impaired children differs from individual to individual depending upon the degree of severity of their visual impairment. However, for understanding about their training and learning requirements and helping them in their adjustment and education, it remains useful to divide them in two major categories: (*i*) Totally blind or nearly so blind children, (*ii*) Low vision and partially blind children. Let us see the types of special learning needs felt by these children for their adjustment and education in their living and inclusive setup of the school along with the possible need redressal.

The Special Learning needs of the Blind Children and their Redressal

1. The blind children need to be trained for becoming independent in terms of carrying out their day to day activities and having, necessary movements related to their social environment and work situations. With the use of stick and their sense of hearing and touch they should be specially trained in their physical movements so much so as to across the busy road as much independently as possible.

2. They need to be trained to carry out the different types of co-curricular activities with the help of special programmes and equipments used in the inclusive setup of the schools. As a result, they should be made to learn many things regarding physical education activities, sports and games, debates and declamation contests, literary activities like poem recitation, dramatisation and acting, music and dancing, working with clay and plasticine, etc.

3. The blind children have special attitude for music, hearing and listening, touching and smell sensational activities. Therefore, much attention should be paid to train and provide curricular and co-curricular experiences to the blind children in the activities related to these sensory experiences.

4. The blind children need to be properly trained in craft activities and vocational works of varying nature for becoming economically independent and usefully employed in the government, and privately managed establishments or even becoming self-employed to earn their livelihood. As a result they may be seen to carry out simple organisational activities like running of telephone system and STD both but also to operate delicate machines and computer working.

The Special Learning Needs of Partially Blind Children and their Redressal

1. The first and most important need of the these children is to help and train them in using their corrective measures like spectacles, eye glasses in a proper safe way and also become habitual in their use with ease and convenience.

2. The second important need of these children is to teach and train them for making wise use of their residual vision with care in the minimum way as possible. Consequently they should never be loaded with unnecessary reading and writing work. Similarly delicate artistic work, geometrical construction, drawing and painting, needle work, minute observation work etc. should be altogether avoided with such students.

3. In terms of their learning these children also need proper modification in the class room and work situations such as need for allotting seats in the front line of the teaching-learning situations and adequate arrangement for lighting etc.

4. In addition these children also need to adopt the measures like below for their proper education and adjustment in an inclusive classroom setup.

(*i*) Paying individual attention for removing their difficulties with regard to their perception of the instructional material written on the black-board, charts, maps, etc.

(*ii*) Taking precaution to speak out the things written on the black-board and other visual aids.

(*iii*) Making much use of the material and devices needing senses other than the vision etc. making use of audio cassettes, radio broad-casting, tape recorder, etc.

(*iv*) Equipping them with the extra vision equipments like hand lens, magnifying glass, etc.

(*v*) Provision of having bold lettered books in the library for the use of these children.

(*vi*) Taking other helpful measures for making the things perceived depending upon their disability e.g. a colour blind or any such perception impaired child may be told about the facts with other ways.

C. Special Needs Of Children Suffering from Orthopaedical Impairment or Locomotor Disabilities and Redressal

The learning needs of the children suffering from orthopaedical impairment or locomotor disabilities are no different from their normal peers since their sense of vision, hearing and mental functioning are not affected with their locomotor impairments or disabilities. The only difference lies in their inability to exercise proper locomotor functioning in their movements restricting the use of their motor organs for engaging into motor activities related to reading, writing and doing practical work, etc. It is here they need special care and training in teams of their proper adjustment and education in inclusive setup of the school. Let us try to analyse some of such learning and adjustment needs of these children along with the possible redressal measures.

1. The prime need of the orthopaedically handicapped is to make them self reliant in terms of the disability and handicapness felt by them in managing their day to day affairs. The essential training for this purpose must be made an integral component of their education. In cases when the help of additional aids and equipments for their proper movements and activities are needed, they should be helped in their acquiring and adapting to their use.

2. They need to have all opportunities through curricular and co-curricular experiences for their proper academic growth and balanced personality development much on the same lines and the way as provided to their normal peers. At no time we must make them feel that they are different or in any way inferior to the normal children in the matter of learning and acquiring curricular facts.

3. The awareness of the self, the acquaintance with the abilities and disabilities is very much essential for any individual for his proper progress. Therefore, there is no harm if the impaired may know the hard facts of their disability and handicapness. However, the main thing is that they should not be allowed to develop any complexes, anxiety and frustrations on account of such handicapness. On the contrary, they should be made to learn to make their life more adaptable, enjoyable and optimistic by using suitable adaptive modes including social maturation, interactive and communication skills.

4. The vocational training and learning of such experiences as to make them economically self-reliant, self-employed or getting suitable employment must be made an integral part of their educational programme.

5. They must be given such concrete experience, knowledge and skills that may successfully equip them for their better adjustment in their future life activities and socio-psycho-physical environment. These experiences may be given through various co-curricular activities and other community and social participation processes.

6. Nature has every compensation for the disabilities and handicapeness and limitations felt by the impaired children in one area by rewarding them to have necessary abilities, interests and aptitudes for excelling them in another areas and venues of life. As a teacher and parents, we must be consciously and deliberately find out the areas and avenues where an individual impaired child may excel with a little motivation, training and educational efforts.

7. These children also need to have adaptation and modifications in the ways of their teaching and training well in tune with the nature of their orthopedical or locomotor impairment *e.g.*

(*i*) The children who face difficulties in writing must be assigned little or no written assignments. The provision of oral tests in stead of written should also be made for them. In some cases where the need arises they should be given more time for completing their assignments or answering the questions.

(*ii*) They need to be provided seating arrangement *i.e.* table, chair and other working seats in the class, laboratory and workshop in tune with the nature of their deformities.

D. Special Needs of Children Suffering from Learning Disabilities Like Dyslexia and Dyscalculia and Their Redressal

The special needs related to learning and adjustment of these two types disabled children in the inclusive setup are centered around their typical learning difficulties arising in the area of language and mathematics. Children suffering from dyslexia are found to exhibit significant problems in terms of language acquisition *i.e.* learning of language skills like reading, writing, listening, and speaking and thus exhibit an urgent special need of being helped in the development of these language skills. The dyscalculia children on the other hand, have significant problems related to the learning of mathematical concepts and their applications and thus are found to exhibit a strong demand for being helped in getting rid of these learning difficulties.

In both these cases of meeting the learning needs of the suffering children, redressal is clearly based on the adoption of suitable ways and means on the part of teachers to help the children in the proper acquisition and development of the needed concepts and skills related to language and mathematics at various levels of their age and mental development.

In brief the dyslexia and dyscalculia children can be helped in the ways summarized as below:

1. Reading difficulties: Children can be helped by:

(*i*) providing phonetic guidance and drill.

(*ii*) providing model reading and ask students to copy or imitate.

(*iii*) taking the help of audio-visual aids, stories narration, etc. or getting away with the difficulty to comprehend the text material.

(*iv*) adopting the strategies like peer tutoring, highlighting texts, passages key words or concepts, etc.

2. Writing difficulty

(*i*) Provide sufficient drill and practice for the proper figuring of letters, writing in straight line and maintaining legibility in its presentation.

(*ii*) Providing a structure or model of writing and getting it copied in a proper way.

(*iii*) Providing sufficient drill and practice work for doing away with spelling mistakes.
(*iv*) Adopting strategies like repeated short writing assignments, using computer for word processing, spelling and grammar checks and learn to practice correctly spelled words.

3. Spoken language or oral communication difficulties

(*i*) Provide model behaviour of speaking and ask student to repeat, record and evaluate by using proper devices.
(*ii*) Use structure language program or take the services of language laboratory for helping the students in his oral communication.
(*iii*) Adopt the strategies like using visuals for description, using cues and prompts, to help the child know when to speak and what to speak, using rhythm or music for incentive and encouragement, proving sufficient practice and opportunities for speaking, and comprehending, etc.

4. Learning difficulties in Mathematics

(*i*) decreasing distractions in the class during teaching-learning of mathematical concepts.
(*ii*) Providing examples and non-examples for the classification of the fundamental concepts and principles of mathematics.
(*iii*) Using concrete aid material, multimedia for understanding the fundamentals and applications of mathematics.
(*iv*) Providing model behaviour at your own level for learning the right way of doing calculation and solving problems and also making use of peers as models.

E. Special Needs of Children Suffering from Mental Retardation or Disabilities and their Redressal

The learning and adjustment needs of the children suffering from mental or intellectual disabilities differ from individual to individual depending upon the degree of severity of their impairments or level of their mental retardation. As a result, it can be quite fruitful to look at the special needs of these children in the light of the level of their mental retardation in our inclusive education setup.

(a) The children suffering from Severe and Profound Mental Retardation: The children suffering from profound mental retardation never attain in adult life an intellectual level greater than that of the average two years child. Therefore, their need is only limited to have their look after and care on the part of their parents and care taker just a baby of two years throughout their life span (which is usually quite shorter in duration).

The children suffering from severe mental retardation also have a distinction not to attain on intellectual level greater than that of the average four year old child. Hence their need is only limited to make them somehow independent for looking after their own physical well being and doing some manual work. They are not fit for being included in the inclusive setup of the school and therefore institutionalization is always recommended for them.

***(b) The children suffering from Moderate Mental Retardation*:** The children suffering from moderate mental retardation are able to attain intellectual level similar to that of the average six year old child. In their cases thus they may not get any much benefit from the education experiences provided in the inclusive setup along with the normal peers. But however they have the ability to get benefitted from the properly organised training for getting some reasonable independence in terms of their living, doing their day to day task, and perform in crafts and vocational activities. Thus in terms of the satisfaction of their learning and adjustment needs, the children suffering from moderate mental retardation need constant encouragement and guided training for attaining independence in performing their day to day task, social adjustment and doing vocational work requiring less stress on their intellectual abilities.

(c) The children suffering from Mild Mental Retardation: The children suffering from mild mental retardation are much better in terms of their intellectual functioning than their peers suffering from moderate, severe or profound mental retardation. They are capable of attaining intellectual levels comparable to that of the average ten years old child and hence can be properly benefitted from the educative as well as training experiences. In terms of the realization of their specific learning needs, therefore, these children require proper care and attention towards their education so that they may be helped to reach a reasonable level of educational attainment at least upto primary level (reading, writing, arithmetic, general knowledge, understanding of their environment, etc.), participation in games and other co-curricular activities and gaining needed proficiency in arts, crafts and vocational activities for leading their life as independently as possible.

5

Assistive and Adaptive Technologies in Inclusive Setup

WHAT IS ASSISTIVE TECHNOLOGY?

Assistive Technology is an umbrella term that includes assistive, adaptive, and rehabilitative devices for people with disabilities and also includes the process used in selecting, locating, and using them. Assistive technology promotes greater independence by enabling people to perform tasks that they were formerly unable to accomplish, or had great difficulty accomplishing, by providing enhancements to, or changing methods of interacting with, the technology, needed to accomplish such tasks. As a formal definition of the term assistive technology we can here cite a definition adopted in "Individuals with Disabilities Education Act (IDEA)", federal law of USA.

> " *Assistive technology device means any item, piece of equipment, or product system, whether acquired commercially off the shelf, modified, or customized, that is used to increase, maintain, or improve the functional capabilities of a child with a disability.*"

Examples of Assistive Technology include (*i*) the screen readers that enable people to hear electronic text as synthesized speech, (*ii*) speech-to-text software that enable people to use their voices to enter text. (*iii*) Text telephones, (*iv*) Accessible keyboards, (*v*) standing frames, (*vi*) Large print, (*vii*) Braille, and (*viii*) speech recognition software, etc.

OBJECTIVES OF ASSISTIVE TECHNOLOGY IN INCLUSIVE SETUP

- To enable them to get adapted or adjusted to the environment of the inclusive setup.
- To enable them to approximate normal fluency, rate, or standards — a level of accomplishment in the classroom teaching-learning which could not be achieved by any other means.
- To provide access for participation in programs or activities which otherwise would be closed to them.
- To increase endurance or ability to persevere and complete tasks that otherwise are difficult to be attempted on routine basis.
- To enable them to concentrate and focus on learning tasks, rather than other objects or activities in the environment.
- To help them in raising their communication activities and skills.

- To provide greater access to information and environmental exposure.
- To help them in making use of the assistive technology including computer technology for their adaptation, education and development.
- To support social interactions with peers, schoolmates, teachers and other school personnel.

ASSISTIVE TECHNOLOGY AND ADAPTIVE TECHNOLOGY

The term adaptive technology is often used as the synonym for assistive technology. However, they are different terms. Assistive technology refers to "Any item, pieces of equipment, or product system, whether acquired commercially, modified, or customized, that is used to increase, maintain, or improve functional capabilities of individuals with disabilities" while adaptive technology covers items that are specifically designed for persons with disabilities and would seldom be used by non-disabled persons. In other words, "assistive technology is any object or system that increases or maintains the capabilities of people with disabilities, "While adaptive technology is "any object or system that is specifically designed for the purpose of increasing or maintaining the capabilities of people with disabilities." Consequently, adaptive technology is a subset of assistive technology.

Adaptive technology often refers specifically to electronic and information technology access.

ASSISTIVE AND ADAPTIVE TECHNOLOGIES (AT) FOR VARYING TYPES OF DISABLED OR DIFFERENTLY ABLED STUDENTS IN THE INCLUSIVE SETUP

A. Assistive Technology for Orthopedically or Mobility Impaired

Orthopedically or mobility impaired students need a wide variety of assistive technologies enabling them to adapt and learn in the inclusive class room setup. With their limited physical capacities and difficulty in movements they essentially need some ways and means of assisting them in a proper way for coping with such deficiencies or deficits. Surely and certainly the assistive technology options should match here with the specific needs associated with the nature of their physical capacities and movability. Let us see how the challenges posed by the impairment deficiencies of these students can be faced with the help of assistive and adaptive technologies in an inclusive classroom setup.

- *Helping the Orthopedically impaired by equipping them with artificial limbs.* Initially attempts should be made to help the orthopedically impaired with the use of prosthesis. Prosthesis, prosthetic, or prosthetic limb is a device that replaces a missing body part. Prostheses are typically used to replace parts lost by injury (traumatic) or missing from birth or to supplement defective body parts. Inside the body, artificial heart valves are in common use. Other devices and aids can be considered prosthetics include artificial leg, foot or hand, hearing aids, artificial eyes, Gastric bands and dentures, etc.

• *Equipping the Orthopedically impaired with mobility devices.* The Orthopedically and mobility impaired students may be helped in their proper mobility with the devices like wheel chairs and walkers. These devices allow them to perform mobility related activities of daily living and necessary movements in the school and classes. The devices come in a number of variations where they can be propelled either by hand or by motors where to occupant uses electrical controls to manage motors and seating control actuators through a joystick, sip-and-puff control, or other input devices.

• *Helping the Orthopedically impaired in providing written responses.* Some of the orthopedically impaired students may feel difficulty in providing written responses on account of their disability or physical incapacities. Such students may be helped (*i*) by asking them to make use of those pens and pencils that require less pressure and are easier to grasp and also have a provision for the hand splinters or holders, *e.g.* for helping the pen, pencil or crayon holding, (*ii*) by a fellow non-disabled student for taking class notes and providing written responses on his behalf, (*iii*) training the child in using the other hand or even legs, etc., if his writing hand (left or right) is impaired, and (*iv*) making provision for the use of computers, laptops, mobiles for written communications and computations by making suitable adoption as per needs and impairments of the affected students.

• *Helping orthopedically impaired in attending to reading tasks.* Some of the orthopedically impaired students feeling difficulty in attending the reading tasks may be helped by making provisions like below.

(*i*) Providing talking books, recorded texts and lectures for helping the disabled who are unable to hold or use books and printed material of reading. It can also be made easy to read for the some on computer screen by adjusting the visibility of the letters/drawings, etc. as per requirements of their convenience.

(*ii*) Providing reading stands, book holders, etc. adapted to their needs — sitting, standing and reclining position at the time of engaging in the reading tasks.

(*iii*) Making provisions of page turners and elastic or rubber bands and larger paper clips for securing pages on either side of the open book as per their need and requirements.

• *Carrying out essential adaptation in terms of material facilities and environmental modifications.* For helping the orthopedically impaired in their proper movements as well as taking parts in the activities of the inclusive setup along the normal peers it is very much essential to bring essential adaptation in material facilities and environmental surroundings related to classrooms, libraries, laboratories, assembly halls, work places, toilets, drinking water places, etc. It may include the adaptations in terms of providing proper ramps and walkways; arrangement of proper seating and working in the classrooms, laboratories, and workshops, and ways for interacting and taking parts in the group activities, etc.

- *Helping Orthopedically impaired in accessing computers, and mobile technology.* Students who are not able to use their hands to interact with a computer, laptop or mobile phones can be helped through alternative access and input assistive technology. Some examples of hardware and software used by students with mobility challenges include switch activation and scanning software, speech recognition software, touch pads and touch screens, on screen (*e.g.* iPad, iPhone and iPod touch) and alternative keyboards, head mouse, foot mouse, joystick, and sip and puff activation technology (allowing a person with substantial disability to make selections and navigate computerized interfaces by controlling inhalations and exhalations).

B. Assistive Technology for Visually Impaired

Visually impaired students while receiving instructions and going through the learning experiences in an inclusive classroom setup may be helped a variety of assistive technology and means in the manner given below.

- *Assistive technology to help in visual assess*: It is meant for increasing the visual assess to printing material or other visionary objects for gaining desired information. It may include the devices and equipment like magnifiers (hand held, stand magnifier, or spectacle magnifier) closed circuit television, and computers (magnifying screen images through specialized hardware and software).
- *Assistive technology to help in auditory access:* Visually impaired children are privileged to have proper auditory access, therefore it remains beneficial for them to have good opportunities and means for the auditory access of the things to be visualized. In a useful auditory access they can make use of synthetic speech technology (production of sound by means of computers.) With its services of converting writing words into speech it can properly assist the visually impaired to have easy auditory access to books, newspapers, typed material and manuscripts, etc. We have at present such advanced reading equipment or machines that can *be* successfully used for scanning and reading printed material to the visually impaired with a synthetic voice. They may also facilitate them to regulate the speed and tone of the voice and can even have the machine spell out words letter by letter if desired. These can safely be used with a personal computer to convert print to speech. Head phones are also available for using these devices/machines on the part of visually impaired without disturbing other students of the inclusive classroom.

• *Assistive technology to help in the tactile access.* Visually impaired are also in a position to have a proper tactile access of the printed material and visionary objects. There is now availability of such devices that can help visually impaired to read regular print effectively by converting print into a tactile mode. Coupled with computer technology now, these devices are now proving helpful both in converting regular print to Braille (tactile access) and Braille to print vice versa. It can help them to take notes and tests along with other students of the inclusive class and prepare assignments and papers at home. With the help of user friendly key-board, visually impaired students can store their work in a pen drive or may produce standard print copies for being used by their teachers or other sighted peers.

• *Assistive technology to help in orientation and mobility.* It includes the use of devices and equipment that may prove helpful to the visually impaired students in their safe, smooth and efficient orientation and mobility with regard to day-to-day living and functioning in inclusive setup. Here they may be trained to make use of canes (made of wood or aluminum) and other electronic travel aids such as laser beam cane and sonic guide. A lesser beam cane is an electronic device that emits three beams of infrared light (one up, one down and one straight ahead). These are converted into sound after hitting the objects in the path of visually impaired and thus enabling them to get proper single of the objects or hurdles in their path. Sonic guide represents a sort of an electronic device which after being born by a visually impaired child on his head is capable of emitting ultrasound and converting reflection from objects lying in the path into audible sound. The characteristic of this sound then may further help the visually impaired child for making judgement in terms of the distance, textures and directions of objects lying in his environment.

• *Assistive technology to help in instructional output.* It includes the use of the devices, equipment and other aid material that may prove helpful to the visually impaired students to gain desired learning experiences through the formal instructional activities of an inclusive setup. As examples of such aid material for teaching various school subjects and content material we may cite the use of (*i*) Cranmer abacus (an special abacus to be manipulated and read more easily by touch) for learning number concepts and making calculations in terms of counting, adding and subtracting, etc., (*ii*) speech plus talking calculator, (*iii*) embossed relief maps and diagrams, (*iv*) three dimensional models, (*v*) electronic probes that give valuable signals in response to light, (*vi*) raised line writing paper and graph paper, (*vii*) talking clocks, (*viii*) talking thermometers and barometers, (*ix*) spelling and grammar aids, and (*x*) talking books and dictionaries, etc.

C. Assistive Technology for Hearing Impaired

Students with hearing impairments benefit from accommodations that may include the use of interpreters, preferential seating, and visual cues. Many of these students also use assistive listening devices such as hearing aids and personal FM systems. Increasingly, schools are experimenting with classroom sound amplification systems to accommodate students with hearing impairments and central auditory processing disorders. There are now some sophisticated, and expensive speech recognition technologies available such as communicator that translates an instructor's voice to text and sign language on a computer screen. Some students who are deaf are discovering this technology quite helpful in classroom settings. Assistive or adaptive technology devices and means employed for assisting and helping the hearing impaired students in one or the other ways in an inclusive classroom setup may include the following:

(*i*) *Preferential seating:* Here the hearing impaired students are made to sit as near as possible to the teacher/instructor. It benefits the students who suffer from the mild or moderate hearing loss.

(*ii*) *Receiving help through the peers*: Hearing impaired students may be helped by the peers sitting next to them in the class or also after the class by the tutor or other friend peers in taking and sharing class notes, attending to the speakers, and helping in other oral communication activities.

(*iii*) *Use of hearing/listening aids:* Hearing impaired students may be made to bear and use the modern electronic hearing aids for picking up sound, magnifying its energy and delivering this louder sound to their ear and brain. There is much development in the field of assistive listening technology used with hearing aids or without for the hearing impaired children summarized as below.

- As an example of such development, we can name the vibro-tectile device. It consists of a microphone (usually clipped to the collar), and electronic sound receiver/analyzer in some type of pocket carrier (often worn at the waist) and a wrist vibrator that is activated when sounds are picked up. With such a setting, the device is quite helpful for the hearing impaired to increase their awareness of sound and improve speed reading skills, reception for speech and quality of expressive language.

As an example of the available group assistive listening devices, we can name the FM sound system (a system enabling to establish a radio link between the teacher and the hearing impaired children). In the classroom setup, the teacher is here required to transmit on an FM frequency through microphone transmitter (often wore on the lapel, near the lips) and the children are receiving the transmitted message through their pre-set individual receivers. Since no wires or separate amplifiers are used in this system. Teachers and students can move freely around the classroom area and the system can be used indoors or outdoors depending upon the needs of inclusive setup.

(*iv*) *Cochlear implants.* In case when the child is unable to be helped much through hearing aids, then the next alternative lies in implanting an electronic device in his cochlear through surgery. It is helpful in stimulating those hearing nerves in the cochlear that are not impaired resulting into the hearing of the sound on the part of the child. This implantation functions in the same way as implantation of a pace maker in the heart.

(v) *Providing captions for the video presentation.* Since the oral communication/dialogues, etc. of a telecast program or video presentation are not accessible by the hearing impaired, the due provision can be made for it accessibility by captioning the subtitle of the communicated feelings and ideas for the desired education and instructional activities of the hearing impaired.

(vi) *Using text message for communication.* For the desired communication, the hearing impaired can make use of mobile phone of sending and receiving text messages to their peers as well as teachers/ instructors regarding the class room instruction, assignments or project activities.

(vii) *Using computer technology.* Use of computer technology can offer a lot of assistance to the hearing impaired for their proper communication, education, and adjustment in the inclusive classroom setup in the ways mentioned below.

- Many useful software programs are now available for the teaching and learning of the curricular subjects to the hearing impaired in an appropriate way.
- Computer technology is able to provide hearing impaired interactive videos for self-instruction, graphic displays of voice production to improve spoken language and online message boards for exchanging information.
- Computer technology is able to provide valuable internet and web services for helping the hearing impaired in their attempts of seeking education, training and any information they need for their adjustment and development.

D. Assistive Technology for children with Speech Disability or Communication Disorder

The children suffering from speech disabilities or communication disorders may be helped through the adoption of Augmentative and alternative communication (AAC) technology. AAC is an umbrella term that encompasses methods of communication for those with impairments or restrictions on the production or comprehension of spoken or written language. AAC systems are extremely diverse and depend on the capabilities of the user. They may be as basic as pictures on a board that are used to request food, drink, or other care; or they can be advanced speech generating devices, based on speech synthesis, that are capable of storing hundreds of phrases and words. There are a number of products, devices, hardware and software available for the adoption of AAC technology to the students suffering from speech and communication problems ranging from low-tech symbol/picture boards and wallets to high-tech portable or handheld computer equipped with AAC software.

E. Assistive Technology for Learning Disabled

Learning Disabilities Students with learning disabilities can be strong candidates for assistive technology support. Some of these learning disabilities include development speech and language disorders (articulation, expressive language and/or receptive language disorders) as well as academic skills disorders (reading, writing and/or arithmetic disorders). The assistive or adaptive technological measures like below may prove quite fruitful in this direction.

- *Use of audio recording devices.* The use of such devices may be able to rectify many of their language learning difficulties particularly related to pronunciation, proper intonation, and way of speaking, etc. Reading, speaking, and conversation skills can be better developed with the help of audio recording devices.
- *Use of video or power point presentations for the instruction.* It may provide high quality visual and auditory presentation of the facts, and principles related to the instruction of school subjects. The learning disabled students can watch useful and interesting academic as well as social presentations on video format and simultaneously listen to the carefully prepared narration for providing useful instruction.
- *Use of Computer Assisted Instruction (CAI).* It can help in doing away with the deficiencies regarding reading, writing, communication, mathematics, sciences and other practical oriented subjects. As examples of the advanced developments in CAI we can cite hypertext and Hypermedia technologies used for the instruction of learning disable.

Hypertext technology use pop-up text windows with a simple press of key, moving of the mouse or touch of the screen. It may give definitions or illustrations of difficult words, may reword or rewrite the confusing or complicated language of the text, provide useful additional hints for solving the problems, give diagrams, pictures, and maps, etc. for proper understanding of the text material, concepts and generalizations on the part of the learning disabled students.

Hypermedia technology makes use of a variety of formats to supplement enrich the text by merging computer and media technologies. The learning disabled thus may be helped to listen, watch, store, locate and search the needed information through the use of the multimedia application of the computer technology.

F. Assistive Technology for students suffering from Autism Disorders

The characteristics of students with Autism disorders (AD) vary considerably. Students with AD process and react to information and other stimuli in unique ways. Some students with AD enhance their communication abilities through Augmentative and alternative communication (AAC) support. The use of computers, specialized software, and other technologies may provide organizational support and improve levels of focus.

In this way necessary efforts can be made for providing help or assistance to the disabled or differently abled students in the inclusive classroom setup along with the other non disabled peers for their adequate adaptation, education and development by resorting to the desired adaptive and assistive technologies and means meant for this purpose.

6

Adaptation and Accommodation according to Various Disabilities

INTRODUCTION

In an inclusive setup of a school there is the presence of diverse learners characterized with diverse learning needs, abilities and capacities for getting adjusted and benefitted through the learning experiences provided to them in the school. It is a glaring fact that many of the diverse learners can't be properly benefitted through the adoption of 'one fit to all sizes' principle. Hence a suitable modification or adaptation is essentially needed for meeting out the needs of the diverse learners for helping them to learn, develop and progress to the tune of the abilities and potential. We have to be sufficiently flexible in providing to the diverse learners of the inclusive setup all that suits them well in relation to their capacities or incapacities, abilities or disabilities, potentials and limitations. We can't prescribe the same instructional objectives, curricular and co-curricular experiences to all the students belonging to an inclusive setup. The goals or objectives of providing instruction /learning experiences to them should essentials reflect diversity and flexibility according to their capacities and needs. In a nutshell, thus an inclusive setup we need to follow the principle of adaptations *i.e.,* making suitable changes in the teaching learning environment according to the demands of the altered circumstances. Such adaptations, in relation to the teaching-learning task going on in the school needs to be planned and organized on three different footings, namely (*i*) Adaptations and accommodation in instructional objectives, (*ii*) Adaptations and accommodation in prescribed curriculum, and (*iii*) Adaptations and accommodation in the planning and organization of co-curricular activities. Let us try to know about all these types of adaptations and accommodation carried out for the benefit of diverse learners belonging to an inclusive setup.

ADAPTATIONS AND ACCOMMODATION IN INSTRUCTIONAL OBJECTIVES

Instructional objectives set the path of instructional work carried out for the learners in a class or school. These objectives decide what is to be carried out in the teaching-learning process for the benefit of the learners and also set the limits of achievements and attainments on the part of learners through the curricular and co-curricular experiences provided to them. We can't expect the same level of attainment or achievements from all types of diverse learners of an inclusive class. It is, therefore, quite essential on our part to allow sufficient flexibility in setting diverse instructional objectives for the diverse learners well in tune with their nature of capacities or incapacities, potentials or limitations. In other words, we need to introduce suitable adaptations and accommodation in the prescribed instructional objectives meant to serve the general population of the students belonging to non-inclusive setup of the regular schools or non-exceptional (normal) or non-disabled students of the inclusive setup. Let us see why and how it should be done.

1. The children suffering from locomotor impairment may not be able to handle or manipulate objects or engage in the activities exercised and controlled through the movements of body organs. In their cases, therefore, while setting instructional objectives for the teaching-learning of school subjects we should take a lot of caution in prescribing instructional objectives that may seem to be a bit non attainable in view of their locomotor limitations. In terms of laboratory work, project work and workshop activities, they should have before them only such objectives the realization of which may be possible (through some amendment or adaptations) on the part of locomotor or orthopaedically impaired children.

2. The children suffering from hearing impairment especially the deaf are unable to get benefitted through any learning experiences delivered through audio channel. Similarly, the children suffering from visual impairment especially the blind remain deprived of the advantages gained through visual learning experiences. Both of them respectively can't engage in the activities and performances dependent upon the sense of hearing and sight. The suitable adaptations should therefore be made to these learners in the setting of instructional objectives in view of their limitations of using their sense of hearing and sight. For example, hearing impaired can't be expected to demonstrate the same level of language understanding and mastery over the pronunciation and use of language as exhibited by their normal peers. Therefore, for them we have to set such instructional objectives in language teaching that may seem proper in view of their felt difficulties or limitations. Similarly for blind children, we should have needed adaptations in setting the instructional objectives related to learning experiences dominated with the use of sight. In the work and activities requiring laboratory work, project work, and workshop activities, we should not be enthusiastic to expect from them in the participation of these activities. Here we should make necessary adaptation in the instructional goals well within the tune of their incapacities.

3. The children suffering from mental retardation can't learn and perform at the intellectual level demonstrated by their non-disabled or disabled

peers. There may be some cases of mentally retarded where we have to seek adaptations of the instructional objectives to the level of almost no scholastic attainments. They are only instructed and helped for making them capable of doing self-help and community living. For the educable mentally retarded we may set the instructional objectives quite in tune with their mental ages and intellectual capacities irrespective of what we are expecting from their non-disabled peers.

4. The children suffering from learning disabilities like dyslexia and dyscalculia suffer from serious limitations in learning, understanding and demonstrating performances in many of the academic task particularly related to the subject mathematics, numerical analysis and languages. The milestones of performances and standard of achievements related to these learning areas should therefore be suitably modified and changed for these children in proper tune with their incapacities and difficulties.

5. In addition to the presence of one or the other types of disabled children, we may also witness the presence of quite capable, talented and gifted children in an inclusive class. They urgently need to learn and perform more than their disabled or non-disabled average peers. In their cases, thus we have to raise the level of expected attainment or performance well in tune with the level of their giftedness or talent in one or the other learning and performance areas. Similarly, where we have the presence of slow learners and scholastically backward children in the inclusive class, we have to seek adaptations in instructional objectives much on the lines as expected from these children in relation to the nature of their slow learning and backwardness in one or the other learning areas.

In this way, we should try to seek diversification in the setting of instructional objectives *i.e.* the expectations from the different types of learners in terms of their scholastic achievements and performances well in tune with the nature of capacities or incapacities, potential or limitations possessed by them for the learning, understanding and performing in one or the other academic areas.

ADAPTATIONS AND ACCOMMODATION IN CURRICULUM

The pedagogical approach named as curriculum adaptations and accommodation for the teaching-learning of CWSN in an inclusive setup is based on the principle and notion that all children can't be benefitted through the learning experiences imparted in the inclusive setup in the same way. They have their own strengths and limitations to learn and understand the things and attain a maximum level of their learning progress. Instead of adapting the children to a fixed and rigid curriculum, the attempts should then be necessarily made to seek adaptation in the school curriculum according to the diverse nature and needs of the children belonging to an inclusive class including CWSN.

In its practical and applied aspect, curriculum adaptation and accommodation in an inclusive education setup may be considered as an on going dynamic process that is aimed to modify and adapt the prescribed curriculum or program of studies (the totality of learning experiences provided to the learners through manifold activities held in the school) for meeting the learning and developmental requirements of the learners including children with special needs or different abilities. It helps in enabling the teachers and administrator of an inclusive school to welcome learners of all abilities and ensures that every student admitted in the school is challenged to learn and progress at his/her maximum in tune with his or her abilities and capacities. As a result, thus curriculum adaptation in an inclusive setup involves differentiation to meet the needs of all students belonging to the inclusive setup. This differentiation involves organization of learning experiences as well as ways and means of imparting them in a proper way, their assessment and evaluation and structuring of learning environment including barrier free physical environment. In other words, not only the curriculum but its implementation also needs proper adaptation for helping all the learners to achieve success through the learning experiences available to them in an inclusive setup. Throwing light on the nature of such curriculum adaptation. The NCTE publication, "Including Children with Special Needs—Upper Primary Stage" (2015) says:

> "*Curriculum adaptation involves differentiation to meet the needs of all students. The content, the teaching process, assessment and evaluation, and the physical environment may be modified to help students to achieve success in the classroom. The kind of activities chosen by the teacher, including group activities, must be flexible and reflect the background knowledge of small groups or individual students.*"

How to carry out Curriculum Adaptation and Accommodation in an Inclusive Setup

As said above the task of curriculum adaptation involves the task of bringing modifications and changes in the contents of the curriculum (curricular and co-curricular experiences to the learners) and the ways and modes of implementing it in a particular teaching-learning environment. In this connection, Deschenes et al (1994) has mentioned about nine types of curriculum adaptations for being tried in an inclusive setup of a school. We are here reproducing them with a little modification.

Nine Types of Curriculum Adaptations and Accommodation

1. *Curriculum adaptation in terms of Quantity*. Adapt the number of items that the learner is expected to learn or number of activities student will complete prior to assessment for mastery.

For example: Reduce the number of social studies terms a learner must learn at any one time. Add more practice activities or worksheets.

2. *Curriculum adaptation in terms of Time.* Adapt the time allotted and allowed for learning, task completion, or testing.

For example: Individualize a timeline for completing a task; pace learning differently (increase or decrease) for some learners.

3. *Curriculum adaptation in terms of Level of Support.* Increase the amount of personal assistance to keep the student on task or to reinforce or prompt use of specific skills. Enhance adult-student relationship; use physical space and environmental structure.

For example: Assign peer buddies, teaching assistants, peer tutors, or cross-age tutors. Specify how to interact with the student or how to structure the environment.

4. *Curriculum adaptation in terms of Input.* Adapt the way instruction is delivered to the learner.

For example: Use different visual aids, enlarge text, plan more concrete examples, provide hands-on activities, place students in cooperative groups, pre-teach key concepts or terms before the lesson.

5. *Curriculum adaptation in terms of Difficulty.* Adapt the skill level, problem type, or the rules on how the learner may approach the work.

For example: Allow the use of a calculator to figure math problems; simplify task directions; change rules to accommodate learner needs.

6. *Curriculum adaptation in terms of Output.* Adapt how the student can respond to instruction.

For example: Instead of answering questions in writing, allow a verbal response, use a communication book for some students, allow students to show knowledge with hands on materials.

7. *Curriculum adaptation in terms of Participation.* Adapt the extent to which a learner is actively involved in the task.

For example: In geography, have a student hold the globe, while others point out locations. Ask the student to lead a group. Allow the student having written output difficulties to use raised line paper etc.

8. *Curriculum adaptation in terms of Alternate Goals.* Adapt the goals or outcome expectations while using the same materials. When routinely utilized, this is only for students with moderate to severe disabilities.

For example: In a social studies lesson, expect a student to be able to locate the colours of the states on a map, while other students learn to locate each state and name the capital.

9. *Curriculum adaptation in terms of "Substitute Curriculum" Sometimes called "functional curriculum".* Provide different instruction and materials to meet a learner's individual goals. When routinely utilized, this is only for students with moderate to severe disabilities.

For example: During a language lesson a student is learning toileting skills with an aide.

Another Approach for classifying the types of Curriculum Adaptation and Accommodation

In this concern, the NCERT Publication "Meeting Special Needs in School – A Manual" (2007:51) has provided two types of curriculum adaptation along with examples. Let us discuss them for getting acquainted with the know-how of the mechanism of curriculum adaptation in an inclusive setup.

A. Curriculum Adaptation allowing Multi-level Curriculum Instructions

A curricular activity or area may have different levels *i.e.* there may be different alternatives for performing this activity or it may have many components of varying level of difficulty. Therefore, attempts may be made to get the learners engaged in the learning of one or the other types of the component related to a common curricular program or activity going on in an inclusive class. It may help in adapting the curriculum as per need and ability of the diverse students for their proper learning and progress. Such provision of curriculum adaptation has been named as "Multi-level Curriculum Instructions". It has been defined by Giangreco, Cloninger and Salcelverson (1998) in the following words.

> "*Multi-level curriculum instructions refer to teach a diverse group of learners within a shared activity in which students have individually appropriate learning outcomes within the same curricular area.*"

Example 1. While teaching 'Law of floating bodies' in a science inclusive class where majority of students may be working on what makes objects float or sink, some CWSN or disabled may be understanding the concept of sinking and floating and the difference between them.

Example 2. While teaching the topic "Multiplication of fractional digits" in an inclusive class some students may be working on the practice of difficult questions related to multiplication of fractional digits, a few may be assigned quite simple problems on fractions multiplications and the others may be doing only a quite limited number of problems (as it takes them longer to complete the computational work).

B. Curriculum Adaptation Allowing Curriculum Overlapping

In such type of curriculum adaptation, the curriculum areas in which students gets engaged during their teaching-learning does not remain the same as happens in the former multi-level curriculum instruction. They may overlap but still then they are found to work on these in a shared activity of the inclusive classroom for remaining busy in the realization of their appropriate learning outcomes or goals through their own efforts.

Example 1. In a social studies inclusive class while working on a unit of the subject social studies in the groups, some may be achieving the learning outcomes for social studies and the others belonging to CWSN group may be targeting on the development of communication skills through the learning experiences planned for a social studies teacher for the development of these skills among the needed CWSN.

Example 2. In a language inclusive class while practising individual spelling words (selected by the teacher or the students) there may be a different number of words for different group of students according to their mental level, previous knowledge and experience. In addition some students may work on fewer words or more words than might be determined as the norms for their grade.

ADAPTATIONS IN CO-CURRICULAR ACTIVITIES

Organization of co-curricular activities is a quite essential component of the learning experiences provided to the learners in the school environment. An inclusive school thus also may be found to organize a number of co-curricular activities for the wholesome development and welfare of the diverse learners belonging to its inclusive setup. These activities may be named and classified as under:

1. Physical activities in the shape of children's play, games and sports, physical exercises, yoga asanas and other yogic activities, mass drill and parade etc.
2. Cultural activities like dance, drama, musical activities, fancy dress show, school band etc.
3. Literary activities like debates and declamation contest, seminars and symposium, poetical recitation. Story and Essay writing competitions. Quiz Competitions etc.
4. Social or civic activities like celebration of social, religious and national festivals, participation in NSS or NCC activities, scouting or girl guiding, community cooking and dining, organization of cleanliness week, etc.
5. Multipurpose or Miscellaneous activities such as excursion of field trips, organization of exhibitions and fairs, working on various types of projects, and organization of subject and activities clubs, etc.

The inclusive environment of school provides valuable opportunities to the diverse learners including disabled for gaining valuable experiences and gaining benefitted in so many ways contributing towards their wholesome development and progress. The inclusion, of the disabled in gaining such experiences invites a lot of challenges for both the teachers as organizers of these co-curricular activities and the different types of disabled or CWDN as participants. In view of the limitations caused by the one or the other types of impairments or disabilities suffered on the part of children with disabilities, there arises an urgent need of applying appropriate adaptations in the organization of one or the other co-curricular activities for them. The things like below may be kept in mind while going through such adaptations in the organization of co-curricular activities.

1. The disabled children should be helped in opting for the

participation in co-curricular activities that may be effectively undertaken by them in view of the functional limitations caused through their impairments or disabilities along with their non-disabled peers.

2. The suitable modifications and adaptations should be undertaken in the means and ways of carrying out the tasks related to one or the other co-curricular activities much in tune with the types of impairments or disabilities of the disabled children in the manner given below.

- The locomotor or orthopaedically impaired as well as hearing and visually impaired children should be equipped with such means, equipments and material that can help them in overcoming the limitations or barriers caused through their particular type of impairment or non-functioning of their sensory or body organs. It can help these children in taking part in play way and sports activities, literary, cultural and social activities according to their own interests and demand of the inclusive setup.
- The nature of the difficulty level of the participation in co-curricular activities should be so adjusted and adapted as to help the intellectually impaired or mentally disabled children for properly participating in one or the other types of co-curricular activities. For example there may be a number of play way activities and games that may fit well in the intellectual capacities possessed by them in relation to their level of mental retardation.
- There should be more emphasis on providing needed facilities and organizing such co-curricular activities including sports and games that may suit the requirements of a number of differently abled students. For example, the indoor games along with barrier free environment and limitations free devices and playing material should be arranged in the inclusive setup of the school. The help of assistive and adaptive technological means should be taken for facilitating the participation of the disabled children in one or the other types of co-curricular activities on the individual or group basis. With the advancement of technological means and the will power and struggle of the disabled for getting success in their participation, we can now witness well the successful organization of various types of co-curricular activities quite challenging ones such as cricket playing on the part of blinds and sports competitions on the regional, national and international basis for the differently abled children and people.

In this way, if appropriate attention is paid towards the suitable adaptations in the ways and means of the organisation of co-curricular activities, then it may certainly pave a proper way for the active participation of the disabled children along with their non-disabled peers of the inclusive setup for getting them benefitted in terms of their proper adjustment and wholesome development.

7

Educational Provision for the Disabled in International Declaration and Conventions

INTRODUCTION

With the proclamation of Human Rights and impact of the philosophy of humanism, there has been a world wide call for providing humane treatments to the disabled and stop their isolation and give up the policies and provisions of seclusion for their education and development. For this purpose a number of organized attempts have been made by the world society and nations from time to time under the banner of UNO in the form of a number of Joint International conventions and conferences. It has resulted into useful declaration of statements, framework for actions or provisions and policies for shaping the education of the disabled. In this chapter, here we would be focusing our discussion in getting acquainted with two of these ventures in the name of (*i*) Salamanca Statement and Frame work of Action, 1994 and (*ii*) UN Conventions on the Rights of Persons with Disabilities (UNCRPD), 2006.

SALAMANCA STATEMENT AND FRAMEWORK OF ACTION, 1994

An International document and declaration in the name of "The Salamanca Statement and Framework for Action on Disability Education (1994)" has come into existence as a result of deliberations held in June 1994 in a World Conference on Special Needs Education. More than 300 participants representing governments of the 92 countries of the world including India and 25 International organizations met in Salamanca, Spain in this conference jointly held by the Ministry of Education and Science Spain and UNESCO.

The conference through its four days deliberations (7-10 June), came up with a report and resolutions in the form of Statement and Framework for action in implementing the policy of inclusive education for the education and welfare of the children with special needs particularly the disabled. We are hereby reproducing views in this regard available in the document issued as the deliberations of this conference.

The Salamanca Statement

(on principles, policy and practice in Special Needs Education)

The statement in original runs as under:

1. We, the delegates of the World Conference on Special Needs Education representing ninety-two governments and twenty-five international organizations, assembled here in Salamanca, Spain, from 7-10 June 1994, hereby reaffirm our commitment to Education for All, recognizing the necessity and urgency of providing education for children, youth and adults with special educational needs within the regular education system, and further hereby endorse the Framework for Action on Special Needs Education, that governments and organizations may be guided by the spirit of its provisions and recommendations.
2. We believe and proclaim that:
   - every child has a fundamental right to education, and must be given the opportunity to achieve and maintain an acceptable level of learning,
   - every child has unique characteristics, interests, abilities and learning needs,
   - education systems should be designed and educational programmes implemented to take into account the wide diversity of these characteristics and needs,
   - those with special educational needs must have access to regular schools which should accommodate them within a child-centred pedagogy capable of meeting these needs,
   - regular schools with this inclusive orientation are the most effective means of combating discriminatory attitudes, creating welcoming communities, building an inclusive society and achieving education for all; moreover, they provide an effective education to the majority of children and improve the efficiency and ultimately the cost-effectiveness of the entire education system.
3. We call upon all governments and urge them to:
   - give the highest policy and budgetary priority to improve their education systems to enable them to include all children regardless of individual differences or difficulties,
   - adopt as a matter of law or policy the principle of inclusive education, enrolling all children in regular schools, unless there are compelling reasons for doing otherwise,
   - develop demonstration projects and encourage exchanges with countries having experience with inclusive schools,
   - establish decentralized and participatory mechanisms for planning, monitoring and evaluating educational provision for children and adults with special education needs,

- encourage and facilitate the participation of parents, communities and organization of persons with disabilities in the planning and decision-making processes concerning provision for special educational needs,
- invest greater effort in early identification and intervention strategies, as well as in vocational aspects of inclusive education,
- ensure that, in the context of a systemic change, teacher education programmes, both pre-service and in-service, address the provision of special needs education in inclusive schools.

4. We also call upon the international community; in particular we call upon:

- governments with international cooperation programmes and international funding agencies, especially the sponsors of the World Conference on Education for All, the United Nations Educational, Scientific and Cultural Organization (UNESCO), the United Nations Children's Fund (UNICEF), United Nations Development Programme (UNDP), and the World Bank:
  - to endorse the approach of inclusive schooling and to support the development of special needs education as an integral part of all education programmes;
- the United Nations and its specialized agencies, in particular the International Labour Office (ILO), the World Health Organization (WHO), UNESCO and UNICEF;
  - to strengthen their inputs for technical cooperation, as well as to reinforce their cooperation and networking for more efficient support to the expanded and integrated provision of special needs education;
- non-governmental organizations involved in country programming and service delivery:
  - to strengthen their collaboration with the official national bodies and to intensify their growing involvement in planning, implementation and evaluation of inclusive provision for special educational needs;
- UNESCO, as the United Nations agency for education:
  - to ensure that special needs education forms part of every discussion dealing with education for all in various forums,
  - to mobilize the support of organizations of the teaching profession in matters related to enhancing teacher education as regards provision for special educational needs,
  - to stimulate the academic community to strengthen research and networking and to establish regional centres of information and documentation; also, to serve as a clearinghouse for such activities

and for disseminating the specific results and progress achieved at country level in pursuance of this Statement,

- to mobilize funds through the creation within its next Medium-Term Plan (1996-2002) of an expanded programme for inclusive schools and community support programmes, which would enable the launching of pilot projects that showcase new approaches for dissemination, and to develop indicators concerning the need for and provision of special needs education.

5. Finally, we express our warm appreciation to the Government of Spain and to UNESCO for the organization of the Conference, and we urge them to make every effort to bring this Statement and the accompanying Framework for Action to the attention of the world community, especially at such important forums as the World Summit for Social Development (Copenhagen, 1995) and the World Conference on Women (Beijing, 1995).

The Framework for Action (on Special Needs Education)

What is needed to be done for meeting the requirements of the education of CWSN has been summarized in the introduction portion of this document in the following way.

1. This Framework for Action on Special Needs Education was adopted by the World Conference on Special Needs Education organized by the Government of Spain in co-operation with UNESCO and held in Salamanca from 7 to 10 June 1994. Its purpose is to inform policy and guide action by governments, international organizations, national agencies, non-governmental organizations and other bodies in implementing the Salamanca Statement on Principles, Policy and Practice in Special Needs Education. The Framework draws extensively upon the national experience of the participating countries as well as upon resolutions, recommendations and publications of the United Nations system and other intergovernmental organizations, especially the Standard Rules on the Equalization of Opportunities for Persons with Disabilities. It also takes account of the proposals, guidelines and recommendations arising from the five regional seminars held to prepare the World Conference.

2. The right of every child to an education is proclaimed in the Universal Declaration of Human Rights and was forcefully reaffirmed by the World Declaration on Education for All. Every person with a disability has a right to express their wishes with regard to their education as far as this can be ascertained. Parents have an inherent right to be consulted on the form of education best suited to the needs, circumstances and aspirations of their children.

3. The guiding principle that informs this Framework is that schools should accommodate all children regardless of their physical, intellectual, social, emotional, linguistic or other conditions. This should include disabled and gifted children, street and working children, children from remote or nomadic populations, children from linguistic, ethnic or cultural minorities and children from other disadvantaged or marginalized areas or groups. These conditions create a range of different challenges to school systems. In the context of this Framework, the term 'special educational needs' refers to all those children and youth whose needs arise from disabilities or learning difficulties. Many children experience learning difficulties and thus have special educational needs at some time during their schooling. Schools have to find ways of successfully educating all children, including those who have serious disadvantages and disabilities. There is an emerging consensus that children and youth with special educational needs should be included in the educational arrangements made for the majority of children. This has led to the concept of the inclusive school. The challenge confronting the inclusive school is that of developing a child-centred pedagogy capable of successfully educating all children, including those who have serious disadvantages and disabilities. The merit of such schools is not only that they are capable of providing quality education to all children; their establishment is a crucial step in helping to change discriminatory attitudes, in creating welcoming communities and in developing an inclusive society. A change in social perspective is imperative. For far too long, the problems of people with disabilities have been compounded by a disabling society that has focused upon their impairments rather than their potential.

4. Special needs education incorporates the proven principles of sound pedagogy from which all children may benefit. It assumes that human differences are normal and that learning must accordingly be adapted to the needs of the child rather than the child fitted to preordained assumptions regarding the pace and nature of the learning process. A child-centred pedagogy is beneficial to all students and, as a consequence, to society as a whole. Experience has demonstrated that it can substantially reduce the drop-out and repetition that are so much a part of many education systems while ensuring higher average levels of achievement. A child-centred pedagogy can help to avoid the waste of resources and the shattering of hopes that is all too frequently a consequence of poor quality instruction and a 'one size fits all' mentality towards education. Child-centred schools are, moreover, the training ground for a people-oriented society that respects both the differences and the dignity of all human beings.

5. This **Framework for Action** comprises the following sections:

- I. New thinking in special needs education
- II. Guidelines for action at the national level
  - A. Policy and organization
  - B. School factors
  - C. Recruitment and training of educational personnel
  - D. External support services

E. Priority areas
F. Community perspectives
G. Resource requirements

III. Guidelines for action at the regional and international level.

Out of the above cited Dimensions related to Framework for Action, we would here concentrate on the first two – New thinking in special needs education and Guidelines for action at the national level (especially related to school children).

I. New Thinking in Special Needs Education
(*Especially related to School Children*)

(*i*) The trend in social policy during the past two decades has been to promote integration and participation and to combat exclusion. Inclusion and participation are essential to human dignity and to the enjoyment and exercise of human rights. Within the field of education, this is reflected in the development of strategies that seek to bring about a genuine equalization of opportunity. Experience in many countries demonstrates that the integration of children and youth with special educational needs is best achieved within inclusive schools that serve all children within a community. It is within this context that those with special educational needs can achieve the fullest educational progress and social integration. While inclusive schools provide a favourable setting for achieving equal opportunity and full participation, their success requires a concerted effort, not only by teachers and school staff, but also by peers, parents, families and volunteers. The reform of social institutions is not only a technical task it depends, above all, upon the conviction, commitment and good will of the individuals who constitute society.

(*ii*) The fundamental principle of the inclusive school is that all children should learn together, wherever possible, regardless of any difficulties or differences they may have. Inclusive schools must recognize and respond to the diverse needs of their students, accommodating both different styles and rates of learning and ensuring quality education to all through appropriate curricula, organizational arrangements, teaching strategies, resource use and partnerships with their communities. There should be a continuum of support and services to match the continuum of special needs encountered in every school.

(*iii*) Within inclusive schools, children with special educational needs should receive whatever extra support they may require to ensure their effective education. Inclusive schooling is the most effective means for building solidarity between children with special needs and their peers. Assignment of children to special schools – or special classes or sections within a school on a permanent basis – should be the exception, to be recommended only in those infrequent cases where it is clearly demonstrated that education in regular classrooms is incapable of meeting a child's educational or social needs or when it is required for the welfare of the child or that of other children.

(*iv*) The situation regarding special needs education varies enormously from one country to another. There are, for example, countries that have well established systems of special schools for those with specific impairments. Such special schools can represent a valuable resource for the development of inclusive schools. The staff of these special institutions possess the expertise needed for early screening and identification of children with disabilities. Special schools can also serve as training and resource centres for staff in regular schools. Finally, special schools or units within inclusive schools – may continue to provide the most suitable education for the relatively small number of children with disabilities who cannot be adequately served in regular classrooms or schools. Investment in existing special schools should be geared to their new and expanded role of providing professional support to regular schools in meeting special educational needs. An important contribution to ordinary schools, which the staff of special schools can make, is to the matching of curricular content and method to the individual needs of pupils.

(*v*) Countries that have few or no special schools would, in general, be well advised to concentrate their efforts on the development of inclusive schools and the specialized services needed to enable them to serve the vast majority of children and youth – especially provision of teacher training in special needs education and the establishment of suitably staffed and equipped resource centres to which schools could turn for support. Experience, especially in developing countries, indicates that the high cost of special schools means, in practice, that only a small minority of students, usually an urban elite, benefit from them. The vast majority of students with special needs, especially in rural areas, are as a consequence provided with no services whatsoever. Indeed, in many developing countries, it is estimated that fewer than 1 per cent of children with special educational needs are included in existing provision. Experience, moreover, suggests that inclusive schools, serving all of the children in a community, are most successful in eliciting community support and in finding imaginative and innovative ways of using the limited resources that are available.

II. Guidelines for Action at the National Level

A. Policy and Organization: The major recommendations in this area are as below.

- To create legislative measures for recognizing the principle of equality of opportunity to the disabled in the field of education.
- To develop parallel and complementary legislative measures in the fields of health, social welfare, vocational training and employment in order to support and give full effect to educational legislation.
- To make educational policies at all levels, from the national to the

local to stipulate that a child with a disability should attend the neighbourhood school that is, the school that would be attended by the child did not have a disability. Exception to this rule should be considered on a case-by-case basis where only education in a special school or establishment can be shown to meet the needs of the individual child.

- The practice of 'mainstreaming' children with disabilities should be an integral part of national plans for achieving education for all. Even in these exceptional cases where children are placed in special schools, their education need not be entirely segregated.

B. School Factors

Schools should be adequately prepared for meeting the needs of inclusive education. For this purpose they should work for

- Adapting curricular to children's needs, not vice-versa.
- Providing additional instructional support to CWSN in the context of the regular curriculum, not a different curriculum.
- Helping the CWSN in participating fully in the school programs meant for wholesome development.
- Incorporating formative evaluation into the regular educational process for getting the needed feedback on a continual basis.
- Arranging a continuum of support to CWSN, ranging from minimal help in regular classrooms to additional learning support programs within the schools and extending, where necessary, to the provision of assistance from specialist teachers and external support staff.
- Arranging the appropriate and affordable technology to enhance success in the school curriculum and to aid communication, mobility and learning.

C. Recruiting and Training of Educational Personnel

The things like below need to be done in this concern.

(*i*) Pre-service training programmes should provide to all student teachers, primary and secondary alike, positive orientation toward disability, thereby developing an understanding of what can be achieved in schools with locally available support services. The knowledge and skills required are mainly those of good teaching and include assessing special needs, adapting curriculum content, utilizing assistive technology, individualizing teaching procedures to suit a larger range of abilities, etc. In teacher-training practice schools, specific attention should be given to all teachers preparing to exercise their autonomy and apply their skills in adapting curricula and instruction to meet pupils needs as well as to collaborate with specialists and co-operate with parents.

(*ii*) A proper system of in service training to all teachers should be established supported well by distance education and other self-instruction techniques.

(*iii*) Specialized training in special needs education leading to additional qualifications should normally be integrated with or preceded by training and experience as a regular education teacher in order to ensure complementarily and mobility.

(*iv*) The training of special teachers needs to be reconsidered with a view to enabling them to work in different settings and to play a key role in special educational needs programmes. A non-categorical approach encompassing all types of disabilities should be developed as a common core, prior to further specialization in one or more disability-specific areas.

(*v*) A recurrent problem with education systems, even those that provide excellent educational services for students with disabilities, is the lack of role models for such students. Special needs students require opportunities to interact with adults with disabilities who have achieved success so that they can pattern their own lifestyles and aspirations on realistic expectations. In addition, students with disabilities should be given training and provided with examples of disability empowerment and leadership so that they can assist in shaping the policies that will affect them in later life. Education systems should therefore seek to recruit qualified teachers and other educational personnel who have disabilities and should also seek to involve successful individuals with disabilities from within the region in the education of special needs children.

D. External Support Services

The things like below may be useful in this concern.

(*i*) Support to ordinary schools could be provided by both teacher-education institutions and by the outreach staff of special schools. The latter should be used increasingly as resource centres for ordinary schools offering direct support to those children with special educational needs. Both training institutions and special schools can provide access to specific devices and materials as well as training in instructional strategies that are not provided in regular classrooms.

(*ii*) External support by resource personnel from various agencies, departments and institutions, such as advisory teachers, educational psychologists, speech and occupational therapists, etc., should be co-ordinated at the local level. School clusters have proved a useful strategy in mobilizing educational resources as well as community involvement. Clusters of schools could be assigned collective responsibility for meeting the special educational needs of pupils in their area and given scope for allocating resources as required. Such arrangements should involve non-educational services as well. Indeed, experience suggests that education services would benefit significantly if greater efforts were made to ensure optimal use of all available expertise and resources.

E. Priority Areas

(*i*) *Early Childhood Education*: The success of the inclusive school depends considerably on early identification, assessment and stimulation of the very young child with special educational needs. Early childhood care and education programmes for children aged up to six years ought to be developed and/or reoriented to promote physical, intellectual and social development and school readiness. These programmes have a major economic value for the individual, the family and the society in preventing the aggravation of disabling conditions. Programmes at this level should recognize the principle of inclusion and be developed in a comprehensive way by combining pre-school activities and early childhood health care.

(*ii*) *Girl's education*: Girls with disabilities are doubly disadvantaged. A special effort is required to provide training and education for girls with special educational needs. In addition to gaining access to school, girls with disabilities should have access to information and guidance as well as to models which could help them to make realistic choices and preparation for their future role as adult women.

(*iii*) *Preparation for Adult life*: Young people with special educational needs should be helped to make an effective transition from school to adult working life. Schools should assist them to become economically active and provide them with the skills needed in everyday life, offering training in skills which respond to the social and communication demands and expectations of adult life.

F. Community Perspectives

The things like below may be attended in this concern.

(*i*) *Parents partnership*: The education of children with special educational needs is a shared task of parents and professionals. A positive attitude on the part of parents favours school and social integration. Parents need support in order to assume the role of a parent of a child with special needs. The role of families and parents could be enhanced by the provision of necessary information in simple and clear language; addressing the needs for information and training in parenting skills is a particularly important task in cultural environments where there is little tradition of schooling. Both parents and teachers may need support and encouragement in learning to work together as equal partners.

(*ii*) *Community Involvement*: Efforts should be made to encourage community participation by giving support to representative associations and inviting them to take part in decision-making. To this end, mobilizing and monitoring mechanisms composed of local civil administration, educational, health and development authorities, community leaders and voluntary organizations should be established in geographical areas small enough to ensure meaningful community participation.

(*iii*) *Public Awareness*: Policy-makers at all levels, including the school level, should regularly reaffirm their commitment to inclusion and promote positive attitudes among children, among teachers and among the public-at-large towards those with special educational needs. In this concern mass media (newspapers, films and television channels, etc.) can play a powerful role in promoting positive attitudes towards the integration of disabled persons in society, overcoming prejudice and misinformation, and infusing greater optimism and imagination about the capabilities of persons with disabilities. The media can also promote positive attitudes of employers towards hiring persons with disabilities. The media should be used to inform the public on new approaches in education, particularly as regards to provision for special needs education in regular schools, by popularizing examples of good practice and successful experiences.

G. Resource Requirements

In this connection Guidelines for Action has commented in the following way.

The development of inclusive schools as the most effective means for achieving education for all must be recognized as a key government policy and accorded a privileged place on the nation's development agenda. It is only in this way that adequate resources can be obtained. Changes in policies and priorities cannot be effective unless adequate resource requirements are met. Political commitment, at both the national and community level, is needed both to obtain additional resources and to redeploy existing ones. While communities must play a key role in developing inclusive schools, government encouragement and support is also essential in devising effective and affordable solutions.

EDUCATIONAL PROVISIONS IN UN CONVENTION ON THE RIGHTS OF PERSONS WITH DISABILITIES (UNCRPD), 2006

Proceedings of the UN convention on the Rights of Persons with Disabilities (UNCRPD), 2006 represents a quite valuable document concerning the adjustment, education and welfare of the persons with disabilities. It begins with a preamble and includes 50 articles. As a matter of educational provisions for the disabled, necessary statements have been provided in the article 24 of this document and the overall purpose of the drafting of the document has been provided in the Article 1. Here at present for the benefit of our readers we would like to present (in original) what has been provided in the preamble, article 1 and article 24 of this document.

PREAMBLE

The States Parties to the present Convention,

(*a*) *Recalling* the principles proclaimed in the Charter of the United Nations which recognize the inherent dignity and worth and the equal and inalienable rights of all members of the human family as the foundation of freedom, justice and peace in the world.

(*b*) *Recognizing* that the United Nations, in the Universal Declaration of Human Rights and in the International Covenants on Human Rights, has proclaimed and agreed that everyone is entitled to all the rights and freedoms set forth therein without distinction of any kind.

(*c*) *Reaffirming* the universality, indivisibility, interdependence and interrelatedness of all human rights and fundamental freedoms and the need for persons with disabilities to be guaranteed their full enjoyment without discrimination.

(*d*) *Recalling* the International Covenant on Economic, Social and Cultural Rights, the International Covenant on Civil and Political Rights, the International Convention on the Elimination of All Forms of Racial Discrimination, the Convention on the Elimination of All Forms of Discrimination against Women, the Convention against Torture and other Cruel, Inhuman or Degrading Treatment or Punishment, the Convention on the Rights of the Child, and the International Convention on the Protection of the Rights of All Migrant Workers and Members of Their Families.

(*e*) *Recognizing* that disability is an evolving concept and that disability results from the interaction between persons with impairments and attitudinal and environment barriers that hinders their full and effective participation in society on an equal basis with others.

(*f*) *Recognizing* the importance of the principles and policy guidelines contained in the World Programme of Action concerning Disabled Persons and in the Standard Rules on the Equalization of Opportunities for Persons with Disabilities in influencing the promotion, formulation and evaluation of the policies, plans, programmes and actions at the national, regional and international levels to further equalize opportunities for persons with disabilities.

(*g*) *Emphasizing* the importance of mainstreaming disability issues as an integral part of relevant strategies of sustainable development.

(*h*) *Recognizing also* that discrimination against any person on the basis of disability is a violation of the inherent dignity and worth of the human person.

(*i*) *Recognizing further* the diversity of persons with disabilities.

(*j*) *Recognizing* the need to promote and protect the human rights of all persons with disabilities, including those who require more intensive support.

(*k*) *Concerned* that, despite these various instruments and undertakings, persons with disabilities continue to face barriers in their participation as equal members of society and violations of their human rights in all parts of the world.

(*l*) *Recognizing* the importance of international cooperation for improving the living conditions of persons with disabilities in every country, particularly in developing countries.

(*m*) *Recognizing* the valued existing and potential contributions made by persons with disabilities to the overall well-being and diversity of their communities, and that the promotion of the full enjoyment by persons with disabilities of their human rights and fundamental freedoms and of full participation by persons with disabilities will result in their enhanced sense of belonging and in significant advances in the human, social and economic development of society and the eradication of poverty.

(*n*) *Recognizing* the importance for persons with disabilities of their individual autonomy and independence, including the freedom to make their own choices.

(*o*) *Considering* that persons with disabilities should have the opportunity to be actively involved in decision-making processes about policies and programmes, including those directly concerning them.

(*p*) *Concerned* about the difficult conditions faced by persons with disabilities who are subject to multiple or aggravated forms of discrimination on the basis of race, colour, sex, language, religion, political or other opinion, national, ethnic, indigenous or social origin, property, birth, age or other status.

(*q*) *Recognizing* that women and girls with disabilities are often at greater risk, both within and outside the home, of violence, injury or abuse, neglect or negligent treatment, maltreatment or exploitation.

(*r*) *Recognizing* that children with disabilities should have full enjoyment of all human rights and fundamental freedoms on an equal basis with other children, and recalling obligations to that end undertaken by States Parties to the Convention on the Rights of the Child.

(s) *Emphasizing* the need to incorporate a gender perspective in all efforts to promote the full enjoyment of human rights and fundamental freedoms by persons with disabilities.

(*t*) *Highlighting* the fact that the majority of persons with disabilities live in conditions of poverty, and in this regard recognizing the critical need to address the negative impact of poverty on persons with disabilities.

(*u*) *Bearing in mind that* conditions of peace and security based on full respect of the purposes and principles contained in the Charter of the United Nations and observance of applicable human rights instruments are indispensable for the full protection of persons with disabilities, in particular during armed conflicts and foreign occupation.

(*v*) *Recognizing* the importance of accessibility to the physical, social, economic and cultural environment, to health and education and to information and communication, in enabling persons with disabilities to fully enjoy all human rights and fundamental freedoms.

(*w*) *Realizing* that the individual, having duties to other individuals and to the community to which he or she belongs, is under a responsibility to strive for the promotion and observance of the rights recognized in the International Bill of Human Rights.

(*x*) *Convinced* that the family is the natural and fundamental group unit of society and is entitled to protection by society and the State, and that persons with disabilities and their family members should receive the necessary protection and assistance to enable families to contribute towards the full and equal enjoyment of the rights of persons with disabilities.

(*y*) *Convinced* that a comprehensive and integral international convention to promote and protect the rights and dignity of persons with disabilities will make a significant contribution to redressing the profound social disadvantage of persons with disabilities and promote their participation in the civil, political, economic, social and cultural spheres with equal opportunities, in both developing and developed countries.

Have agreed as follows:

Article 1
Purpose

The purpose of the present Convention is to promote, protect and ensure the full and equal enjoyment of all human rights and fundamental freedoms by all persons with disabilities, and to promote respect for their inherent dignity.

Persons with disabilities include those who have long-term physical, mental, intellectual or sensory impairments which in interaction with various barriers may hinder their full and effective participation in society on an equal basis with others.

Article 24
Education

1. States Parties recognize the right of persons with disabilities to education. With a view to realizing this right without discrimination and on the basis of equal opportunity. States Parties shall ensure an inclusive education system at all levels and lifelong learning directed to:

(*a*) The full development of human potential and sense of dignity and self-worth, and the strengthening of respect for human rights, fundamental freedoms and human diversity;

(*b*) The development by persons with disabilities of their personality, talents and creativity, as well as their mental and physical abilities, to their fullest potential;

(*c*) Enabling persons with disabilities to participate effectively in a free society.

2. In realizing this right, States Parties shall ensure that:

(*a*) Persons with disabilities are not excluded from the general education system on the basis of disability, and that children with disabilities are not excluded from free and compulsory primary education, or from secondary education, on the basis of disability;

(*b*) Persons with disabilities can access an inclusive, quality and free primary education and secondary education on an equal basis with others in the communities in which they live;

(*c*) Reasonable accommodation of the individual's requirements is provided;

(*d*) Persons with disabilities receive the support required, within the general education system, to facilitate their effective education;

(*e*) Effective individualized support measures are provided in environments that maximize academic and social development, consistent with the goal of full inclusion.

3. States Parties shall enable persons with disabilities to learn life and social development skills to facilitate their full and equal participation in education and as members of the community. To this end, States Parties shall take appropriate measures, including:

(*a*) Facilitating the learning of Braille, alternative script, augmentative and alternative modes, means and formats of communication and orientation and mobility skills, and facilitating peer support and mentoring;

(*b*) Facilitating the learning of sign language and the promotion of the linguistic identity of the deaf community;

(*c*) Ensuring that the education of persons, and in particular children, who are blind, deaf or deaf blind, is delivered in the most appropriate languages and modes and means of communication for the individual, and in environments which maximize academic and social development.

4. In order to help ensure the realization of this right, States Parties shall take appropriate measures to employ teachers, including teachers with disabilities, who are qualified in sign language and/or Braille, and to train professionals and staff who work at all levels of education. Such training shall incorporate disability awareness and the use of appropriate augmentative and alternative modes, means and formats of communication, educational techniques and materials to support persons with disabilities.

5. States Parties shall ensure that persons with disabilities are able to access general tertiary education, vocational training, adult education and lifelong learning without discrimination and on an equal basis with others. To this end, States Parties shall ensure that reasonable accommodation is provided to persons with disabilities.

8

Educational Provisions for the Disabled in Acts and Policies

INTRODUCTION

The world society and nations through their various meets, conventions and international agreements has recognized the right to education for all with no discrimination of any kind. The Salamanca Statement and UN convention on the Rights of Persons with Disabilities-2006 discussed in Chapter Seven of this text provide a valid testimony for such understanding about the adjustment and mainstreaming of the disabled in the regular school.

For ensuring education for all and protecting the rights of the children with disabilities to attend the schools nearest to their locations along with their non-disabled peers, the state parties were urged (as well as commonly agreed) to frame the needed educational policies and make constitutional provisions for the same. Accordingly, the nations signatories to these international agreements and understanding tried to frame educational policies and made constitutional provision for safeguarding the interest of the disabled at their own level in their respective countries. India has also taken adequate measures on this account. It has made adequate provision, for the education and care of the disabled children and brought out a number of constitutional provisions in the name of acts and national policies. In this chapter we would like to focus on such policies and provisions meant for the education and welfare of the disabled.

EDUCATION OF THE DISABLED IN NPE, 1968

The National Policy of Education brought out by Government of India in 1968 was aimed to improve the quality of education in the country and focussed on providing educational facilities to all the citizens. It provided following statement for the education of the disabled under Section 4 maintaining equalization of educational opportunities in the school education system.

> "*Educational facilities for the physically and mentally handicapped children should be expanded and attempts should be made to develop integrated programs enabling the handicapped children to study in regular schools.*"

EDUCATION OF THE DISABLED IN NPE, 1986

Indian parliament during the budget session in 1986 discussed and adopted the National Policy on Education, 1986.

It has provided the things like below for the education of the disabled under the title 'Handicapped' in Part IV of its description "Education for Equality". The original version in this connection is reproduced below:

Handicapped

4.9 The objective should be to integrate the physically and mentally handicapped with the general community as equal partners, to prepare them for normal growth and to enable them to face life with courage and confidence. The following measures will be taken in this regard:

- (*i*) Wherever it is feasible, the education of children with motor handicaps and other mild handicaps will be common with that of others.
- (*ii*) Special schools with hostels will be provided, as far as possible at district headquarters, for the severely handicapped children.
- (*iii*) Adequate arrangements will be made to give vocational training to the disabled.
- (*iv*) Teachers training programmes will be reoriented, in particular for teachers of primary classes, to deal with the special difficulties of the handicapped children; and
- (*v*) Voluntary cffort for the education of the disabled will be encouraged in every possible manner.

EDUCATION FOR DISABLED IN POA (1992)

Education of the disabled in Program of Action, 1992 according to a written document belonging to Ministry of Human Resource Development, Department of Education, Government of India (discussed under Chapter 4 under the title "Education of the Handicapped") is reproduced below.

4. Education of the Handicapped

1. Present Situation

4.1.1 It is estimated that about 12.59 million children with disabilities are to be provided education in the school system.

Out of these, about half a million require vocational training.

4.1.2 The educability of another two million disabled children is to be improved through early intervention and services by ECCE.

4.1.3 At the end of 1991-92 about 30,000 children with disability were availing special benefits under the scheme of Integrated Education for Disabled Children (DBDC). In addition, about 60,000 children with mild disabilities received resource support without special benefits. A large number of children with disability are also receiving education in special schools which number about 1035.

4.14 The Project Integrated Education for Disabled (PIED) is being implemented, as a field demonstration, in one block each in ten States and Union Territories.

4.1.5 The innovative multi-category training of resource teachers has been found to be effective and has been institutionalised in the Regional Colleges of Education, the universities offering special education courses and the training programmes organised by Non-Governmental Organisations.

4.1.6 Each DIET has been provided a resource centre for orienting elementary teachers and establishing field demonstrations in lab areas. Faculty from 102 DIETs have so far received induction training at the NCERT.

4.1.7 The Ministry of Welfare had taken steps to ensure supply of trained manpower to special schools and improve standards in these schools through the National Institutes for the Handicapped (NIHs) and increased support to NGOs.

4.1.8 The Ministry of Labour manages 17 Vocational Rehabilitation Centres (VRCs) for the handicapped and helps in their placement also. About 66,000 persons with disability have been rehabilitated under this scheme by September, 1991. Three per cent of seats for admission to ITIs and under the Apprenticeship Training Scheme are available for handicapped persons. These seats are being fully utilised.

4.1.9 The evaluation of special schools and the scheme of IEDC has revealed some grey areas. General education system is not yet mobilized to a noticeable extent, for education of the handicapped, either at the Central or State level. Inputs from different schemes like CBR, DRC, ECCE, non-formal education, adult education, vocational and technical education, etc. are not being brought together for the education of the physically handicapped. Some States are still reluctant to implement IEDC while some are implementing it rather indifferently. Few NGOs are active in rural area's. The standard of education in special schools needs improvement. Facilities for the education of children with multiple handicaps are yet to be developed. The early detection and intervention programmes so essential for education of these children have yet to be started. The goal of UEE for this disadvantaged group would remain an unachievable dream unless concerted and urgent measures are taken.

2. NPE Review Perspective

4.2.1 As part of its concern for equalisation of educational opportunities, the NPE, 1986 focuses on the needs of children with disabilities. The NPE, 1986 recommended an integrated education in general schools for children with locomotor handicaps and with other mild disabilities, orientation and pre-service training of general teachers to meet special needs of these children, provision of vocational training, establishment of special schools for severely disabled children and encouragement of voluntary organisations in these tasks. The PoA suggested a pragmatic placement principle. It postulated that a child with disability who can be educated in a general school should be educated in a general school only and not in a special school. Even those children who are initially admitted to special schools for training in plus curriculum skills should be transferred to general schools once they acquire daily living skills, communication skills and basic academic skills.

3. Targets

4.3.1 For achieving equalisation of educational opportunities, children with disability should have access to quality education comparable to other children. However, considering the financial resources likely to be available during the 8th Plan the targets for education of disabled children would be as follows:

(*i*) Children who can be educated in general primary schools
  (*a*) Universal enrolment by the end of 9th Five Year Plan.
  (*b*) Ensuring achievement of minimum level of learning through adjustment and adaptation of curriculum and teaching to special needs.

(*ii*) Children who require to be educated in special schools or special classes in general schools
  (*a*) Universal enrolment by the end of the 9th Five Year Plan.
  (*b*) Ensuring achievement of level of learning commensurate with their potential.

(*iii*) Reduction of drop out rates on par with other children.

(*iv*) Providing access to disabled children to secondary and senior secondary schools with resource support and making special provision for vocational training of these children, particularly those with intellectual disabilities.

(*v*) Reorienting pre-service and in-service teacher education programmes including pre-school teachers training programmes to meet special needs in the classroom.

(*vi*) Reorienting adult and non-formal education programmes to meet educational and vocational training needs of persons with disability.

4. Implementation Strategies

4.4.1 The strategy of area-specific and population-specific micro-planning for UEE is equally relevant for this disadvantaged group. Planning for UEE and adult literacy at all levels – Centre, State, District, Block and Project – should provide for the educational needs of this category of children.

4.4.2 Education of children with disability will be a component in the training of educational planners and administrators as well as pre-service and in-service teachers. DIETs, CTEs and IASEs which have been provided facilities for this component will have to pay particular attention to this aspect of teacher training. While drawing up schemes for strengthening SCERTs, cells for education of the handicapped may be considered as envisaged, in IEDC.

4.4.3 The material supplied under Operation Blackboard will have to take into consideration special needs of these children. School buildings will have to take note of architectural adjustments needed to ensure access to children with disability, at the construction stage itself so as to avoid expenditure on modifications later on. Special schools need to be opened in the districts which have no special school facilities. The education of the handicapped should form an essential component in all externally assisted basic education projects being implemented or proposed to be implemented.

5. Integrated Education for Disabled Children (IEDC)

4.5.1 The PoA, 1986 target of increasing enrolment of children by 25 per cent per year was achieved as enrolment of disabled children in general schools increased from 15,000 to 30,000. Subject to availability of resources, the cumulative enrolment would reach 50,000 by the end of the 8th Plan. However, an additional 1,00,000 children with mild disabilities will be provided resource support from teachers and learning aids and equipment.

4.5.2 The following actions are needed for achieving the targets laid down:

(*i*) Adequate allocations of resources.

(*ii*) Provision for education of persons with disability should be made an integral component in externally assisted basic education projects.

(*iii*) Provision for education of disabled children should be made in the Centrally Sponsored Schemes of Operation Blackboard, Vocationalisation of Education and Non-Formal Education.

(*iv*) Co-ordinated implementation of schemes like Community Based Rehabilitation, ECCE, VRCs and IEDC so as to reduce cost and achieve higher coverage. This would require coordination among the Ministries/Departments of Health, Welfare, Education, Women & Child Development and Labour.

(*v*) The NGOs have to be encouraged to implement IEDC, particularly in rural areas. The NGOs involved in other educational activities will be encouraged to work in this area also and assisted in developing their expertise.

6. Special Schools

4.6.1 The PoA envisaged provision of an additional 400 special schools at the district headquarters. However, because of resource constraints no new special school has been established. The Ministry of Welfare has identified 240 districts without any special schooling facility. Efforts would be made to provide special schools in these districts by the end of 9th Five Year Plan.

7. Vocational Training

4.7.1 The Ministry of Labour is providing vocational training to the handicapped through the Craftsman Training Scheme (CTS), the Apprenticeship Training Scheme and separate Vocational Rehabilitation Centres (VRCs). Three per cent of the seats for admission to ITIs under the Craftsman Training Scheme and Apprenticeship Training Scheme are reserved for candidates who are handicapped but have aptitude and are otherwise fit to undergo the required training. The States/UTs have been advised from time to time to implement this reservation for the handicapped which will be continued during the 8th Plan also. Seventeen VRCs will continue to provide training to a larger number of handicapped persons during the 8th plan. The instructors in ITIs will receive orientation to meet special needs of handicapped persons. This component will be added in ITI instructor's training programme. Adjustment and adaptation of equipment to provide full access to disabled persons will be ensured.

4.7.2 The National Institutes for the Handicapped under the Ministry of Welfare will continue their efforts to provide vocational training to the handicapped.

4.7.3 The Department of Education will also encourage voluntary organisations working in the area of vocational education and training for the handicapped. The CIVE will provide support to vocational training programmes for the handicapped through teacher training material and other resources.

8. Orientation and Training of Teachers

4.8.1 All the DIETs to be established by the end of the 8th Plan will have a resource room and trained faculty to teach the essential component of education of children with disability. They will also run orientation programmes for teachers at least from lab areas and practising schools to establish field demonstration of IEDC programme. The SCERTs will support field demonstrations under the scheme of IEDC. Similar action is suggested for the 250 CTEs and 50 IASEs. The budget provision is available in the scheme itself. The pre-service training curriculum will induct essential components in these areas, wherever it has not been done so far.

4.8.2 All in-service teachers should receive awareness input on education of children with disability in orientation programmes. In each area/ institution where IEDC is implemented all teachers will receive orientation as envisaged in the scheme of IEDC. The heads of institutions and educational administrators will also receive training. Considering the large numbers to be covered, the Indira Gandhi National Open University and NCERT should plan credit courses on special education to equip general teachers to meet special needs. The NCERT will provide training to the IEDC cell staff. Multicategory training of resource teachers will be encouraged in UGC supported programmes.

9. Training of Educational Administrators

4.9.1 The NIEPA in collaboration with NCERT should develop programmes for training educational administrators and making them aware of the needs of this group. The IGNOU should design and offer courses for this target group also.

10. Special Teachers

4.10.1 The NIHs and its regional training centres have built up capacity to train single disability special teachers for special schools. Besides meeting demands of the new special schools, the existing untrained teachers will be trained and backlog cleared by the end of the 8th Plan. In service training of special teachers will be planned in a way that each teacher receives a three-week course every four years.

4.10.2 Efforts will be made to promote special education units in university departments of education for training teachers to handle multicategory disabilities.

11. Educational and Vocational Guidance Personnel

4.11.1 The existing educational and vocational guidance counsellors should be provided training in dealing with disabled children and their parents. Essential component should also be added to their preservice training programmes. The NCERT and NIHs should design and offer in-service course for in-service counsellors.

12. Content and Process

4.12.1 Curriculum flexibility is of special significance for these children. Special needs of these children will be met, if child centred education is practised. The curriculum adjustment and adaptation of teaching methods and material will be waked out, field tried and provided to the users. The following actions will be taken:

(*i*) Guidelines for child centred education, including special needs in the classroom, being developed at the NCERT will be made available by mid 1993.

(*ii*) Guidelines for adjustment of curriculum and instructional material and methods for visually and hearing handicapped at primary level have been developed. These will be made available to teachers. Work for upper primary and secondary school level will be started and completed by the end of 1994.

(*iii*) The achievement of minimum levels of learning by children with mild disabilities should be ensured through resource support and alternative learning material, wherever needed,

(*iv*) The Boards of Examination should make adjustment and adaptations in examination for the handicapped children.

(*v*) Study of more than one language should not be compulsory for deaf children.

(*vi*) Teaching of Science and Mathematics is either not available to handicapped children or they opt for an easier substitute. Special efforts should be made by the NIHs and the NCERT to develop an action programme to improve access of disabled children to these important areas.

(*vii*) Child-to-child help in education of children with disability is an effective resource in view of large classes and multigrade teaching. NCERT should develop a package and make it available to teachers by the end of 1993.

(*viii*) The special learning aids and equipment like Braille books, Braille kit, audio visual material will be developed and made available to schools by NIHs and NCERT.

13. Use of Mass Media

4.13.1 Radio and television are being used in a limited way both for advocacy as well as educational purposes. The CIET, SIETs, NIHs and other organisations will develop a variety of programmes so that they can be regularly telecast/broadcast The MHRD will approach the Ministry of Information and Broadcasting for providing adequate time for this purpose.

4.13.2 The CIET, SIETs and NIHs will also develop software in non-telecast mode and make it available to DIETs, other training centres and NGOs working with disabled persons.

4.13.3 Field publicity units should be utilised by States for advocacy programmes. Newspapers and magazines have started popular advocacy and educational writing in this area. The NCERT and the NIHs will develop packages and hand over to journalists in workshops.

14. Availability of Special Learning Material and Aids

4.14.1 Learning material in Braille is still not available to all children. Same is the case with aids like Braille slate, Taylor frame, etc. Similarly language training material for speech and hearing handicapped is not available in regional languages. Steps will be taken by the NIVH, AYJNIHH, NIMH and the NCERT to ensure the availability of such material.

15. Monitoring and Evaluation

4.15.1 The availability of a reliable data base is essential for proper monitoring and evaluation of educational programmes for persons with disability. Towards this end the District Education Office, must, with the help of other agencies, collect data about the number of disabled persons in the District – disability wise, sex wise and age group wise; beneficiaries under IEDC, special schools, ITIs, VRCs, etc., number of special and resource teachers, their qualifications and pay scale, and budget utilisation. Similar information should also be included in the statistics collected by MHRD as also the Educational Surveys conducted by NCERT.

4.15.2 The MHRD and the Ministry of Welfare should make grants under IEDC and special schools contingent on the periodic returns giving the information. An interdepartmental Committee should be setup at the State and Central levels for monitoring. In addition, regular visits by the officers of the MHRD, NCERT, Regional Colleges of Education and field offices, should lead to status reports.

4.15.3 Evaluation studies by external agencies, universities conducting courses on education and rehabilitation of persons in specific geographical areas will be commissioned by MHRD and the Ministry of Welfare.

EDUCATION OF THE STUDENTS WITH DISABILITIES IN PWD ACT, 1995

The Persons with Disabilities (Equal opportunities, Protection and Full Participation) Act, 1995 is an act enacted by Parliament of India. It provides legislative support and protection to the education, adjustment and welfare of the persons with disabilities (including disabled children studying in the schools). It clearly stands for legal protection to provide equal opportunities for their education and development in an inclusive setup with their full participation in all the programs of the school attended by them.

In its documentary form (published in Part II, Section I of the Extraordinary Gazette of India, Ministry of Law, Justice and Company Affairs, Government of India New Delhi) the PWD Act, 1995 has been divided into 14 chapters named as below.

I. Preliminary
II. The Central Coordination Committee
III. The Slate Coordination Committee
IV. Prevention and Early Detection of Disabilities
V. Education
VI. Employment
VII. Affirmative Action
VIII. Non-Discrimination
IX. Research and Manpower Development
X. Recognition of Institutions for Persons with Disabilities
XI Institution for Persons with Severe Disabilities
XII. The Chief Commissioner and Commissioners for Persons with Disabilities
XIII. Social Security
XIV. Miscellaneous

As far as the education and welfare of the children with disabilities is concerned, it has been well described in chapters IV and V of this document.

Accordingly, we here are reproducing what has been provided in these two chapters for the well being and education of the children with disabilities.

Chapter IV. Prevention and Early Detection of Disabilities

Within the limits of their economic capacity and development, the appropriate governments and the local authorities, with a view to preventing the occurrence of disabilities, shall:

(*a*) Undertake or cause to be undertaken surveys, investigations and research concerning the cause of occurrence of disabilities;

(*b*) Promote various methods of preventing disabilities;

(*c*) Screen all the children at least once in a year for the purpose of identifying "at-risk" cases;

(*d*) Provide facilities for training to the staff at the primary health centers;

(*e*) Sponsor or cause to be sponsored awareness campaigns and is disseminated or, cause to be disseminated information for general hygiene. Health and sanitation;

(*f*) Take measures for pre-natal, parental and post-natal care of mother and child;

(*g*) Educate the public through the pre-schools, schools, primary health centers, village level workers and anganwadi workers;

(*h*) Create awareness amongst the masses through television, radio and other mass media on the causes of disabilities and the preventive measures to be adopted.

Chapter V. Education

1. The appropriate governments and the local authorities shall-
   (*a*) Ensure that every child with a disability has access to free education in an appropriate environment till he attains the age of eighteen years;
   (*b*) Endeavour to promote the integration of students with disabilities in the normal schools;
   (*c*) Promote setting up of special schools in government and private sector for those in need of special education, in such a manner that children with disabilities living in any part of the country have access to such schools;
   (*d*) Endeavour to equip the special schools for children with disabilities with vocational training facilities.
2. The appropriate governments and the local authorities shall by notification make schemes for-
   (*a*) Conducting part-time classes in respect of children with disabilities who having completed education up to class fifth and could not continue their studies on a whole-time basis;
   (*b*) Conducting special part-time classes for providing functional literacy for children in the age group of sixteen and above;
   (*c*) Imparting non-formal education by utilizing the available manpower in rural areas after giving them appropriate orientation;

(*d*) Imparting education through open schools or open universities;

(*e*) Conducting class and discussions through interactive electronic or other media:

(*f*) Providing every child with disability free of cost special books and equipments needed for his education.

3. The appropriate Governments shall initiate or cause to be initiated research by official and non-governmental agencies for the purpose of designing and developing new assistive devices, teaching aids, special teaching materials or such other items as are necessary to give a child with disability equal opportunities in education.

4. The appropriate governments shall setup adequate number of teachers' training institutions and assist the national institutes and other voluntary organizations to develop teachers' training programmes specializing in disabilities so that requisite trained manpower is available for special schools and integrated schools for children with disabilities.

5. Without prejudice to the foregoing provisions, the appropriate governments shall by notification prepare a comprehensive education scheme which shall make Provision for-

(*a*) Transport facilities to the children with disabilities or in the alternative financial incentives to parents or guardians to enable their children with disabilities to attend schools.

(*b*) The removal of architectural barriers from schools, colleges or oilier institution, imparting vocational and professional training.

(*c*) The supply of books, uniforms and other materials to children with disabilities attending school.

(*d*) The grant of scholarship to students with disabilities.

(*e*) Setting up of appropriate fora for the redressal of grievances of parent, regarding the placement of their children with disabilities.

(*f*) Suitable modification in the examination system to eliminate purely mathematical questions for the benefit of blind students and students with low vision.

(*g*) Restructuring of curriculum for the benefit of children with disabilities.

(*h*) Restructuring the curriculum for benefit of students with hearing impairment to facilitate them to take only one language as part of their curriculum.

6. All educational institutions shall provide or cause to be provided amanuensis to blind students and students with or low vision.

EDUCATION AND WELFARE OF THE CHILDREN WITH DISABILITIES IN RCI ACT, 1992

The Rehabilitation Council of India Act, 1992 is an act or legislative measure enacted by the Parliament of India. It was aimed to make provision for the constitution of the Rehabilitation Council of India for regulating the training of rehabilitation professionals and the maintenance of a Central Rehabilitation Register and for matters connected therewith or incidental thereto.

As a document, it has been published in the Gazette of India Extraordinary Part II-Section I by the Legislative department of the Ministry of Law, Justice and Company Affairs, Government of India, New Delhi. It is comprised of three chapters named as Preliminary, The Rehabilitation Council of India and Functions of the Council. The latest version also contains Amendment carried out in the act in the year 2000. For the angle of the education and rehabilitation of children with disabilities, the Chapter I (Preliminary) and Chapter III (Functions of the Council) are hereby reproduced leaving the Chapter II which almost describes the constitution and organization of the RCI.

Chapter I
Preliminary

1. (1) This Act may be called the Rehabilitation Council of India Act, 1992.

(2) It shall come into force on such date as the Central Government may, by notification in the Official Gazette, appoint.

2. (1) In this Act, unless the context otherwise requires–

(*a*) "Chairperson" means the Chairperson of the Council appointed under sub-section (3) of Section 3;

(*b*) "Council" means the Rehabilitation Council of India constituted under Section 3;

(*c*) "handicapped" means a person:

(*i*) visually handicapped;

(*ii*) hearing handicapped;

(*iii*) suffering from locomotor disability; or

(*iv*) suffering from mental retardation;

(*d*) "hearing handicap" means deafness with hearing impairment of 70 decibels and above, in the better ear or total loss of hearing in both ears;

(*e*) "locomotor disability" means a person's inability to execute distinctive activities associated with moving, both himself and objects, from place to place, and such inability resulting from affliction of either bones, joints, muscles or nerves;

(*f*) "member" means a member appointed under sub-section (3) of Section 3 and includes the Chairperson;

(*g*) "Member-Secretary" means the Member-Secretary appointed under sub-section (1) of Section 8;

(*h*) "mental retardation" means a condition of arrested or incomplete development of mind of a person which is specially characterized by sub-normality of intelligence;

(*i*) "notification" means a notification published in the Official Gazette;

(*j*) "prescribed" means prescribed by regulations;

(*k*) "recognised rehabilitation qualifications" means any of the qualifications included in the Schedule;

(*l*) "Register" means the Central Rehabilitation Register maintained under sub-section (1) of section 23;

(*m*) "regulations" means regulations made under this Act;

(*n*) "rehabilitation professionals" means-

(*i*) audiologists and speech therapists;

(*ii*) clinical psychologists;

(*iii*) hearing aid and ear mould technicians;

(*iv*) rehabilitation engineers and technicians;

(*v*) special teachers for educating and training the handicapped;

(*vi*) vocational counsellors, employment officers and placement officers dealing with handicapped;

(*vii*) multi-purpose rehabilitation therapists, technicians; or

(*viii*) such other category of professionals as the Central Government may, in consultation with the Council, notify from time to time;

(*o*) "visually handicapped" means a person who suffers from any of the following conditions, namely:

(*i*) total absence of sight;

(*ii*) visual acuity not exceeding 6/60 or 20/200 (Snellen) in the better eye with the correcting lenses; or

(*iii*) limitation of the field of vision subtending and angle of degree or worse.

(2) Any reference in this Act to any enactment or any provision thereof shall, in relation to an area in which such enactment or such provision is not in force, be construed as a reference to the corresponding law or the relevant provision of the corresponding law, if any, in force in that area.

The Chapter II. Rehabilitation Council of India, contains Section 3 to Section 10 of the RCI Act. Here we are not presenting it as it pertains to organization and staff of the RCI.

Chapter III
Functions of the Council

(1) The qualifications granted by any University or other institution in India which are included in the Schedule shall be recognized qualifications for rehabilitation professionals.

(2) Any University or other institution which grants qualification for the rehabilitation professionals not included in the Schedule may apply to the Central Government to have any such qualification recognized, and the Central Government, after consulting the Council may, by notification, amend the Schedule so as to include such qualification therein and any such notification may also direct that an entry shall be made in the last column of the Schedule against such qualification only when granted after a specified date.

12. The Council may enter into negotiations with the authority in any country outside India for settling of a scheme of reciprocity for the recognition of qualifications, and in pursuance of any such scheme, the Central Government may, by notification, amend the Schedule so as to include therein any qualification which the Council has decided should be recognized, and by such notification may also direct that an entry shall be made in the last column of the Schedule declaring that it shall be the recognized qualification only when granted after a specified date.

13. (1) Subject to the other provisions contained in this Act, any qualification included in the Schedule shall be sufficient qualification for enrolment on the Register.

(2) No person, other than the rehabilitation professional who possesses a recognized rehabilitation qualification and is enrolled on the Register-

(*a*) shall hold office as rehabilitation professional or any such office (by whatever designation called) in Government or in any institution maintained by a local or other authority;

(*b*) shall practice as rehabilitation professional anywhere in India;

(*c*) shall be entitled to sign or authenticate any certificate required by any law to be signed or authenticated by a rehabilitation professional;

(*d*) shall be entitled to give any evidence in any court as an expert under section 45 of the Indian Evidence Act, 1872 on any matter relating to the handicapped:

Provided that if a person possesses the recognized rehabilitation professional qualifications on the date of commencement of this Act, he shall be deemed to be an enrolled rehabilitation professional for a period of six months from such commencement, and if he has made an application for enrolment on the Register within said period of six months, till such application is disposed of.

(3) Any person who acts in contravention of any provision of sub-section (2) shall be punished with imprisonment for a term which may extend to one year, or with fine which may extend to one thousand rupees, or with both.

14. Every university or institution in India which grants a recognized qualification shall furnish such information as the Council may, from time to time, require as to the courses of study and examinations to be under gone in order to obtain such qualification, as to the ages at which such courses of study and examinations are required to be undergone and such qualification is conferred and generally as to the requisites for obtaining such qualification.

15. (1) The Council shall appoint such number of inspectors as it may deem requisite to inspect any university or institution where education for practising as rehabilitation professionals is given or to attend any examination held by any university or institution for the purpose of recommending to the Central Government recognition of qualifications granted by that university or institution as recognized rehabilitation qualifications.

(2) The Inspectors appointed under sub-section (1) shall not interfere with the conduct of any training or examination but shall report to the Council on the adequacy of the standards of education including staff, equipment, accommodation, training and other facilities prescribed for giving such education or of the sufficiency of every examination which they attend.

(3) The council shall forward a copy of the report of the Inspector under sub-section (2) to the University or institution concerned and shall also forward a copy, with the remarks of the university or the institution thereon, to the Central Government.

16. (1) The Council may appoint such number of Visitors as it may deem requisite to inspect any university or institution wherein education for rehabilitation professionals is given or attend any examination for the purpose of granting recognized rehabilitation qualifications.

(2) Any person, whether he is a member of the Council or not, may be appointed as a Visitor under sub-section (1) but a person who is appointed as an Inspector under sub-section (1) of section 15 for any inspection or examination shall not be appointed as a Visitor for the same inspection or examination.

(3) The Visitor shall not interfere with the conduct of any training or examination but shall report to the Chairperson on the adequacy of the standards of education including staff, equipment, accommodation, training and other facilities prescribed for giving education to the rehabilitation professionals or on sufficiency of every examination which they attend.

(4) The report of a Visitor shall be treated as confidential unless in any particular case the Chairperson otherwise, directs:

Provided that if the Central Government requires a copy of the report of a Visitor, the Council shall furnish the same.

17. (1) When upon report by the Inspector or the Visitor it appears to the Council—

(*a*) that the courses of study and examination to be undergone in or the proficiency required from candidates at any examination held by any University or institution, or (*b*) that the staff, equipment, accommodation, training and other facilities for instruction and training provided in such University or institution,

do not conform to the standard prescribed by the Council, the Council shall make a representation to that effect to the Central Government.

(2) After considering such representation, the Central Government may send it to the University or institution with an intimation of the period within which the University or institution may submit its explanation to that Government.

(3) On the receipt of the explanation or where no explanation is submitted within the period fixed then, on the expiry of that period, the Central Government after making such further inquiry, if any, as it may think fit, may, by notification, direct that an entry shall be made in the Schedule against the said recognized rehabilitation qualification declaring that it shall be the recognized rehabilitation qualification only when granted before a specified date or that the said recognized rehabilitation qualification if granted to students of a specified University or institution shall be recognized rehabilitation qualification only when granted before a specified date, or as the case may be, that the said recognized rehabilitation qualification shall be recognized rehabilitation qualification in relation to a specified University or institution only when granted after a specified date.

18. The Council may prescribe the minimum standards of education required for granting recognized rehabilitation qualification by Universities or institutions in India.

19. The Member-Secretary of the Council may, on receipt of an application made by any person in the prescribed manner enter his name in the Register provided that the Member-Secretary is satisfied that such person possesses the recognized rehabilitation qualification.

20. Subject to the conditions and restrictions laid down in this Act regarding engagement in the area of rehabilitation of the handicapped by persons possessing the recognized rehabilitation qualifications, every person whose name is for the time being borne on the Register shall be entitled to practice as a rehabilitation professional in any part of India and to recover in due course of law in respect of such practice any expenses, charges in respect of medicaments or other appliances or any fees to which he may be entitled.

21. (1) The Council may prescribe standards of professional conduct and etiquette and a code of ethics for rehabilitation professionals.

(2) Regulations made by the Council under sub-section (1) may specify which violations thereof shall constitute infamous conduct in any professional respect, that is to say, professional misconduct, and such provision shall have effect notwithstanding anything contained in any other law for the time being in force.

(3) The Council may order that the name of any person shall be removed

from the Register where it is satisfied, after giving that person a reasonable opportunity of being heard, and after such further inquiry, if any, as it may deem fit to make—

(*i*) that his name has been entered in the Register by error or on account of misrepresentation or suppression of a material fact;

(*ii*) that he has been convicted of any offence or has been guilty of any infamous conduct in any professional respect, or has violated the standards of professional conduct and etiquette or the code of ethics prescribed under sub-section (1) which, in the opinion of the Council, renders him unfit to be kept in the Register.

(4) An order under sub-section (3) may direct that any person whose name is ordered to be removed from the Register shall be ineligible for registration under this Act either permanently or for such period of years as may be specified.

22. (1) Where the name of any person has been removed from the Register on any ground other than that he is not possessed of the requisite rehabilitation qualifications, he may appeal, in the prescribed manner and subject to such conditions, including conditions as to the payment of a fee, as may be prescribed to the Central Government whose decision thereon shall be final.

(2) No appeal under sub-section (1) shall be admitted if it is preferred after the expiry of a period of thirty days from the date of the order under sub-section (3) of section 21:

Provided that an appeal may be admitted after the expiry of the said period of thirty days if the appellant satisfies the Central Government that he had sufficient cause for not preferring the appeal within the said period.

23. (1) It shall be the duty of the Member-Secretary to keep and maintain the Register in accordance with the provisions of this Act and any order made by the Council and from time to time to revise the Register and publish it in the Official Gazette.

(2) The Register shall be deemed to be a public document within the meaning of the Indian Evidence Act, 1872 and may be proved by a copy thereof.

24. (1) The Council shall furnish such reports, copies of its minutes, abstracts of its accounts, and other information to the Central Government as that Government may require.

(2) The Central Government may publish in such manner as it may think fit, any report, copy, abstract or other information furnished to it by the Council under this section or under section 16.

25. Notwithstanding anything contained in the Code of Criminal Procedure, 1973, no court shall take cognizance of an offence punishable under this Act except upon a complaint, in writing, made by any person authorized in this behalf by the Council.

26. No suit, prosecution or other legal proceeding shall lie against the

Central Government, Council, Chairperson, members, Member-Secretary or any officer or other employee of the Council for anything which is in good faith done or intended to be done under this Act.

27. The Chairperson, members, Member-Secretary, officers and other employees of the Council shall, while acting or purporting to act in pursuance of the provisions of this Act or of any rule and regulation made there under, be deemed to be public servants within the meaning of section 21 of the Indian Penal Code.

28. The Central Government may, by notification, make rules in carry out the purposes of this Act.

29. The Council may with the previous sanction of the Central Government, make, by notification, regulations generally to carry out the purposes of this Act, and without prejudice to the generality of the foregoing power, such regulations may provide for—

(*a*) the management of the property of the Council;

(*b*) the maintenance and audit of the accounts of the Council;

(*c*) the resignation of members of the Council;

(*d*) the powers and duties of the Chairperson;

(*e*) the rules of procedure in the transaction of business under sub-section (3) of section 4;

(*f*) the function of the Executive Committee and other committees, constituted under section 7;

(*g*) the powers and duties of the Member-Secretary under sub-section (1) of section 8;

(*h*) the qualifications, appointment, powers and duties of, and procedure to be followed by, Inspectors and Visitors;

(*i*) the courses and period of study or of training, to be undertaken, the subjects of examination and standards of proficiency therein to be obtained in any University or any institution for grant of recognized rehabilitation qualification;

(*j*) the standards of staff, equipment, accommodation, training and other facilities for study or training of the rehabilitation professionals;

(*k*) the conduct of examinations, qualifications of examiners, and the condition of the admission to such examinations;

(*l*) the standards of professional conduct and etiquette and code of ethics to be observed by rehabilitation professionals under subjection (1) of section 21;

(*m*) the particulars to be stated, and proof of qualifications to be given, in application for registration under this Act;

(*n*) the manner in which and the conditions subject to which an appeal may be preferred under sub-section (1) of section 22;

(*o*) the fees to be paid on applications and appeals under this Act;

(*p*) any other matter which is to be, or may be, prescribed.

EDUCATION OF THE CHILDREN WITH DISABILITY IN RIGHT TO EDUCATION ACT, 2009

Right to Education Act, 2009 is a legislative measure and act enacted by Parliament of India aimed to provide for free and compulsory education to all children of the age of six to fourteen years. It received the assent of the President on 26th August, 2009 and published in the Gazette of India on 27th August, 2009. Its enforcement and functioning rests with the Legislative department of the Ministry of Laws and Justice, Government of India.

As a written document, RTE Act, 2009 is divided into seven chapters named as below.

I. Preliminary (providing legal meanings to the terms used in the act)
II. Right to Free and Compulsory Education
III. Duties of Appropriate Government, Local Authorities and Parents
IV. Responsibilities of Schools and Teachers
V. Curriculum and Completion of Elementary Education
VI. Protection of Rights of Children
VII. Miscellaneous

In the end a schedule has also been provided enlisting norms and standards for a school supposed to implement the RTI.

For a detailed description of the provisions of the act, readers may go through all the 13 pages of this written document available on internet at the Website of the Ministry of Law and Justice, Government of India or may get a printed copy from the publication department of Government of India. However, the main provisions lying in this act, particularly in reference to the education of the children with Disability may be outlined as below.

1. *Right of Child to Free and Compulsory Education*: Every child of the age six to fourteen years shall have a right to free and compulsory education in a neighbourhood school till completion of elementary education.

Here it should also be clear that

(*i*) no child shall be liable to pay any kind of fee or charges or expenses which may prevent him or her from pursuing and completing the elementary education.

(*ii*) a child suffering from disability, as defined in clause (*i*) of section 2 of the Persons with Disabilities (Equal Opportunities, Protection and Full Participation) Act, 1996, shall have the right to pursue free and compulsory elementary education in accordance with the provisions of Chapter V of the said Act (The same as given to non-disabled peers).

2. *Special provision for children not admitted to, or who have not completed Elementary Education*: Where a child above six years of age has not been admitted in any school or though admitted, could not complete his or her elementary education, then, he or she shall be admitted in a class appropriate to his or her age.

Provided that where a child is directly admitted in a class appropriate to his or her age, then, he or she shall, in order to be at par with others, have a right to receive special training, in such manner, and within such time-limits, as may be prescribed.

Provided further that a child so admitted to elementary education shall be entitled to free education till completion of elementary education even after fourteen years.

3. ***Right of Transfer to other School***:

(*i*) Where in a school, there is no provision for completion of elementary education, a child shall have a right to seek transfer to any other school, excluding the school belonging to a specified category and an unaided school not receiving any kind of grants to meet its expenses from the appropriate Government and local authority.

(*ii*) Where a child is required to move from one school to another either within a state or outside for any reason whatsoever, such child shall have the right to seek transfer to any other school excluding the school belonging to specific category or an unaided school.

4. ***Duty of Appropriate Government or Local Authority to Establish a School***: For carrying out the provisions of this act the appropriate Government and local authorities shall establish, within such area or limits of neighbourhood as may be prescribed a school where it is not so established within a period of three years from the commencement of this act.

5. ***Sharing of Financial and other Responsibilities***: The Central Government and the State Government shall have concurrent responsibility for providing funds for carrying out the provision of this act.

6. ***Duty of Parents and Guardians***: It shall be the duty of every parent or guardian to admit or cause to be admitted his or her child or ward, as the case may be, to an elementary education in the neighbourhood school.

7. ***Appropriate Government to provide for Pre-school Education***: With a view to prepare children above the age of three years for elementary education and to provide early childhood care and education for all children until they complete the age of six years, the appropriate Government may make necessary arrangement for providing free pre-school education for such children.

8. ***Extent of School's Responsibility for Free and Compulsory Education***: For the purpose of this act, a school

(*a*) established, owned and controlled by the appropriate government or local authority shall provide free and compulsory elementary education to all children admitted therein.

(*b*) receiving aid or grants to meet whole or parts of its expenses from the government or local authority shall provide free and compulsory elementary education to such proportion of children admitted therein as its annual recurring aid or grants so received bears to its annual recurring expenses, subject to minimum of twenty-five per cent.

(*c*) belonging to specific category (such as Kendriya Vidyalaya, Sanik School, Navodaya, or owned by minorities) or unaided shall admit in class 1 to the extent of at least twenty-five per cent of the strength of that class; children belonging to weaker section and disadvantaged group (including disabled) in the neighbourhood and provide free and compulsory elementary education till completion.

Provided further that where any school government, non-government, aided or unaided imparts pre-school education, the provision of clauses (*a*) to (*c*) mentioned above shall apply to admission to such pre-school education.

9. ***No Capitation Fee and Screening procedure for admission*:**

(*i*) No school or person shall, while admitting a child, collect any capitation fee and subject the child or his or her parents or guardian to any screening procedure.

(*ii*) Any school or person, if in contravention of the provisions of sub-section (1) —

(*a*) receives capitation fee, shall be punishable with fine which may extend to ten times the capitation fee charged.

(*b*) subjects a child to screening procedure, shall be punishable with fine which may extend to twenty-five thousand rupees for the first contravention and fifty thousand rupees for each subsequent contraventions.

10. ***Proof of Age for Admission*:**

(*i*) For the purposes of admission to elementary education the age of a child shall be determined on the basis of the birth certificate issued in accordance with the provisions of the Births, Deaths and Marriages Registration Act, 1886 or on the basis of such other document, as may be prescribed.

(*ii*) No child shall be denied admission in a school for lack of age proof.

11. ***No Denial of Admission*:** A child shall be admitted in a school at the commencement of the academic year or within such extended period as may be prescribed.

Provided that no child shall be denied admission if such admission is sought subsequent to the extended period.

Provided further that any child admitted after the extended period shall complete his studies in such manner as may be prescribed by the appropriate Government.

12. ***Prohibition of Holding back and Expulsion*:** No child admitted in a school shall be held back in any class or expelled from school till the completion of elementary education.

13. *Prohibition of Physical Punishment and Mental Harassment to Child:* No child shall be subjected to physical punishment or mental harassment. Person breaking this rule shall be liable to disciplinary action.

14. *No school to be established without obtaining Certificate of Recognition*: No school other than a school established owned or controlled by the appropriate Government or the local authority shall after the commencement of this act be established or function without obtaining a certificate of recognition from such authority by making an application in such form and manner, as may be prescribed. Provided that no such recognition shall be granted to a school unless it fulfils norms and standard specified for this purpose.

15. *School Management Committee*: A school (leaving the schools specified or unaided) shall constitute a School Management Committee consisting of the elected representatives of the local authority, parents or guardians of children admitted in the school and teachers.

16. *School Development Plan*: Every school committee shall prepare a school development plan, in such manner as may be prescribed. The plan so prepared will work as the basis for grants sanctioned by the appropriate Government or local bodies.

17. *Qualifications for Appointment and Terms and Conditions of Service of Teachers*:

(*i*) Any person possessing such minimum qualification, as laid down by an academic authority; authorized by the central government, by notification, shall be eligible for appointment as a teacher.

(*ii*) The salary and allowance payable to, and terms and conditions of service of, teachers shall be such as may be prescribed.

18. *Duties of Teachers and Redressal of their Grievances*:

(*i*) A teacher in the school shall perform the following duties, namely:

- (*a*) maintain regularity and punctuality in attending school.
- (*b*) conduct and complete the curriculum in accordance with the provisions laid down in this act.
- (*c*) complete entire curriculum within the specified time.
- (*d*) assess the learning ability of each child and accordingly supplement additional instructions, if any, as required.
- (*e*) hold regular meetings with parents and guardians and appraise them about the regularity in attendance, ability to learn, progress made in learning and any other relevant information about the child, and
- (*f*) perform such other duties as may be prescribed.

(*ii*) A teacher committing default in performance of duties shall be liable to disciplinary action under the service rules applicable to him or her.

(*iii*) The grievance, if any, of the teacher shall be redressed in such manner as may be prescribed.

19. *Pupil-Teacher Ratio*: Within six months from the date of commencement of this act, the appropriate government and the local authority shall ensure that the pupil-teacher ratio as specified in the schedule (of this act) is maintained in each school.

20. *Prohibition of Deployment of Teachers for Non-educational Purposes*: No teacher shall be deployed for any non-educational purpose other than the decennial population census, disaster relief duties or duties relating to elections to the local authority or the state legislatures or parliament, as the case may be.

21. *Prohibition of Private Tuition by Teacher*: No teacher shall engage himself or herself in private tuition or private teaching activity.

22. *Curriculum and Evaluation Procedure*: The curriculum and evaluation procedure for elementary education shall be laid down by an academic authority to be specified by the appropriate Government, by notification.

23. *Monitoring of Child's Rights to Education*: In this regard, the National Commission for Protection of Child Rights or the State Commission for Protection of Child Rights as the case may be, shall perform the following functions, namely-

(*a*) examine and review the safeguards for rights provided by or under this Act and recommend measures for their effective implementation;

(*b*) inquire into complaints relating to child's right to free and compulsory education; and

(*c*) take necessary steps as provided under sections 15 and 24 of the said Commissions for Protection of Child Rights Act.

EDUCATION OF THE CHILDREN WITH DISABILITY IN NATIONAL POLICY FOR PERSONS WITH DISABILITIES, 2006

A National Policy For Persons with Disabilities was brought out in the year 2006 as to fulfill an essential demand or need of having a comprehensive document or policy statement for the care, education and well being of the persons with disabilities on a national basis. The official document on National Policy for Persons with Disabilities was released on 10th February, 2006 by the Minister of Social Justice and Empowerment, Government of India, New Delhi.

The Document is mainly divided into four major sections.

A. Introduction
B. National Policy Statement
C. Principal Areas of Intervention
D. Responsibility for Implementation

In introduction, the present available measures and efforts made for the care, education and wellbeing of the disabled have been highlighted in brief and the need of having a national policy for disabled has been emphasized. The second section entitled as 'National Policy Statement' provides a mention and essential description of the areas that have been targeted by the "National Policy for Persons with Disabilities" by concluding that the focus of the policy shall be on the following.

I. Prevention of Disabilities
II. Rehabilitation Measures – Physical rehabilitation, educational rehabilitation and economic rehabilitation
III. Women with Disabilities
IV. Children with Disabilities
V. Barrier-free environment
VI. Issue of Disability Certificates
VII. Social Security
VIII. Promotion of Non-Government Organizations (NGOs)
IX. Collection of Regular Information on Persons with Disabilities
X. Research
XI. Sports, Recreation and Cultural life
XII. Amendments to existing Acts dealing with the Persons with Disabilities

The third section entitled as 'Principal Areas of Intervention' provides the action plan to be carried out for the care, education and well-being of the persons with disabilities (including children) under the following heads.

I. Prevention, Early Detection and Intervention
II. Programmes of Rehabilitation
III. Human Resource Development
IV. Education of Persons with Disabilities
V. Employment
VI. Barrier-Free environment
VII. Social Protection
VIII. Research
IX. Sports, Recreation and Cultural activities

The fourth section entitled as 'Responsibility for Implementation' discusses the measures taken for looking after the progress and getting feedback about matters relating to the implementation of the policy.

As far as the present text is concerned we will be focusing our attention for looking into what has been laid down in the National Policy for persons with disabilities, 2006 about the education of the disabled. Let us thus reproduce what has been prescribed in the policy document about the education of the disabled.

Education of Persons with Disabilities

It will be ensured that every child with disability has access to appropriate pre-school, primary and secondary level education by 2020. Special care will be taken to—

(*i*) Make schools (building, approaches, toilets, playgrounds, laboratories, libraries etc.) barrier free and accessible for all disability.

(*ii*) Medium and method of teaching will be suitably adapted to the requirements of most disability conditions.

(*iii*) Technical/supplementary/specialized system of teaching/learning will be made available within the school or at a common center easily accessible to a cluster of schools.

(*iv*) Teaching/learning tools and aids such as educational toys, Braille/talking books, appropriate software etc. will be made available. Incentives will be given to expand facilities for setting up of general libraries, e-libraries, Braille-libraries and talking books libraries, resource rooms, etc.

(*v*) National Open School and distance learning programmes will be popularized and extended to other parts in the country.

(*vi*) Sign language, Alternative and Augmentative Communications (AAC) and other modes as a viable medium in inter personal communication will be recognized, standardized and popularized.

(*vii*) Schools will be located within easy traveling distance. Alternatively, viable travel arrangements will be made with the assistance of the community, State and NGOs.

(*viii*) Parent-Teacher counseling and grievance redressal system will be setup in the schools.

(*ix*) There will be separate mechanism to review annually the intake and retention of the girl child with disability at primary, secondary and higher levels of education,

(*x*) Many children with disabilities, who cannot join inclusive education system, would continue to get educational services from special schools. Special schools shall be appropriately re-modelled and re-oriented based on technological development. These schools will also help prepare children with disabilities to join mainstream inclusive education,

(*xi*) In some cases due to the nature of disability (its type and degree), personal circumstances and preferences, home-based education will be provided.

(*xii*) Course curriculum and evaluation system for children with various disabilities shall be developed keeping in view their capabilities. Examination system will be modified to make it disabled friendly by exemptions such as learning mathematics, learning only one language, etc. Further, facilities like extra time, use of calculators, use of Clarke's tables, scribes, etc would be provided based on the requirement.

(*xiii*) Model Schools of Inclusive Education will be setup in each State/U.T. to promote education of persons with disabilities.

(*xiv*) In the era of knowledge society, computers play very important role. Efforts will be made so that every child with disability gets suitably exposed to the use of computers.

(*xv*) Children with disabilities upto the age of six years will be identified and necessary interventions made so that they are capable of joining inclusive education.

(*xvi*) Educational facilities will be provided in psychosocial rehabilitation centres for mentally ill persons,

(*xvii*) Many schools discourage enrollment of students on account of their disability due to lack of awareness about the capabilities of disabled persons. Programmes will be taken for sensitization of teachers, principals and other staff members in all schools,

(*xviii*) Special Schools presently being supported by the Ministry of Social Justice & Empowerment will incrementally become resource centres for inclusive education. Ministry of Human Resource Development shall open new special schools depending upon the requirement,

(*xix*) Adult learning/leisure centers for adults with severe learning difficulties will be promoted.

(*xx*) Three per cent reservation for persons with disabilities in admission to higher educational institutions shall be enforced. Universities, colleges and professional institutions will be provided financial support to establish Disability Center to take care of educational needs of students with disabilities. They will also be encouraged to make classrooms, hostels, cafeterias and other facilities in the campus accessible to students with disabilities.

(*xxi*) Include a module in induction and in-service training programmes of teachers on issues relating to management of children with disabilities.

The Ministry of Human Resource Development will be the nodal Ministry to coordinate all matters relating to the education of persons with disabilities.

9

Organisation and Management of an Inclusive School

CONCEPT OF AN INCLUSIVE SCHOOL

The concept of an inclusive school is well linked with the concept of "inclusion and inclusive setup". Inclusion as we have already discussed in the Chapter Two of this text means non-exclusion *i.e.* including or embracing all the intended learners in the mainstream or the teaching-learning setup of the school without having any differential or discrimination on any ground whatever it may be. It is the latest concept and trend in providing care and education to the differently abled or disabled along with the non-disabled peers in line with the special education measures and concepts previously known as segregation (having provision for institutionalization and special schools for the disabled) and integration (accommodating the disabled somehow in the normal school setup without getting prepared for their proper education and development). Here in the inclusive setup we take it for granted that all children irrespective of their abilities or disabilities are part and parcel of any system of school education. It is the responsibility of the regular schools to include all children in the main stream along with their non-disabled peers by making adequate provisions for their education and all round development. The differences between the school education setups related with the philosophies of separation. Integration and inclusion can be explained well by the comparison used below.

- A school advocating separation may say to the disabled students, "Sorry this school is not meant for you."
- Another school believing in the philosophy of integration may be found to say to the disabled students seeking admission; "Well you may come here, we have no arrangement for you but we will try to accommodate you somehow."
- Another school running on the philosophy of inclusion must say "Well you are most welcome. We will try to provide you all what is needed for your education and development along with the other students of the school."

In this way, an inclusive school and its setup is found to differ in a variety of ways from the normal or integrated education providing schools meant for the normal student population or the schools having provision for including children with special needs/disabled in its mainstream with no proper facilities and positive attitude towards their proper education and wholesome development.

In fact, an inclusive school and its inclusive setup may be found to be characterised with: (*i*) positive attitude and warm feelings towards disability and disabled children, (*ii*) provision of adequate infrastructural facilities, men-material facilities for the adjustment, education and wholesome development of the disabled along with their normal peers, (*iii*) the provision of adequate support services for helping the disabled in their proper education and development, (*iv*) Training facilities for the teaching and non-teaching personnel for helping the disabled in adjusting and getting proper opportunities for their education and development along with the peers.

Looking in this way, we may now define and understand an inclusive school and its setup as a school and setup that is capable of embracing all the learners and providing them facilities, infrastructure, human resources, means and methods for their proper adjustment, education and all round development with no discrimination of any nature well in tune with their capacities and individualities.

ORGANISATION AND MANAGEMENT OF AN INCLUSIVE SCHOOL FOR ITS PROPER FUNCTIONING

It is a hard fact that inclusive schools can exercise their responsibility well only when sufficient attention is given for managing and organizing them well to serve the cause of inclusive education. In general, the things discussed ahead may help much in this direction.

A. Working for the Proper Infrastructure and Accessibility

The first and foremost requirement for the establishment and running of an inclusive school is to get it equipped with the needed infrastructural facilities in terms of its building, material facilities, and their proper accessibility to all the users with no discrimination of any kind.

The measures like below may prove quite beneficial in this concern.

1. Regular school building including the pathways and stairs, etc. need to be constructed or modified by keeping in mind the accessibility to all types of students – disabled and non-disabled. It must provide needed entrance, mobility and functioning for all including orthopedically or locomotor disabled, as well as visually impaired. The need for the use of the wheel chair on the part of orthopedically impaired, and cane travelling on the part of visually impaired should also be given due consideration. Therefore, the building and pathways of the inclusive school should not only be free from

architectural barriers but should also be quite accessible to all by having provisions of simple ramps, hand-rails, wide doorways, proper toilet and water arrangement, etc.

2. Adequate attention should also be paid over the suitability of accommodation, seating arrangement and working facilities in all the learning and working places of the school like classes, assembly hall, laboratories, workshops, playgrounds, canteen and boys/girls common rooms so that the students with disabilities may not feel any accessibility problem regarding their mobility, adjustment and functioning,

3. To facilitate needed accessibility of the learning and working experiences to the children with disabilities, there should be proper provision of their sitting and working in tune with the nature of their impairment or disability. The hearing and visually impaired, children with locomotor or multiple disabilities, autism, etc. should thus be provided needed spacing, front seats, nearness to the teacher and the support systems for accommodating their learning or working difficulties etc. We should see that inclusion of the disabled does not mean to get them excluded from special supports, they need for their proper adjustment, education and development and it should always be available to them in an inclusive setup.

B. Developing Awareness and Positive Attitude towards Disability

The policy of inclusion and its implementation in the shape of the proper and useful functioning of the inclusive schools can't be carried out on sound footing unless there comes a change in the environment of the regular schools towards disabilities and the disabled. The school authorities, teachers and other personnel working in the school, non-disabled students and their parents are needed to give up the age old notion of remaining away from the disabled. The school should welcome and embrace the disabled as it welcomes the other non-disabled students and try to provide them education and other developmental facilities with no discrimination of any kind. There should be proper awareness among the school authorities and teachers about the needs and problems of the disabled (general and specific) and efforts should be earnestly made to address these problems for facilitating proper adjustment and development of the disabled along with the non-disabled students population. In fact, there is a need to develop a desirable positive attitude towards disability and disabled on the part of school authorities and teachers on the lines suggested below.

- Diversities and differences are bound to exist on this earth. We all differ from each other in so many things.
- The children may possess different types of abilities and capacities and it is quite natural to have some students differing or deviating much from the normal level of abilities or capacities found in

majority of children in one or the other attributes of their development/ personality. The disabled children thus should be treated as differently abled having differences or deviation from the non-disabled student in terms of the possession of some traits or unique characteristics rather than being considered hopeless, problem creators, and misfit in the mainstream of the regular schools.

- The school authorities and teachers should be well informed about the legislative measures *i.e.* right to education and the need of creating an environment in the school in favour of the policy of inclusive education. There should be a clear understanding on their part that equal access to education for all the students is a matter of right and not a privilege and they should work for the success of inclusive education in their school with their all sincerity and efforts.
- School authorities and teachers should believe in the uniqueness of the disabled and consider that every child has a unique potential for being developed in an unique way. Simply he or she wants proper help, guidance and timely feedback/encouragement for doing so and it is their duty for meeting the learning needs of every child (disabled or non-disabled) with no discrimination of any kind.

C. Building Proper Human Resources

The third essential requirement for making disabled friendly environment in the school is concerned with empowering it with the needed appropriate human resources. In this regard, the things like below need to be cared well.

- There should be an appropriate teacher-student ratio in the school so that proper individual attention can be paid over the students population belonging to an inclusive setup.
- The staff appointed in the school should be properly oriented towards the philosophy of inclusion and expectations from them in fulfilling their duties in an inclusive setup.
- Every teacher appointed in the school should be properly equipped with the knowledge, skills, interests and attitudes necessary for working in the inclusive setup. Their preparation in this regard may be well organized through pre-service and in-service teacher education well designed programs and only competent teachers capable of working in the inclusive setup should be appointed and continued to serve in the inclusive schools.
- Since every regular school need to work as inclusive school as a result of the implementation of Right to Education Act, there should be an intensive efforts on the part of schools and education authorities at the State and Central level for providing needed

attention towards the orientation and preparation of the teachers to face the challenge of the inclusive setup.

- There is a need of appointing a teacher in the capacity of special education teacher who can be entrusted with the task of.
  - (*i*) establishing and managing a resource room for the children with disability or special needs.
  - (*ii*) providing guidance and help to the subject teachers, laboratory assistants/instructors, physical education teachers in dealing with the disabled or differently abled children.
  - (*iii*) providing help and guidance to the disabled and differently abled population of the school in meeting their special needs and getting them properly adjusted and developed according to their capacities and interests.
  - (*iv*) providing guidance and seeking cooperation from the parents of the differently abled for their adjustment and welfare.
- In Addition to the special teacher there should be proper arrangement of availing the services of other experts helpful in the proper adjustment, and development of the differently abled students (on part time or call basis) like below.

  —Psychologist/Clinical psychologist

  —Eye and Ear specialist

  —Speech therapist and audiologist

  —Physiotherapist

  —Occupational therapist and Counselor

  —Orthoptist and Prosthetist

  —Orientation and mobility specialist

  —Rehabilitation Counsellor/psychologist
- The staff working in school office, library, sports grounds, workshops and laboratories should also be properly oriented towards the need and requirement of functioning in an inclusive setup, particularly towards keeping a proper attitude towards disability and special needs of differently abled students.

D. Building Appropriate Material Resources

In the inclusive setup, there arises need of arranging for a variety of material resources in the manner given below.

(*i*) Inclusive schools have to equip them with the necessary teaching-learning material for helping the teachers and learners in executing the teaching-learning tasks in an effective and convenient way. Disabled children may need a variety of aid material depending up on the nature of their disability, learning needs and learning styles. Accordingly, inclusive schools should make proper arrangement of the audio, video, kinesthetic, and multi-sensory teaching-learning aid material.

(*ii*) Children with special needs or disabilities need a variety of assistive and adaptive resource materials and equipments for the adequate adjustment, learning and participation in the curricular and co-curricular programs of inclusive education. As examples of the aids and equipments we may name, the aids and equipments helping in their locomotor movements and activities, visual and hearing aids, and advanced technology based assistive devices (already discussed in the chapter Five of this text). Hence, adequate efforts should be made to procure these devices and equipment with the full knowledge of their use and applications.

E. Adoption of Whole School Approach

Adoption of whole school approach may also prove quite beneficial in the successful organization and management of an inclusive school. The question here may arise what do we mean by the whole school approach and how does it help in the success of an inclusive setup?

Whole school approach towards inclusive education is a term that is generally employed for utilizing all the resources, efforts, links and connections owned by the school along with building a positive climate and healthy relationships among all the stakeholders (students, teachers, school personnel, school administration, parents and community people) to join hands for the success of the system of inclusive education.

In fact as a philosophy thus a whole school approach is nothing but to do on the part of the school whatever it can do at its utmost through the resources, efforts and relationships at its disposal for building a healthy positive climate in the school to achieve its desired mission or goal *i.e.* providing education to all in an inclusive setup.

The whole school approach to inclusive education thus may be found to work towards a shared and committed efforts on the part of all the stakeholders (students, teachers, school personnel, school administration, parents and community) for building a positive healthy climate and engage in the purposeful activities for the education, adjustment, development and progress of all the students in an inclusive setup. For this purpose, in the whole school approach, the duties and responsibilities are properly shared among the stakeholders and functioning of the school system is well geared for achieving the mission *i.e.* the successful running of the inclusive setup. Let us see how it can be done and what type of activities and responsibilities are shared by the various stakeholders.

The Role of the School Administration and Authorities

- To believe and accept the philosophy of inclusion as a way of doing justice for all the intended learners irrespective of their being disabled or non-disabled.

- To arrange for all the needed infrastructural facilities aimed: (*i*) to provide restriction free environment to all learners, (*ii*) facilitating accessibility to all types of learning experiences-curricular and co-curricular with no discrimination.
- To arrange for all types of human resources needed for the appropriate functioning of inclusive education curricular and co-curricular programs including caring and meeting of the individual specific needs of the differently abled students.
- To arrange for the aids and equipments, means and devices, resource room facilities, etc. for the use of the teachers and students in their teaching and learning as well as meeting the adjustment and specific learning needs of the disabled.
- To provide means and facilities for the proper orientation of the staff about their functioning and role in an inclusive setup.
- To provide the services of special education teacher and other supporting staff like educational psychologist, clinical psychologist, guidance personnel, medical professionals, rehabilitation professional, etc.
- To take care of building positive attitude and healthy climate in the school about inclusive education and especially towards disability. No children in the school should be harassed or discriminated on account of his being differently abled.
- To arrange for the type of continuous and comprehensive evaluation, timely feedback and reinforcement, early diagnosis and remedial measures needed for the success of the programs and activities run for the education, adjustment and progress of all the learners belonging to inclusive setup.
- To seek active cooperation and involvement of the school staff, parents, students and community for making inclusive practice a success.

The Role of Teachers

- To have proper pre-preparation and orientation for fulfilling their responsibilities well in an inclusive setup.
- To work for demonstrating a quite positive unbiased healthy attitude towards the learning and capacities of the differently abled.
- To learn and practice needed methodology, aid material equipments and devices for meeting the needs of differently abled in the inclusive setup.
- To work for providing individual attention and care for meeting the learning needs of all learners in the inclusive setup with no discrimination of any kind.
- To seek cooperation of the non-disabled peers for adjustment, education and development of the disabled.

- As a outside partner to seek involvement of the parents, community people and NGO for the education, adjustment rehabilitation and welfare of the differently abled.
- To encourage, stimulate, train the differently abled for their full participation in the curricular and co-curricular activities according to their capacity and limitations.

The main responsibility for the successful functioning of an inclusive setup in the adoption of whole school approach lies on the shoulders of school administration and teaching staff. Both of these functionaries, then may attempt to seek involvement and cooperation of all other stakeholders in the manner and ways outlined below for the success of inclusive education practice.

(*i*) Parents are the main stakeholders in the work and tasks related to the education and welfare of their children. The whole school approach towards inclusive education demands that their active cooperation and involvement is quite essential for success of this program. They themselves are quite worried for the adjustment and education of their children especially for the differently abled. They have all fear that the child may be ridiculed, harassed, side lined or get depressed on account of his or her disability. All such concerns can be successfully handled by getting the parents involved in the welfare of the children through the parent-teacher organization meetings, seeking their cooperation in the organization of co-curricular activities or paying individual attention to the learners with special needs.

(*ii*) The whole school approach also needs active cooperation and involvement of the community people through their varying functions and roles. Therefore, earnest attempts should be made by the school authorities and staff for establishing needed rapport with the community in which school is functioning. Community people may provide their valuable services and contributions in the form of donations, doing away with discrimination and negative feelings towards the disabled in the community, providing their services as professionals, experts, counsellors, clinical and therapists and working as volunteers and the members of NGO's for the assistance, adjustment and education of the differently abled in the inclusive setup.

(*iii*) In the whole school approach to inclusive education it is the cooperation, collaboration and group work of the children that is most valued for the successful functioning of an inclusive classroom or work situation. Peer caring and peer tutoring may play wonder in meeting out the special adjustment, caring and learning needs of the disabled peers of the inclusive setup. Thereby deliberate attempts are made in the whole school approach for utilizing the cooperation and contributions of non-disabled peers for taking along with them their disabled peers in relation to the execution of a number of curricular and co-curricular activities of the inclusive setup in tune with their potential and capabilities.

(*iv*) The whole school approach to inclusive education also seriously asks for the full scale involvement, motivation, enthusiasm and participation of all the learners irrespective of their abilities and disabilities in all the curricular and co-curricular programs and activities planned in the inclusive setup. The disabled and differently abled learners should themselves be well prepared and ready for getting benefitted through the experiences of the inclusive setup. Their hesitation or fear of getting along with others and facing the odds of the school situation must be properly removed and their confidence in their abilities (irrespective of their limitations) should be so built as to get duly benefitted from the processes and outcomes of the inclusive setup.

In addition to seeking active involvement and cooperation of all the stakeholders, the whole school approach also asks for doing necessary efforts and adopting desirable measures like below for the success of the inclusive education program.

- The needed flexibility in providing curricular and co-curricular learning experiences should be adopted in an inclusive setup depending upon the needs of the situation and type of children present in the inclusive setup.
- The teaching-learning style should be accommodated according to the teaching-learning needs of the inclusive group.
- The evaluation tasks and activities be so designed as to provide needed timely feedback and assessment measures according to the demands of the inclusive setup.

In this way whole school approach tries to seek active cooperation and involvement of all the stakeholders, including restructuring the teaching-learning environment in a suitable way for providing a total effect aimed to bring the needed desirable outcomes of the processes and product of the inclusive education.

ADDRESSING INEQUALITY AND DIVERSITY IN THE CLASSROOM–PEDAGOGICAL AND CURRICULUM CONCERNS

An inclusive classroom is very much characterized with widespread inequality and diversity among the learners. Where inequality is perceived in terms of locale, gender roles, caste, colour, racial, cultural and language differences among the learners, the diversity is visible in the form of the differences in the abilities, capacities, potential, interest and goals of learning and development lying before the learners. In a more clear term diversity among the learners is very much noticed in the form of the presence of disabled and non-disabled peers in the class. Now the question may arise what steps or measures should be taken for getting addressed the issues or problems raised on account of such inequality or diversity present in inclusion class. The measures suggested in the chapter in the name of: (*a*) Proper infrastructure and accessibility, (*b*) Awareness and positive attitude towards disability, (*c*) Organisation of proper human resources, (*d*) Organisation of appropriate material resources, and (*e*) Adoption of whole

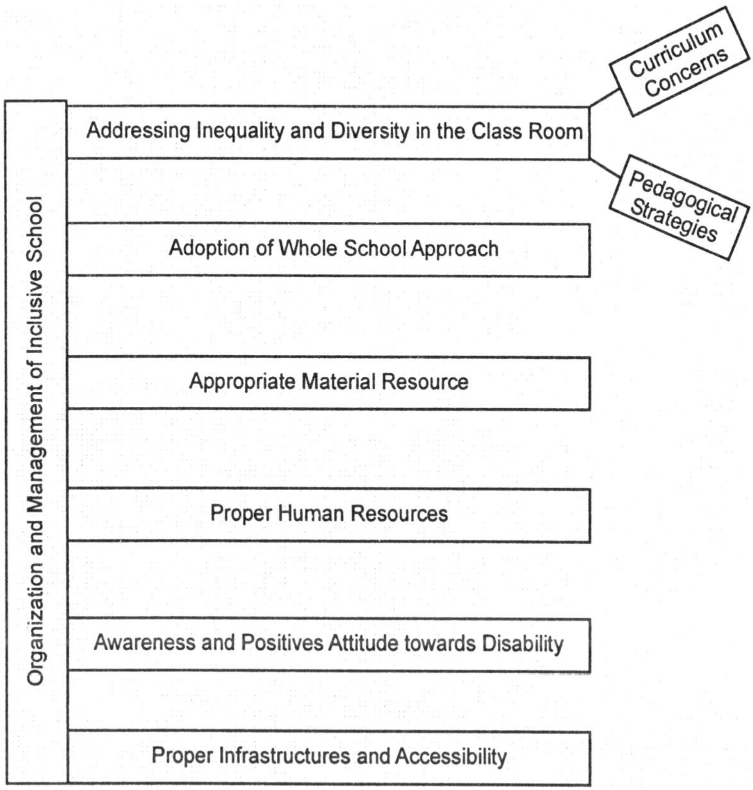

Fig. 9.1 : Organization and Management of an Inclusive School

school approach may help a lot in addressing the issues related to inequality and diversity of the inclusive classroom.

However, it also needs to be supported further by taking into account some more useful considerations like (*i*) The use of appropriate pedagogy accompanied with needed curriculum adaptation and (*ii*) Using special measures for dealing with the inequality related to gender bias or other types of marginalization. Let us first concentrate over the pedagogical use and curriculum adaptation for addressing the presence of inequality and diversity in an inclusive classroom.

Pedagogy Concerns

The principle "one method or strategy fits for all" does not work at all in the inclusive class. Inequality and diversity found here demands the maintenance of too much flexibility and diversity in the use of teaching, learning methods and strategies. As the learners and their learning needs and styles so the method or strategies used for helping them in the attainment of their learning goals, this basic principle is the real corner stone of making use of pedagogical concerns for addressing in inequality and diversity of an inclusive classroom. A teacher has to adopt a particular teaching style or strategy and make use of different sensory material or teaching aids and appliances in consideration with the nature of their inequality and diversity, ability or disability for one or the other type of learning or performance in curricular or co-curricular areas. We will be discussing in detail in the Chapter Thirteen of this text a number of diverse pedagogical strategies for dealing with the teaching-learning issue raised on account of the inequality and diversity of the inclusive classroom. In general, a teacher has to employ a particular teaching style such as auditory, visual, kinaesthetic, etc. depending upon the auditory, visual, kinaesthetic learning styles of the disabled or non-disabled students of the class.

Curriculum Concerns

The principle "The same contents, subject matter or learning experiences for all learners" does not hold any ground in an inclusive class. How can we have same expectation from the mentally retarded, as targeted for the students of normal or average intelligence in terms of the acquisition of one or the other type of learning experiences. The curriculum needs modifications and adaptation according to the learning needs, abilities and disabilities and learning goals set for them in one or the other situation. We have already discussed such adaptation and accommodation in curriculum in the Chapter Seven of the text.

ADDRESSING INEQUALITY RELATED TO GENDER IN THE SCHOOL

The girls have to suffer from a typical type of exclusion and discrimination in the society, school and classroom on account of gender bias or stero-types as discussed in the Chapter One of this text. Now question here may arise what measures can be taken for doing away with such gender inequality in the schools and classrooms?. In general, the measures or provisions like below may work well in bringing desired attitudinal or behaviour changes among the interactions.

A. Measures involving Curriculum Inputs

School curriculum should be so constructed as well as brought into implementation as to help in achieving gender equality in schools and classrooms. For this purpose due care is taken for the following.

- No bifurcation or division of the subjects, curricular or co-curricular areas in terms of the distinctive separate fields meant for boys or girls should be made in the prescribed curriculum. There should be a common curriculum consisting of core and options providing uniform choices for both boys and girls.
- For doing away with gender stereotypes and discrimination against girl children, a free choice should be given to girls to opt for the curricular subjects and co-curricular activities including sports considered to be only meant for boys. Similarly, boys should also

not be discouraged or denied for choosing the curricular subject and co-curricular activities traditionally considered as the female dominated areas.

B. Text Books as a means of achieving Gender Equality

Proper efforts should be made to produce/publish such text books on the different subjects of the school curriculum that may prove helpful in eliminating gender bias and discrimination against females by taking measures like below:

(*i*) Text books must stop to show females usually as week, oppressed and pitiable figures obeying their male counterparts at all the stages of their life.

(*ii*) Text books should stop highlighting the characters and authors as males. Similarly, sentences beginning with he and using adjectives him in place of she and her should be get balanced by providing due importance to both the genders.

(*iii*) The characters used and incidence narrated in the text books should not reflect male bias in any way. Rather they must by to encourage or reinforce equality and dignity of both sex – males and females in social life.

C. Student-teacher Interactions as a means of achieving Gender Equality

Many times in the school gender bias and discrimination to girls is reflected through the nature of student-teacher interactions occurring in the school and classroom setup. The things like below should be property considered for achieving gender equality in schools and classroom.

- Teacher should try to provide equal and fair treatment to the girls students in their interaction and dealing will them in the classroom on other work situations.
- They should try to do away with a number of stereotypes in distributing work or assigning duties to the students.
- For example, girls should be well entrusted for providing leadership to the group projects, community work and other team work held in the school. They should be encouraged to participate in the co-curricular and outdoor activities traditionally considered mainly for the boys.
- Teacher should encourage female students to participate in the curricular and co-curricular activities of the school at par with their male peers with the needed confidence by helping them to side away the traditional stereotypes related to such participation.
- Male and female students should be made to do away with their male and female stereotype and get engaged in cooperative learning and social interaction with due respect of each other's individuality and freedom.

10

Support Services available in an Inclusive School

INTRODUCTION

In an inclusive school there is a provision for including all the learners in the mainstream of its education with no discrimination of any kind with a commitment of providing equal opportunities for their wholesome development in tune with their capabilities and learning needs. It is a great challenge before the school administration and teachers for meeting the adjustment and learning needs of the non-disabled and disabled children of wide variety through the limited resources at their disposal in the inclusive setup of their school. Here arises the need of calling for the assistance of essential support services and partnership with those who can provide valuable help and assistance in the needed adjustment and wholesome development of the learners belonging to inclusive setup specially the differently abled or disabled. Let us see what type of support services can be available or arranged with the efforts of school for this purpose.

A. SUPPORT SERVICES AVAILABLE THROUGH EXTERNAL SPECIALIZED AGENCIES

There are many external agencies (working on the local, state and national level) that stand for serving the cause of disabled in terms of providing help to them in their proper identification, adjustment, rehabilitation, education and development in one or the other ways. We may name them:

(*i*) Composite Resource Centres (CRCs), District Resource Centres (DRCs) and Block Resource Centers (BRCs) working at the Regional, District, and Block level.

(*ii*) District Disability Rehabilitation Centres (DDRCs) funded under the "Scheme for the implementation of Persons with Disabilities (Equal opportunities, Protection of Rights and Full participation) Act 1995" and another scheme namely "Deen Dayal Disabled Rehabilitation scheme".

(*iii*) National level institutes for the care and Rehabilitation of different disabilities such as:

- All Yavar Jung National Institute for the Hearing Handicapped (AYJNIHH), Mumbai.
- Pandit Deen Dayal Upadhyaya Institute for the Physically Handicapped (IPH), New Delhi

- National Institute of Mentally Handicapped (NIMH), Secundrabad,
- National Institute of Visually Handicapped (NIVH), Dehradun.
- National Institute for Orthopaedically Handicapped, (NIOH), Kolkata.
- Swami Vivekanand National Institute for Rehabilitation, Training and Research (SVNIRTAR), Cuttack.
- National Institute for Empowerment of Persons with Multiple Disabilities (NIEPMD), Chennai.
- Indian Sign Language Research and Training Center (ISLRTC), New Delhi.
- Artificial Limbs Manufacturing Corporation of India (ALMCON, Kanpur)
- National Handicapped Financial Development Corporation, (NHFDC), Faridabad.
- Indian Spinal Injury Center (ISIC), New Delhi.

(*iv*) Support Services available through the provisions made and programs implemented in National Policy on Disability 2006, Sarva Shikha Abhiyan, 2000, PWD Act 2001, and RTE, 2009 etc.

(*v*) Support services available from DIETs, SCERTs, NCERT and Special education departments of Universities.

B. SUPPORT SERVICES AVAILABLE THROUGH PARENTAL COOPERATION AND COMMUNITY INVOLVEMENT

Parents and the Community to which the disabled children belong are the major stakeholders in their welfare and progress. It is why their active cooperation and involvement may provide valuable support service for the identification, adjustment, education, rehabilitation and progress of the disabled children in the inclusive setup. Let us see how?

- Parents, family members and community persons may help well in the identification, and diagnosis of the problems associated with the impairments or disabilities of the suffering children. In case, the difficulty is pointed out by the teacher and school authorities, the necessary support for its follow up, remediation and treatment is also properly availed through the active cooperation of the family and community.
- Parents and community personnel may help well in the transportation of the disabled children to the places of learning. In many cases, the community may come forward for arranging buses and vehicles for the daily transportation of the disabled students to the inclusive schools.
- The support of the parents and community is also available in terms of financing the efforts of the school in building necessary infrastructure, creating essential men-material resources and helping

the disabled children for the purchase and maintenance of the needed assistive and adaptive appliances.

- They can contribute in the proper running of an inclusive school by registering their presence and participation in parent-teacher associations, working of a community center in the school campus, and their representation in the managing committee/administration of the school. They can help in the preparation of individual as well as combined education plans for the education and adjustment of the disabled children and provide active help and assistance for the solution of the problems and difficulties encountered in the implementation of inclusive education.
- Parents and Community people may provide valuable support services in building a quite positive and healthy attitude towards disability and disabled. They can also help in building the self-confidence of the disabled and encouraging their learning efforts and outcomes.
- Help of the parents and community members may be properly secured for the organization of a number of co-curricular activities in the school involving disabled children. The parents/community members of the disabled (well acquainted with the type of support, assistance and encouragement needed for the children suffering from a particular impairment) may prove quite helpful in handling the work and activities related to the disabled. They may feel delighted in watching and supporting the activities of their differently abled children and in turn school may also get due benefit of getting their support and assistance for the education and welfare of the differently abled in the inclusive setup.
- Many of the parents and community members may provide their valuable services for the success of an inclusive education setup on account of their being experts in special education for the CWSN, professional in the form of physiotherapist, occupational therapist, clinical psychologist, speech therapist, medical professional, guidance provider or counsellor etc. In this concern it becomes essential on the part of the school to take initiative for inviting them to deliver talks, participating in seminars/workshop and providing interaction or service facilities as a supporting team and professionals for the adjustment, education and welfare of the differently abled.

In this way, by taking care of the necessary measures for making the school ready or prepare for inclusive education and securing essential support services from the available various corners, necessary milestone can be achieved for providing appropriate inclusive setup for the children with special needs or disabled.

C. SUPPORT SERVICES PROVIDED BY PROFESSIONALS AND EXPERTS

In the inclusive setup a school may need the support of a number of professionals and experts for the education, adjustment and welfare of the disabled like below:

- The special education experts and professionals who can provide proper guidance for the teaching-learning of one or the other types of children with special needs or disabilities.
- Medical professionals like Eye and Ear specialist, audiologist, orthoptist and prosthetist, general physician, etc. for diagnosing and treating the medical problems of the disabled children.
- Orientation and mobility specialists providing orientation and help to the children with locomotor impairments.
- Guidance and counselling personnel for providing needed educational, vocational and personal guidance to the children with special needs.
- The therapists professionals like speech therapist, occupational therapist, physiotherapist, psychotherapist for providing needed therapy at the proper time in a proper way.
- The psychologists like educational psychologist and clinical psychologist providing psychological help and assistance to the suffering children.
- Rehabilitation professional providing rehabilitation and assistive aid services for the disabled.
- Social workers including social organization helping differently abled children in their physical and social adjustment in a variety of ways like providing adaptive devices and assistive technology, artificially limbs, mobility and hearing aids, etc.

For availing the services and support from the above professionals and experts school can adopt a variety of ways according to its convenience and funds for the same.

(*i*) It can have their services on part time basis

(*ii*) They can be called off at the time of need

(*iii*) Their services may be availed through the cooperation and courtesy of the composite Regional Centres (CRCs), District Resource Centres (DRC's), SCERTs. State rehabilitation centres and National institutes established for the education and welfare of the disabled etc.

Let us discuss now the role played by the specials personnel usually involved in providing support services in the inclusive schools.

Role of Special Education Teacher

Adjustment and education of the children especially the children with special needs or disabilities becomes a quite big challenge for the teachers and administrators of an inclusive school. Teachers and school personnel experience a lot of difficulty in meeting the adjustment and Special learning needs of the diverse learners, on account of their lack of experience, knowledge and skill required for dealing with differently abled children, It is why, there arises a need of appointing a special education or resource teacher in an inclusive education for helping in facing the challenges of an educational setup. The functions and responsibilities like below are expected to be performed by these special or resource teachers working in the inclusive schools.

1. *Resource Room Functions*: Establishing and managing a resource room for the Children with Special Needs (CWSN) or disabled. In this room they can have various aids and appliances, teaching-learning material, ICT based equipments and devices, assistive and adaptive devices, diagnostic tools, guidance and counselling literature and aid material etc. for carrying out the activities with the students, staff and student's parents.

2. *Diagnostic Functions*: Diagnosing the nature of impairments and learning difficulties faced by the child in his adjustment, learning and progress along with its possible causes and ways of rectification.

3. *Teaching or Instructional Functions*: Here the special resource teacher may share its responsibilities in two separate ways. On one front he directly performs the task of teaching a differently abled or group of them with the use of special education methods and techniques suiting to their requirements *i.e.* using sign language method, braille scripst, multisensory and ICT means, etc. On the other side, he may sit besides students in the class taken by the subject teacher and provides one-on-one help to the differently abled in grasping and learning of what is conveyed by the class teacher through his words and demonstrations. He may also provide additional instruction or help them in their drill, practice, project or assignment work and thus supplementing and filling up the gaps left in their learning on account of their impairments and limitations.

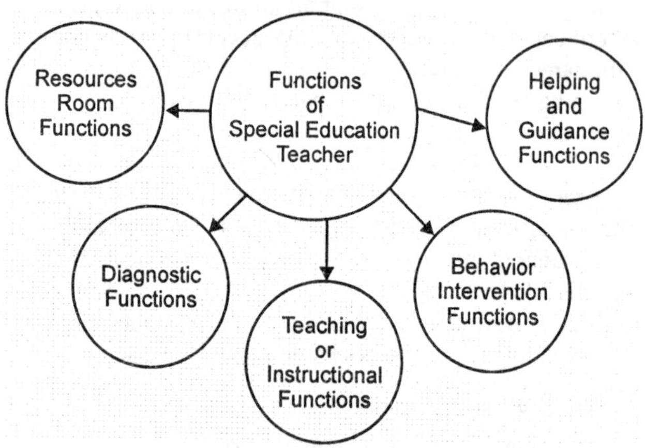

Fig. 10.1: Functions of Special Education Teacher

4. *Behaviour Intervention Functions:* There may arise an urgent need of paying attention towards the behaviour intervention in the case of one or the other differently abled children facing behaviour related psychological problems. For example, a child suffering from autism may be found to get panic as a result of a sudden change of class routine or increase of the level

of loudness in the classroom interaction. It is the special or resource teacher who may then be called for calming down the child and set him on his normal behaviour. Similar is the case with other children who lose their control, demonstrate their resentment and frustration in the class with their study and engage in indisciplinary behaviour. These children also need to be controlled with the help of special or resource teacher.

5. *Helping and Guidance Functions:* A special or resource teacher is found to carry on these functions in the ways described below:

(*i*) He may help and guide the classroom or subject teachers by suggesting:

— ways and means, methods and strategies, aids and device used for the teaching-learning of the differently abled in tune with the nature and types of their impairments/disability in one or the other areas of their development.

— ways and means as well as demonstrating the skill of meeting the learning needs/styles of diverse learners belonging to inclusive setup.

(*ii*) Helping the school authorities and staff by working as a liaison person for taking benefits of the schemes and programs for disabled and inclusive education.

(*iii*) Besides the class room or subject teacher he may also guide and help the other school functionaries like laboratory assistants/ instructors, physical education teachers, music art and craft teachers etc. in dealing with the disabled or differently abled children.

(*iv*) For helping the disabled and differently abled children of the inclusive setup of the school in their adjustment, education and development he may

— Work for creating a positive and favourable attitude towards disabilities and disabled children

— Work for removing the feelings of inferiority, depression and worthlessness from the minds of the disabled children and instilling or infusing necessary confidence and sense of worthwhileness among them for their learning and progress.

— suggest and help in the use of assistive devices on the part of the differently abled for their adjustment, living as well as meeting their learning needs *i.e.* training blinds for the use of braille, hearing impaired for the use of hearing device, orthopaedically impaired for becoming comfortable on wheel chair and using technological means for his learning and living etc.

(*v*) Helping the parents in getting their fears, anxieties and depressions about the well being and future of their disabled child removed or lowered by assuring them that he is there for looking after their interests and welfare. For this purpose he is supposed to keep a good rapport and level of interaction and communication with the parents of the disabled children.

(*vi*) Helping in utilising the services of the experts and professionals like medical personnel, therapists, clinical psychologist, rehabilitation professionals for the adjustment, education and welfare of the disabled children by (*a*) providing them necessary information or data regarding the problems and difficulties of the suffering child (*b*) calling them at the urgency (*c*) assisting them in their intervention and follow up.

In this way, the services rendered and role played by the special or resource teacher in an inclusive school may prove quite beneficial to other functionaries of the school and the disabled children in a variety of ways for realizing the aims and objectives of the inclusive education.

Role of Guidance and Counselling Personnel

In an inclusive school we may have the presence of guidance and counselling personnel in two different ways – (*i*) appointment of a guidance and counselling teacher in the staff of the school, (*ii*) utilising the services of a guidance and counselling professional on part time or call basis. Whatever the case may be the professional responsibilities or functions carried out by them in the inclusive education setup of a school are mainly addressed to the needs of the following functionaries.

1. Students
2. Teachers and other school personnel
3. Parents and family members.

Let us see what type of guidance and counselling may be provided by them to the above functionaries in the context of inclusive education setup.

(*a*) *Guidance and Counselling to the Students*

The work related to guidance and counselling to the students in an inclusive school may cover the following aspects.

1. Many times, the students without disabilities are found to carry the notion that it is not appropriate for them to learn or study along with the disabled. They are thus found to possess a quite negative attitude and antagonistic feelings about their disabled peers. Here guidance and counselling may be provided to them to give up their ill conceived notions and negative attitude towards their disabled peers. For this purpose, necessary opportunities should be created by the guidance providers for the non-disabled to accept differences and have normal healthy interactions with their disabled peers. They should be made to work in a cooperative and friendly environment and learn from the different and unique abilities possessed by each of them.

2. Attempts should be made to assist students with disabilities to give up their hesitation, fear and anxiety of getting adjusted and learn along with their non-disabled peers. They must be provided opportunities to imbibe the sense of belongingness to diverse culture of the school and learn to adjust in the school's inclusive setup as independently as possible.

Many times the disabled children feel depressed, and disturbed on account of their impairments and learning difficulties or remarks passed/behaviour shown towards them by their non-disabled peers or teachers. In such a situation necessary healing touch needs to be provided on the part of guidance and counselling personnel. They should try to help the disabled children to come out from the depression and build necessary confidence and expectations in them for their learning and future development with in their capacity and limitations.

3. The disabled children should be helped to set their individualized learning and progress goals with in their potential and limits. They should be helped to take recognition of their unique and differential capacities along with their impairments and incapacities and learn to capitalize on them as fully as possible. In this connection necessary guidance should be provided for them to excel in one or the other co-curricular field, vocational area or career building venture.

4. The children with disabilities should be helped in developing positive attitude and adaptability towards bearing or using assistive and adaptive technologies/devices for their learning and living.

(b) Guidance and Counselling to the Teachers and School Personnel

The professional colleagues – teachers and other school staff working in the inclusive school also need a variety of guidance and counselling services for developing necessary awareness attitudes, and competencies among them in relation to the thing pointed out below.

1. Guidance and Counselling may be needed for the teachers and other school staff for giving up their wrong notions and negative attitude towards disabilities and disabled children. They should be made to respect or celebrate diversities present in the inclusive school and have a faith in the unique abilities or capacities of the differently abled inspite of their well exposed limitations.

2. The teachers and other school personnel must be trained to interact and behave with the disabled children in a desirable way, neither to become too indifferent, intolerant and harsh to them nor showing unnecessary favour and help for making them too much dependent or a pitiable figure unable to adjust and work in a normal way in the real life.

3. Many teachers have an inherent learned fear, hesitation or anxiety for dealing with the children with disabilities and teaching in an inclusive setup. The same may also be true for many of the laboratory instructors, physical education teachers or trainers and arts and crafts teachers. Necessary guidance and counselling should be provided to all of them for the removal of their hesitation, fear or anxiety of interacting and instructing the disabled children or diverse learners in the inclusive setup.

For serving the more useful purpose in this regard, guidance and counselling personnel with the active assistance of special/resource teachers should also try for training the teachers to orient them about a number of essentials such as special learning needs and learning styles of the diverse learners, organization and management of an inclusive classroom setup, identification and assessment of the difficulties and impairments of the disabled children, monitoring and assessment of the disabled students' learning and progress and dealing with their behavioural and adjustment problems, etc. Moreover teachers and other staff members may also be given opportunities for learning pedagogical approaches, skills and use of necessary adaptive and assistive technologies and ICT means for dealing with the diversities of an inclusive classroom or work situations.

(c) Guidance and Counselling to the Parents and Family Members

Parents and members of the family are found to play a quite key role in the adjustment, education and development of the children with special needs or disabilities. In this way, their active cooperation and involvement is quite necessary for an inclusive education program. In doing so, guidance and counselling personnel of an inclusive education an required to perform the following types of functions:

- They may help the parents for the early identification and awareness about the impairments and difficulties of the disabled children. In case something in this concern is reported by the parents and family members, they may work for its follow-up in collaboration with teachers and special/resource teachers or other support services professionals available to the school.
- They may approach the parents and other family members for providing needed information about the impairments, behavioural problems faced by the child, the child's case history about its educational background, adjustment and learning problems, their views and experiences about the strengths and limitations of the child and other necessary information as needed by guidance and counsellor for the education, adjustment and welfare of their child.
- They may help the parents and family members to have a positive and healthy attitude towards the disability of their child, accept him with his impairments and limitations and hope for its future by capitalizing on his strengths.
- They may help and train the parents and family members for working with the child to make use of the needed assistive and adaptive devices such as hearing aids, crutches, artificial limbs, communication aids, auto-wheel chair, etc.
- They may help and train the parents and family members to help their disabled child in his homework, assignments and project work.
- They may provide necessary knowledge and awareness to the parents and family members about the various schemes, programs, aids and assistance, and legal provisions available from the central

and state governments as well as local authorities and NGO's for the education, adjustment, rehabilitation and welfare of the disabled children. They can also provide active assistance, advice and guidance for availing such facilities to their needy children.

- They may provide valuable help, assistance and advice to the parents and family members for seeking medical, psychological or therapic treatment of the impairments or problems of their children. In this concern, they may also act as a good intermediatory to supply the needed history and information to the concerned professionals for the cure and treatment of the suffering children.
- They may provide needed feedback about the learning and behavioural progress of the children with disabilities to the parents and family member for their active involvement and necessary follow up activities in the interests of the disabled children.

In this way, the guidance and counselling services provided in the school may help the children with disabilities in their adjustment, education, rehabilitation and welfare in the required ways.

Role of Specialized Therapists

An inclusive schools need the services of a few specialized therapists like audiologist cum speech therapist, physiotherapist and occupational therapist. Let us know about the specific roles played by these personnel for the welfare of disabled in an inclusive education setup.

Role of Audiologist cum Speech Therapist

Support services of a special medical professional designated as audiologist cum speech therapist are required for an inclusive school either as part time or on call basis to carryout various responsibilities towards the adjustment, care and treatment of the disabled children suffering from hearing and/or speech related problems. Such audiological cum speech therapist may be found to provide quite useful support services by getting engaged in the following types of activities.

Audiology related Services

(*i*) Diagnosing and assessing the type and degree of hearing impairment among the hearing impaired children.

(*ii*) Suggesting as well as practising ways and means related to care, adjustment and treatment of the hearing impaired such as equipping them with the use of hearing aids, recommending operation and other medical treatments of the defective hearing organs, etc.

(*iii*) Counselling parents and teachers for dealing with hearing impaired in terms of the status of their hearing impairment, use of hearing aids and possible care for the treatments and medication of the hearing impaired.

Speech Therapy related Services

(*i*) Diagnosis and assessment of the type and degree of speech and language related problems among the speech impaired children.

(*ii*) Arranging appropriate therapeutic sessions for the speech impaired children for helping them in getting rid of their speech problems or disorders caused on account of psychological or habitual response grounds.

(*iii*) Suggesting or providing referral for the possible medical treatment of the speech related problems, among the suffering children.

(*iv*) Guiding parents and teacher in relation to dealing with the children suffering from speech disorders.

The Role of a Physiotherapist

The support services of a professional physiotherapist on a part time or call basis are also needed in an inclusive school for taking care of children with disabilities especially those suffering from locomotor or orthopaedically impairment or difficult movement on account of illness/diseases. The main objective served by the services of a physiotherapist is to help the suffering children reach their full potential in terms of their movements and adjustment through the needed provisions of physical interventions, advice and support. The services provided or activities performed by a physiotherapist in this concern may be outlined below:

(*i*) To provide needed diagnosis and assessment of the nature of the difficult movement or locomotor/orthopaedically impairment of a suffering child especially in relation to:

- Strength and co-ordination
- Motor Development
- Posture and balance
- Quality of movement
- Function and workability

(*ii*) Acquainting teacher and parents with the nature of the difficulties faced by the children as well as the seriousness of their movement difficulty for the needed care, adjustment and treatment.

(*iii*) Providing interventions of the following nature

- Direct therapy to the suffering children individually or in a group for attaining their full physical potential.
- Suggesting and helping the suffering children in terms of their equipping with special equipments, appliances and assistive devices.
- Recommending exercise and programs of work and ways of supporting the child in different learning and work environment.

- Providing needed training and advice for the parents, teachers, care takers, etc. for dealing with and helping them in their adjustment and workability in different situations.

The Role of an Occupational Therapist

Many of the children with impairments or disabilities of one or the other nature experience difficulty and problems for their adjustment and learning in the inclusive environment of the school. It can affect their occupation or work performance skills in a quite negative way. It may happen to any child belonging to the inclusive setup found to be grippled with one or the other physical, developmental, sensory, attentional and /or learning challenges. The role of an occupational therapist available on part time or call basis is mainly focused on improving the student's performance of tasks and activities associated with his successful school functioning, i.e. to make him adjusted to his school's learning and work environment and help him to do work and activities related to curricular and co-curricular tasks of the inclusive school at his or her full potential. In this concern the task and activities performed by an occupational therapist may be outlined as below:

(*i*) To diagnosis or assess the problems or difficulties faced by differently abled in their adjustment and learning/work performance in the inclusive setup.

(*ii*) To recommend schools the task adaptations, task modification and assistive or adaptive devices for the use of differently abled considered necessary for optimitizing their performance/working in the inclusive setting.

(*iii*) To provide direct intervention through occupational therapy to the affected children for improving, restoring, maintaining or prevent deterioration in one or the other skills (such as visual—motor coordination, gross motor and fine motor abilities, visual-perceptual skills) required for their performance and working in the inclusive setup.

(*iv*) To provide medical, physical and developmental information and guidance to teachers and parents in a quite clear educational and institutional terms for enabling them to cope with working or functioning limitations of the differently abled caused through their physical developmental, sensory, attentional and/or learning challenges.

(*v*) To work with teachers (special as well as general) for enhancing student's ability to perform/learn and eliminating difficulties or problems that interfere with his/her ability to profit from the curricular and co-curricular experiences organized in the inclusive setup.

(*vi*) To make attempt for ensuring or understanding of and match between the differently abled child's skills and abilities and the expectations placed on his/her in the inclusive school setting.

11

Making Learning More Meaningful to the Differently Abled

INTRODUCTION

A teaching-learning process for a set of learners in a given situation becomes successful only when the learners are fully involved in the process, by taking genuine interest in their learning. The key to capture and maintain interest of the learners in a teaching-learning process lies well in their understanding that have what is being taught or acquired by them is quite meaningful in serving their own interests and welfare. A little different situation arises in an inclusive setup, where the differently abled face some learning difficulties on account of their impairments or disabilities of one or the other nature. They have their own specific needs for learning, development and adjustment. These needs have to be addressed properly for making them involved in the ongoing teaching learning process for turning their acquired learning experience meaningful to them. For this purpose the teachers concerned have to make use of some useful strategies like below:

(*i*) Strategies helpful in differentiating content

(*ii*) Strategies helpful in curricular adaptation

(*iii*) Resorting to proper lesson planning

(*iv*) Use of appropriate Teaching-Learning Method (TLM).

Let us discuss them one by one.

USE OF STRATEGIES HELPFUL IN DIFFERENTIATING CONTENT

Teachers may make use of one or the other strategies for redressing the special needs of differently abled for making them absorbed in the learning resulting in a quite meaningful or purposeful learning to them. One category of such strategies may involve the task of differentiating contents quite in tune with the nature of the impairment, disability or difficulty faced by them in their learning, adjustment and development. We know that in the process of teaching-learning useful contents/learning experiences are provided to the learners for helping them in their process of adjustment and development. Since a lot of differentiation exists among the learners of an inclusive setup, in terms of the special needs related to their adjustment and development, it becomes necessary on our part to adopt proper strategies for bringing differentiation in the contents/ learning experiences provided to them as illustrated below.

- Visually impaired children should be provided with needed instruction/learning experiences helpful in equipping them with the necessary life skills related to their movements independence in performing their daily routines and using Braille, touch screens, especially designed computers, laptops, mobiles, etc. for their adjustment, living and participation in teaching-learning process. They should be presented with the learning contents or experiences requiring the use of the senses (such as hearing, smell, touch, taste, etc.) other than the sense of sight.
- Hearing impaired should be presented with the learning contents or experiences that are governed through the senses (visual, kinaesthetic, smell, touch, etc.) other than their sense of hearing. Their learning material thus may be loaded with visual pictures and sound less presentations and demonstrations and they may be encouraged to acquire learning experiences through the practical and project work independently or in the groups.
- The content material or learning experiences given to the orthopaedically impaired or locomotor disabled children may be both visual and auditory depending upon the learning situation. Here, care is taken that that the movement difficulty should not come in the way of acquiring learning experiences. Therefore, we should avoid to provide such learning experiences to them that require some such movements (i.e. turning of pages, doing practical project work, movements of their one or the other organs, doing some physical, manual work or exercise etc.) that may pose a lot of difficulty for them on account of their locomotor disability.
- The content material or learning experience presented to a dyslexic or dyscalculia student must reflect a lot of differentiation in comparison to the children not affected by these learning disabilities. Even in the learning contents presented to the dyslexic and dyscalculia attempts should be made to have proper differentiation. 'While easy to go' approach needs to be adapted for the dyslexic in the learning of language, the same is repeated with the dyscalculia in the learning of the subject requiring calculation or computation.
- For the slow learners backward or mentally retarded children care is taken to have differentiation in the learning contents or experiences presented to them in tune with the deficiencies related to their previous knowledge for the subject being learned, cognitive abilities, pace of learning, lack of interest or achievement motivation, etc. In the sharp contrast, on the other hand, the learning material presented to the gifted and creative children should be of a quite challenging nature, rich in learning experiences and capable enough to nurture their talent in a proper way.

USE OF STRATEGIES HELPFUL IN CURRICULAR ADAPTATION

Curriculum is regarded as an organized course or means to achieve the stipulated objectives or learning goals in a teaching-learning context. These objectives or learning goals may differ from learner to learner in relation to their own special needs linked to their adjustment and development. The learning goals or requirements for the mentally retarded, learning disabled, hearing, visual or orthopaedically impaired can't match the learning goals set for the normals. These should essentially differ in their formulation as well as implementation. As a result there is actually a need of having different curriculum or curricular experience set for the learners having differentiation in their abilities, potential or capacities. However, practically it is not feasible for having diverse curricular to diverse learners of an inclusive setup. The solution lies in adopting strategies for carrying out needed adaptation or accommodation in the prescribed curriculum for a particular class or grade. How such curricular accommodation or adaptation can be carried out for meeting the special needs of the differently abled to make learning quite meaningful to them has already been discussed in the Chapter Six of this text. Readers are advised to go through the relevant pages of the chapter.

RESORTING TO PROPER LESSON PLANNING

Lesson planning as we know represents a well chalked out efforts by a teacher for drawing a road map of the journey travelled along with the students for the teaching learning of a topic subject in a fixed duration. Here he decides and lay down in his plan—

(*i*) The objectives for the students learning (i.e. what the students of the class are supposed to learn)

(*ii*) The teaching learning activities to be done for the realization of the laid objectives and

(*iii*) Strategies to checkout the progress of the students in terms of the realization of the laid objectives for proper feedback and follow up.

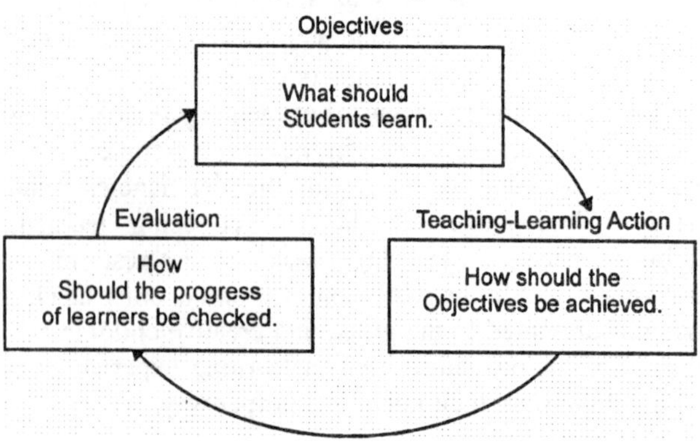

Fig. 11.1: Three Main Elements of Lesson Planning

The development of suitable lesson plan for the teaching-learning of a particular topic subject is really a great challenge for a subject teacher of an inclusive class. Here he needs to take care of the special needs of the diverse learners of varying abilities, capacities, potentials, backgrounds, interests, strengths and limitations. More specifically planning has now to be done for the realization of the objection set for the children with disabilities of varying nature such on visually impaired, hearing impaired orthopaedically or locomotor disabled, learning disabled, mentally challenged, etc. but focussing on the common topic to be dealt in the inclusive class. For this purpose a teacher has to take care of the things below:

1. While setting objectives for the teaching of a particular topic/subject to the inclusive class, the teacher should also keep in mind the learning difficulties of the differently abled for the realization of these common objectives. He should make necessary adaptation in the learning objectives set for these children in accordance with the limitations imposed on them on account of their disabilities.
2. The main body of a lesson plan in concerned with the: (*i*) selection of content/learner/experiences for the teaching of a particular topic, (*ii*) the methodology and strategies used for presenting the content or subject material, (*iii*) the aid, equipment used and activities performed at the hands of both the teacher and students. Here a teacher has to take care of the needs, problems, learning capacity and styles of the diverse learners of the inclusive class for addressing all of these curricular, methodology and teaching-learning aids concerns. He has to mention clearly the adaptation, accommodation and strategies utilized for addressing the special needs of the differently abled learners.
3. Third important thing in the development of lesson plan is planning about the needed assessment or evaluation of the ongoing teaching-learning process so that a continuous mechanism of feedback can be maintained. The type of questions asked in the drill and practice work to be done, opportunities for participating in discussion and demonstration given all should be carefully planned as to provide evidences for the understanding reached on the part of diverse learners about the topic being taught during the classroom period. What type of evaluation devices, strategies and feedback mechanism will remain appropriate for the diverse learner of differential abilities and limitations should be properly cared for planning about such evaluation and feedback mechanism by a teacher in developing the lesson plan.

USE OF APPROPRIATE TEACHING-LEARNING MATERIAL (TLM)

A teacher is supposed to make use of a wide variety of teaching-learning material (called TLM in short) at the various junctures of his teaching learning journey set out in a classroom period along with his students. A lesson plan developed by the teacher on this account specifically mention, the type of teaching-learning material (TLM) used by teacher for the purpose at the various points of his teaching while interacting with his students or making a point graspable to them. The use of such teaching-learning material on the part of a teacher helps much in making the learning more meaningful to the learners, so a teacher has to be quite careful in the selection and use of teaching, learning material. It should invariably meet the specific learning needs, abilities, capacities learning problems and limitations of the diverse learners including the differently abled. For doing this with the differently abled is really a big challenge before an inclusive class teacher. He has to keep in mind a wide variety or spectrum of teaching-learning material at his disposal for addressing the peculiar learning needs and limitations of the disabled. Let us see what type of teaching-learning material can be utilized for making the learning meaningful to various types of differently abled in view of their special learning and adjustment needs.

(*a*) Teacher Learning Material (TLM) for Visually Impaired

(*i*) Use of real objects concrete material, improvised apparatus, toys, models or specimen helpful for learning and experiencing through non-visual senses such as hearing, touch, smell or taste.

(*ii*) Use of tactile graphs, raised diagrams, globes, maps and other learning and working material.

(*iii*) Use of talking books, tape recorders, talking calculators, talking watches and clocks, computers, etc.

(*iv*) Use of specialized material available (Braille, Taylor Frame, Abacus, subject kits, etc.)

(*v*) Use of recorded instructions and texts.

(*vi*) Use of the other developed assistive and adaptative teaching learning devices, specially meant for visually impaired such as screen readers, voice synthesizers, scanners etc.

(*b*) Teaching Learning Method (TLM) for Hearing Impaired

(*i*) Use of real objects concrete material improvised apparatuses toys, models, specimen, etc. helpful for learning and experiencing through non-learning senses such as seeing, touching smelling or tasting.

(*ii*) Use of visual graphic aids such as charts, pictures, graphs, flash cards, cartoons, newspapers, maps and globes.

(*iii*) Use of silent or speechless video recording of the instructions and texts.

(*iv*) Use of visual/graphic organizers like time lines.

(*v*) Use of activity aids visuals demonstration and experimentation.

(*vi*) Use of the developed assistive and adaptative teaching-learning material specifically meant for hearing impaired learners.

(*c*) Teaching Learning Material (TLM) for Mentally Retarded

(*i*) Use of real objects, concrete material, models and specimen improvised apparatuses, toys, playing and amusement articles, etc. for learning and experiencing things involving the use of all sensory abilities but simple and easy to grasp on the part of the mentally disabled.

(*ii*) Use of graphic aids like pictures, charts, and reading text developed carefully to match the intellectual level of the mentally retarded.

(*iii*) Use of multi-sensory aids involving visual, kinaesthetic, tactile and auditory senses.

(*iv*) Use of playing material, amusement activities and repeated demonstration of actions.

(*v*) Use of the developed assistive and adaptation teaching-learning material specifically meant for the intellectually impaired.

(*d*) Teaching-learning Material (TLM) for orthopaedically impaired or locomotor disabled.

Orthopaedically impaired or children with locomotor disabilities are focused to suffer from the movements related problems, difficulties and limitation of their one or the other body organs. However, it does not essentially make them handicapped in terms of the use of their sensory abilities. Usually these children are found to make use of their senses—sense of right, hearing, smell, touch and taste for gaining useful experiences for the realization of their learning objectives. In the use of teaching learning material involving multi-senses thus these children are much alike to the non-disabled normal children. Hence, we can make use of a variety of audio-visual aids and offer multi-sensory material involving the use of their one or the other senses. The only difficulty, problem or limitation arises for them in the use of those aids and equipments, activities and interactions where their locomotors difficulty or limitations come into the way of using them on their part.

12

Pedagogical Strategies in Inclusive Set up

WHAT ARE PEDAGOGICAL OR TEACHING STRATEGIES?

In simple words the term pedagogical or teaching strategy stands for the type of strategy employed by the teacher in carrying out his teaching task in a way most helpful for him to attain the desired teaching-learning objectives. The term strategy in its own way slightly differs from the commonly used terms methods and devices employed by a teacher for carrying out the task of teaching. It stands for specific plans and ways designed and employed by the teacher for attaining his teaching goals or objectives much in the same way as used by a chess player or operation incharge of a warfare. A teaching strategy is so planned and designed as to provide maximum help to the learners in getting them engaged in a learning task as effectively as possible for the realization of the set goals. A strategy used by the teacher must help a learner (*i*) in remaining motivated, interested and absorbed in the process of learning (*ii*) to acquire necessary knowledge, skill, attitude etc. for bringing desired changes in his behaviour (*iii*) to discover or construct the knowledge with his own independent efforts, guided learning or cooperative and group learning. Whatever strategies may be employed by the teacher for his teaching in a particular teaching-learning environment, the goal is to seek best output for the learners through their creative and meaningful learning efforts and endeavours. There are number of teaching strategies available for the teachers for their teaching which can help their learners to learn well (*i*) with the assistance of a teacher or peer tutor or (*ii*) in a group involving cooperative and collaborative spirit and (*iii*) in a reflective way or with the use of multisensory aids. In this chapter, we would be focusing our discussion on the few of these pedagogical or teaching strategies.

PEER TUTORING

You must have heard about the terms tutors and tutorial classes and also must be acquainted with their use in day to day life. A tutor is usually differentiated from a teacher on the ground that he is relatively more nearer to the student than the teacher teaching in the classrooms situation. He can establish more rapport with the student. Students can communicate more comfortably and inhesitantly with their tutors and can avail their cooperation, guidance and help more easily in comparison to teachers. It is this image of a tutor that helps much in drawing necessary benefits on the part of students from their tutors. Its value and impact gets more enhanced when a student finds an opportunity to avail the services of one of his peer as a tutor in place of a particular teacher of the school playing the role of a tutor. Such tutorial services provided by a peer to his fellow student or students are referred to as peer tutoring.

In practice in peer tutoring, a fellow student is seen to help one or more of his fellow students in their learning and development. It is quite natural for a peer tutor to have more rapport, nearness and simplicity in relationship with his fellow students on account of their being of the same age and grade. There is no much difference in their status in respect of experience, abilities and educational status. The only difference that can be seen in a peer tutor and a fellow student is that the former knows a little more or is somewhat more skilled than the later and by virtue of his nearness and acceptability can help the fellow student in a more desirable way.

In this regard the famous Russian Psychologist Lav Vygotsky has tried to convey through the concept of 'Zone of Proximal development' (ZPD) that a child can be helped well in getting instruction from the peers who are near to him in respect of the possession of desired knowledge and experience. They can enjoy more rapport, nearness and trust between them and it results in appropriate instruction and cooperation much helpful for the success in instructional process. It is why the peer tutoring proves a better alternative from many of the students in their instruction and training in comparison to the help rendered by parents, teachers and experts in this regard.

In the inclusive setup peer tutors can play a quite significant role in carrying out the teaching-learning activity. The adoption of peer tutorial system here can help well in realising the dreams of individualised instruction in a better way.

Regarding the role of a peer tutor, it can be played by a non-disabled peer who may be seen to help his or her disabled peer in one or the other task or activity aimed for better adjustment, explanation and illustration of a concept, demonstration of a skill, providing help in performing one or the other task by working as a model or manually helping him or her imitate and practice the model behaviour. It is not essential that a non-disabled peer should always act as a peer tutor. This role can also be played by a disabled peer to his or her disabled counter parts, who has reached to a better level of performance and excellence (in one or the other scholastic or non-scholastic areas) a little earlier than the other disabled peers.

A student whether disabled or non-disabled while playing the role of a peer teacher in the inclusive setup may be found to perform the following four types of activities (Dash, 2001).

(*i*) ***Monitoring*** *i.e.* supervision and regulation of the performance of a tutee.

(*ii*) ***Reinforcing*** *i.e.* providing appropriate contingencies for approved behaviour (such as praising the tutee if he/she has completed the work to a required standard).

(*iii*) ***Modelling*** *i.e.* the demonstration of a particular activity or behaviour by the peer tutor.

(*iv*) ***Explaining*** *i.e.* exposing the relationships on a topic and providing appropriate examples to clarify doubts.

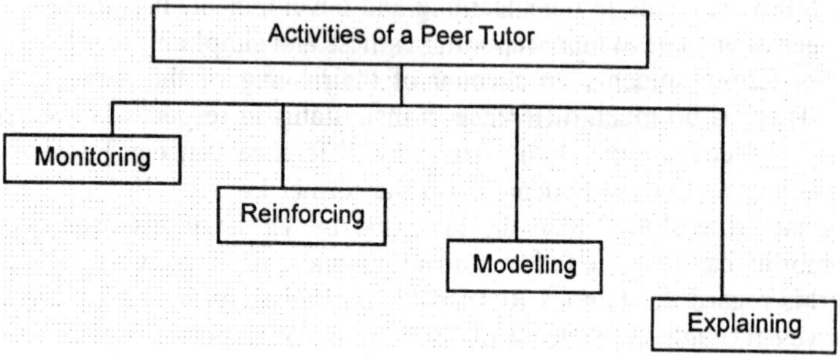

Fig. 12.1: Activities of a Peer Tutor

The role played by peer tutors in the ways mentioned above may prove quite beneficial to the slow learners, backward and differently abled or disabled students in their proper adjustment, education and wholesome development. In an inclusive setup where there is a need of too much individualization in respect of addressing the needs of the variety of students characterized with too much diversity and differences the peer tutoring system may help well in a fruitful way. Moreover, peer tutoring as the research evidences show has all possibilities of many extra advantages over the traditional mode of instruction and guidance services provided to the differently abled in an inclusive setup in the manner outlined below.

— While engaging in the process of instruction and guidance along with their peer tutors students do not experience the hesitation, fear or uneasiness as experienced by them in the interaction with their teachers. Here in this system they feel more confident and ready to learn and definitely it results in knowing and learning the things that they were unable to learn and to know from their teacher and other experts.

— The peer tutors are in a position to provide instruction to their fellow students by coming to their level or status. It can happen because after all they are also the students like their fellow beings. They have no fear for their self-dignity and status like an usual classroom teacher. As a result, the fellow students may come quite nearer to them for attending what they say or show in comparison to the classroom or subject teachers.

— Peer Tutors are in a position to get the fellow students acquainted with their own experiences. They can tell them that they have also been passed through the difficulties and hurdles in learning as felt by the fellow students at this stage. How did they get away from these difficulties, the narration of such experiences may prove quite beneficial to the fellow students in their learning tasks.

— The type of help and guidance that can be availed in the practice work and training activities from the peer tutors is many times prove unmatched. We can't expect it from the teachers in the usual classroom teaching situation. Student are not troubled by a bitter criticism and frequent testing work performed by the classroom teachers but contrarily get timely help and assistance in a very friendly and cordial way from their fellow peer tutors.

COOPERATIVE LEARNING

The Concept of Cooperative Learning

Cooperative learning as the name suggests stand for a learning process or learning strategy in which students are provided opportunities to learn by themselves in a group in a cooperative way. They share each and every information among themselves and help each other for having required knowledge, understanding and application of one or the other aspects of the content material, or course units included in their syllabus. It seems quite contrary to the practice of teaching-learning prevalent in our current educational system. Our on going classroom teaching is totally teacher dominated and content centered. Here teachers are regarded as the repositories of subject knowledge and their role is simply to pour into the open, empty and willing (or non-willing) minds of students their vast reservoir of knowledge. They do not trust their students to learn. They think that they must tell them what to learn and provide all the structure for the learning to take place. This structure of learning provided by them to their students is highly individualistic. It encourages individual as well as competitive learning in place of group and cooperative learning. Here students are tempted to learn more and more in order to gain good grades, divisions, certificates, appreciation or attractive prizes etc. by excelling their own peers or reaching the set target of excellence. Cooperative learning says no to such practices. It advocates cooperative learning (*i.e.* the learning in group by cooperating with one another) in place of the competitive and individualistic approach (encouraging cut throat competition and immoral practices of getting ahead) prevalent in our present system of education and evaluation.

Cooperative Learning in the Context of Inclusive Setup

In the inclusive setup there is the presence of a wide variety of learners with significant divergence in their learning capacities and learning needs. All have to grow and develop according to their own individual capacities and limitations. There is less competition and more emphasis on mutual adjustment and cooperation in an inclusive setup in comparison to the normal regular classrooms. There seems no point for the non-disabled peers to have unnecessary competition with their disabled counterparts. Here, they are naturally driven towards cooperative learning instead of getting engaged in competitions with each other. The teacher should take advantage of this spontaneity for organizing the classroom activities of the inclusive setup on cooperative footings.

How to make use of the Strategy of Cooperative Learning

In inclusive setup we find the presence of diverse groups of learners with diversified learning interests, abilities and capacities. While make use of cooperative learning the teachers should be quite cautious about the formation of groups. A class consisting of 30 students may be broken down into 5 or 6 sub-groups or teams each consisting of equal number of students with different abilities. In these groups (called mixed ability groups) then teaching or instruction is carried out on the reflective level mode instead of the memory or understanding levels of mode.

For proceeding in this concern the teacher may put the students of an inclusive class in a situation: (*i*) to work out the solution of a problematic situation, (*ii*) to collect data and information about getting acquainted with some facts, (*iii*) to seek application and truth value of a generalized principle, (*iv*) to construct, create and produce something new or of some use at their own while working alone or in group.

Putting them in such problematic, self-learning and pushing situations, every learner in the inclusive setup has sufficient freedom to reflect upon his own abilities, previous experiences, skills and potential for proceeding on his learning path. No one has to wait for others as he or she is free to utilize his/her capacities or potential at the utmost for his highest learning or development. Intellectually superior, normal, slow or backward, and the variety of disabled such as hearing, visually, locomotor disabled, learning disabled and mentally sub-normals all can strive and gain the desired milestones in such reflective level teaching-learning setup well in tune with their strengths and limitations.

The fears that only capable, non-disabled and intellectually superior students can benefit from reflective teaching is unfounded or baseless. The reverse is more true as everybody has the opportunity and access for getting proper return of his striving well in tune with his own potentials, and differential abilities. Moreover, there is more cooperation and collaboration in the reflective teaching setup instead of the mutual rivalries and unhealthy competitions as would otherwise possible in memory and understanding level teaching.

A blind child may enjoy fine and rich imagination, the strength and utilization of his all other senses than the sight for reflecting upon in the confronting learning, creative, and constructive work situation. The same is true for the hearing disabled who can focus more in the minute observations of the details of the observed phenomenon and thus reflect well in knowing and applying the things in a better way. The learning disabled although feeling difficulty in some particular learning area may be found to possess extraordinary potential of learning and doing so many things and thus may be found to show quite encouraging results in facing the challenges of reflective teaching. In this way, if analyzed properly there is nothing that may hamper or provide major hurdles on the path of adopting reflective teaching strategy on the part of teachers for the education and development of the students in an inclusive education setup. It help in individualizing the process of instruction as well as benefiting from the collaborated efforts if challenges of reflective thinking in learning one or the other things are thrown to groups comprising of non-disabled and disabled peers.

MULTISENSORY TEACHING

Multisensory teaching as the name suggests, is a teaching that is executed or performed with the adopting ways and means resting on the use of a number of sensory organs (*i.e.* senses of sight, hearing, smell, taste and touch). Since senses are termed as the gate way of knowledge and key means for the acquisition of valuable learning experiences, multisensory teaching has a great potential for proving beneficial and useful in any scheme or program of teaching-learning planned and organized for the school children. Its importance, use and significance is much enhanced in the case of its employment for the adjustment and education of the children belonging to inclusive education setup for the reasons outlined below.

In inclusive setup we have the presence of diverse learners with their diverse needs, potential and capacities for learning. Where non-disabled students, as happens in the usual classroom setup, can be taught by making use of any one or two available sensory means (such as only through lecturing, demonstrating, lecture cum demonstration or experiences given through the senses of smell and touch in the laboratory or workshops), the group of disabled or differently abled present in the inclusive setup need the use of a variety of senses for their adjustment and education depending upon the nature of their impairment and special learning needs. For example,

(*a*) The hearing impaired remain in loss in terms of getting benefitted from the use of their hearing sense, visually impaired suffer this loss in terms of the use of the sense of sight. In their cases thus it becomes quite essential to compensate their losses by making use of their other available senses for the learning and adjusting to the demands of the inclusive setup.

(*b*) The children with intellectual impairment, suffering from autism and one or the other type of learning disabilities may be properly benefitted through the provision of multisensory experiences in the teaching-learning process specially in the form of concrete visualization and manipulation of the things by themselves.

(*c*) The children suffering from locomotor disability or orthopedical impairments may be unable to manipulate the things on account of some impairments in their action organs. While sitting on the wheel chair, they may gain advantages from the display of audio-visual experiences, sensing and smelling the things in their environment as well as taking parts in conversations and dialogues.

(*d*) The children suffering from communication disorders on account of language problems, being deaf and dumb, or suffering from emotional disturbances or intellectual impairments may get necessarily benefitted through the multisensory means and ways available for them for the acquisition of the required learning experiences.

In the inclusive classroom setting thus a subject teacher may be seen to be engaged in the multisensory teaching for providing all the learners belonging to inclusive setup the sensory experiences suitable to their abilities or disabilities, learning styles and learning requirements. In the adoption of such multisensory approach in his teaching the use of multimedia technology of the modern age may also prove quite helpful and beneficial to him. The use of multimedia in the inclusive classroom setup may include a combination of text, audio, still images, animation, video or interactive content forms. Multimedia is usually recorded and played, displayed, or accessed by the computerized and electronic devices, but can also be part of a live performance. Thus, what is presented by the teachers in the classroom as multimedia presentations for the teaching-learning of the subjects may be recorded or live. A recorded presentation may allow interactivity via a navigation system. A live multimedia presentation may allow interactivity via an interaction with the presenter or performer.

In addition to seeing and hearing, the developments in the field of computer and technology have made it possible to provide feeling sensations and illusion of taste and smell to the virtual objects. In this way, utilization of multimedia in the inclusive setup has opened every possibility of providing useful multi-sensory experiences to the learners with the utilization of the multiple senses, (senses of hearing, sight, smell, taste, and touch).

Characteristics Features of Multimedia used in the Inclusive Classroom for Multisensory Teaching

- Multimedia contents are very rich in the sense that they may involve a combination of a variety of media contents-audio, visual, audio-visual, text, pictures, graphs, animation and interactive format.
- Multimedia presentations may require from the teachers to make use of the traditional and computerized electronic devices.
- Multimedia presentations may be viewed by the students in person alive on stage, as well as projected, transmitted or played locally with a media player.

- A teacher may make use of a live or recorded multimedia presentation for helping in his instructional task.
- A teacher may make use of either analog or digital electronic media technology for preparing and presenting his multimedia presentations.
- In the case of making use of the Digital online multimedia on the part of a teacher he may go for its own loading from the related websites or may try to receive it alive or on demand through the respective agencies broadcasting useful educational programs.
- There is specific provision of multimedia presentation in all the modern available electronic and computer applications such as personal computer, laptop, tablet and smart phones. Microsoft corporation also provides the power point software program along with its MS office package for producing power point presentation in the classroom setting. The laptops, PC's and Tablets also have provision of the display of CDS loaded with multimedia teaching learning material for devising necessary benefit on the part of learners for realizing the set learning objectives.

SOCIAL LEARNING

Social learning in its word meaning stands for a type of learning that results from the consequences of observational experiences gained on the part of developing children in the social company of others (elders and more knowledgeable peers). Such observational experiences and their imitation and practice may help a lot to the differently abled or disabled children receive from their non-disabled peers or structured social experiences arranged for them in an inclusive education set up.

Social learning as an approach and theory of learning was first brought into existence by the social psychologist Albert Bandura (1977). As proposed by Bandura through his social learning theory most of what we learn is acquired through simply watching and listening to other people. The children from the very beginning keenly observe the behaviour of others, most commonly of the people nearest to them like parents, members of the family, teachers, the older members of society, etc. In turn, they try to imitate and do what they observe. The power of observational learning can be confirmed through laboratory experiments as well as through observation in our daily life. A child who sees his father throwing utensils around simply because he has not been served food of his taste, learns such behaviour and reproduces it in similar circumstances. He may also incorporate and imitate the behaviour of the characters he reads about in novels, hears about over the radio or sees on TV or in movies. The persons whose behaviour he observes and often imitates are known as models and observational learning is referred to as *modelling.*

Social Learning as a Teaching Strategy in Inclusive Setup

Social learning as an approach and strategy can be quite effectively utilized in inclusive set up for the learning of the differently abled/disabled children. Here the teacher, trainer, non-disabled peers as well as the more capable or an early disabled peer may work as a model for helping and meeting the learning needs of the differently abled. The steps given below suggested by Bandura (1977) may be followed in making use of the social learning strategy for the teaching and learning of the students belonging to inclusive classroom set up.

Step 1. *Attending to and perceiving the behaviour*: In this step the learner is made to observe the behaviour of the person acting as a model. Here the total behaviour or a particular aspect of it may attract attention and become the subject of close attention.

Step 2. *Remembering the behaviour*: In this step, what the learner observes is stored in his memory in the form of mental images.

Step 3. *Converting the memory into action*: In this step, a behaviour observed and remembered by the learner is analysed in terms if its acceptability to the learner with reference to the demands of him self and his environment. It is transformed into action only afterwards and thus the observed relevant and accepted aspects of the model's behaviour are imitated by the learner.

Step 4. *Reinforcement of the imitated behaviour:* In this final step, the behaviour of the model imitated by the learner is reinforced for proper adoption and further continuance.

In this way, by following the above mentioned stages or steps involved in one's social learning, the children belonging to inclusive set up may be helped to acquire a number of skills, applications and understanding of one or the other concepts/principles essential for their adjustment, education and development.

BUDDY SYSTEM

In the inclusive set up paying of individual attention is utmost needed specially for caring and meeting the special needs of the differently abled to their adequate adjustment education and wholesome development along with their non-disabled peers. The task is quite challenging for the classroom/subject teacher. There is the presence of locomotor/ orthopaedically impaired learners in the classroom who may need a variety of assistance and help for their proper mobility in one or the other types of learning situations *i.e.* turning the pages of their texts, holding the things in their hands or placing on the table, performing one or the other activities associated with practical tasks related to curricular or co-curricular needs. Similarly, the children with hearing impairment may need the help of providing them lecture notes/ instructions in writing form or convey what has been required by the teacher in the form of home work, assignment or project work. Visually handicapped on the other hand may need to be helped in getting audio description or translation of the learning events of the classroom alongwith necessary assistance for their proper mobility. Similarly children suffering from intellectual impairment, autism and learning disabilities may need to be assisted and helped in getting adjusted in the inclusive set up alongwith the satisfaction of their learning and developmental requirements. We can't have so many hands and minds to assist and help them at the time of the need unless the cooperation from the fellow students present in the class is not secured. Moreover, it should be availed in proper form from the persons who are properly trained in meeting these special needs of the differently abled at the proper time in a proper way.

The adoption of buddy system is advocated for meeting out the demands of the above narrated situations arising frequently and necessarily in the learning set up of inclusive classrooms. The question arises what do we mean by the buddy system? Who are buddy and what type of roles they need to play in helping and assisting their needy peers?

Buddies in relation to inclusive set up are the student volunteers, mostly the peers of the same age and grade, selected from the group of non-disabled students who are further trained for understanding the needs of their differently abled peers and providing help and assistance to them at the proper time in a proper way.

Mostly the system known as peer-to-peer buddy system (pairing two or more students acting as buddies) is adopted for helping and assisting the disabled or differently abled for their adjustment and education in the inclusive set up. In this system a differently abled peer is looked after by a peer or small group of the students called buddies (of the same class in the classroom situations) or by the senior students (in or out of the class school situations). This small group may vary in size but every time there must be someone present from the non-disabled buddies for assisting and helping the particular disabled student belonging to their buddy circle in his adjustment and learning.

Regarding their functions, buddies have the opportunities to play their roles both in curricular and co-curricular life of the school. Buddies in the classroom *i.e.* (the non-disabled volunteers alongwith the disabled peer of their buddy circle) may work together, share equipments and participate together in cooperative group work or project activities. In the games and other co-curricular activities, the students belonging to a buddy circle (comprising non-disabled volunteers and the disabled peer) may work and participate in a cooperative way. Their activities may also be extended to beyond school boundary such as attending social gatherings in the community or inviting each other in family functions, etc.

The Essentials for Successful Employment of Buddy System

The things like below may prove quite helpful in the successful employment of buddy system for the realization of its objectives in an inclusive education set up.

1. While initiating the buddy system in an inclusive set up, the teacher/school authorities may have an orientation talk and dialogue with the students acquainting them with the nature of difficulties faced by their differently abled peers in their adjustment and education alongwith them in the inclusive set up. They may call then the students volunteering them for the running of the buddy system in the school.
2. The selection of the non-disabled peers as buddies should be made with a great care. Usually, the students selected for playing the role of buddies to the disabled students should be chosen for their maturity, kindness and voluntary spirit of giving their time and efforts for taking away the disabled alongwith them in the performance of curricular and co-curricular activities by providing help and assistance according to their special needs.
3. The non-disabled students volunteers playing the role of helping buddies must be provided appropriate training for exercising their responsibilities in the most appropriate way possible so that (*i*) they don't try and do everything for their disabled buddy turning him/her heavily dependent upon them. (*ii*) they should learn and be made competent to meet the special needs of the disabled buddy in adjusting them to the inclusive set up and joining hands with them in their learning.
4. In the buddies circle, the members should see each other as competent human beings irrespective of the differences in their abilities. The differently abled may be imbibed with a number of unique abilities (irrespective of their impairment in one or two developmental areas) and the non-disabled buddies should also try to learn a number of specialties owned by the differently abled buddy belonging to their buddy circle. For example a hearing impaired may be a good photographer, cartoonist, poet or craftman, a visually impaired may be a good musician, a philosopher, creative genious, etc. The relationship in the buddy circle thus may be on mutually sharing and helping basis for each other's progress in curricular and co-curricular areas.
5. There should be rotation system applied in the inclusion of non-disabled peers assisting and helping a disabled peer in the buddies groups working in an inclusive class since there is a possibility of growing resentment among the non-disabled volunteers that they "have to" work with a particular disabled child.

Benefits of Buddy System

As you know in friendship both the parties remain in a win-win situation. The same is true with a buddies group working in an inclusive set up.

According to Convey (2008), the use of buddies in and out of the classrooms can benefit children with or without disabilities in the manner like below.

Benefits for Non-disabled

Non-disabled children budding the disabled children may be benefitted in terms of

(*i*) getting experiences of interacting with children who they may have not interacted with before.

(*ii*) developing an awareness and respect for diversity, thus helping themselves to develop socially and emotionally.

(*iii*) Developing a deeper understanding of the task or activity (related to curricular and co-curricular areas) as they help clarify ideas and rules for their disabled buddy.

(*iv*) Learning positive skills from their disabled buddy, learn to see things from a different perspective, or learn the value of something they take for granted (*i.e.* value of the sense of hearing, vision, sound intellectual development, locomotor ability that has been denied to the disabled buddy).

Benefits for Disabled

Children with disabilities can benefit from a well-planned, well-implemented buddy system properly through:

(*i*) Seeing social and academic skills modelled

(*ii*) Hearing things explained in "child" language

(*iii*) Getting more one-on-one support than adults can provide in a busy school environment.

(*iv*) Becoming more independent, connected and confident.

REFLECTIVE TEACHING

Teaching in the classroom is generally found to be organized at the three levels known as memory level, understanding and reflective level of teaching. Memory level teaching based on the traditional behaviouristic theories of learning is aimed to pour information directly in the minds of the students for getting it memorized with least care of its proper comprehension, understanding or application on their parts. Understanding level teaching represents relatively a high level in the teaching-learning process as compared to memory level. It provides meanings to what is being taught or learned in a learning situation. Students can properly understand, grasp and apply the learned generalizations in other learning or working situations. However, such type of teaching also does not carry much benefit on account of being too much teacher centered and its inability to develop the power to reflect characterized with independent problem-solving ability, creativity and constructiveness demonstrated by the students in their learning and acquisition behaviour.

For serving this purpose, the teaching needs to be organized at the reflective level instead of the traditional memory or understanding levels. Let us know what we mean by teaching organized at reflective level ?

Meaning and Definition

According to the dictionary meaning the word 'reflecting' stands for the act of reflection (turning back), contemplating or paying serious consideration etc. Consequently, teaching at reflecting level must have its association with the process of reflecting or turning back the existing idea or knowledge for more careful consideration or critical examination to derive fresh conclusion. It is in this sense that Morris L. Bigge has defined it as: "*careful, critical examination of an idea or supposed article of knowledge in the light of the testable evidence which supports it and the further conclusions towards which it points.*" (1967, p. 324)

A careful examination of this definition may reveal the following facts about the nature of the reflecting level of teaching:

- It provides opportunities to the learners for the close, careful and critical examination of the existing facts, ideas, insights and generalizations.
- The learners try to test them in the light of the relevant evidences.
- They are free to set independent hypothesis, test them and draw their own conclusion for learning new facts or acquiring new insight.

Looking into the above cited nature, it is the must that teaching at the reflecting level be organized at some quite advanced level providing opportunities for the utilization of the learner's cognitive abilities. Such opportunities may be best provided if the teaching-learning situations are turned into problematic one and the students are made to discover the solution of problem in the light of their own thinking and independent pursuit of the knowledge. They enjoy freedom of choosing their learning path, devise their own means and ways for arriving at the conclusions, and construct or create knowledge and its applications in their own ways.

Reflective Teaching and Inclusive Classrooms

In inclusive classroom set up we have the presence of diversified learners having diversified interests, potential and abilities for their learning and development. No single prescription in the form of direct telling of the information or training them in one or the other arts and skills can serve the purpose of inclusive education *i.e.* providing equal access and opportunities to all the learners for their wholesome development according to their learning needs and potential with no discrimination of any kind. The reflective level teaching here can work as most suitable alternative in place of direct teaching or instruction mode adopted in the memory or understanding level of teaching.

For proceeding in this concern the teacher may put the students of an inclusive class in a situation, (*i*) to work put the solution of a problematic situation, (*ii*) to collect data and information about getting acquainted with some facts, (*iii*) to seek application and truth value of a generalized principle, (*iv*) to construct, create and produce something new or of some use at their own while working alone or in group.

Putting them in such problematic, self-learning and pushing situations, every learner in the inclusive set up has sufficient freedom to reflect upon his own abilities, previous experiences, skills and potential for proceeding on his learning path. No one has to wait for others as he or she in free to utilize his/her capacities or potential at the utmost for his highest learning or development. Intellectually superior, normal, slow or backward, and the variety of disabled such as hearing, visually, locomotor disabled, learning disabled and mentally sub-normals all can strive and gain the desired milestones in such reflective level teaching-learning set up well in tune with their strengths and limitations.

The fears that only capable, non-disabled and intellectually superior students can benefit from reflective teaching is unfounded or baseless. The reverse is more true as everybody has the opportunity and access for getting proper return of his striving well in tune with his own potentials, and differential abilities. Moreover, there is more cooperation and collaboration in the reflective teaching set up instead of the mutual rivalries and unhealthy competitions as would otherwise possible in memory and understanding level teaching.

A blind child may enjoy fine and rich imagination, the strength and utilization of his all other senses than the sight for reflecting upon in the confronting learning, creative, and constructive work situation. The same in true for the hearing disabled who can focus more in the minute observations of the details of the observed phenomenon and thus reflect well in knowing and applying the things in a better way. The learning disabled although feeling difficulty in some particular learning area may be found to possess extraordinary potential of learning and doing so many things and thus may be found to show quite encouraging results in facing the challenges of reflective teaching. In this way, if analyzed properly there is nothing that may hamper or provide major hurdles on the path of adopting reflective teaching strategy on the part of teachers for the education and development of the students in an inclusive education set up. It help in individualizing the process of instruction as well as benefitting from the collaborated efforts if challenges of reflective thinking in learning one or the other things are thrown to groups comprising of non-disabled and disabled peers.

13

Continuous and Comprehensive Evaluation: Concept and Implications to Facilitate Inclusion

WHAT IS CONTINUOUS AND COMPREHENSIVE EVALUATION OR CCE?

Evaluation is a very essential part of any teaching-learning process as it forms the basis for feedback about the extent of success or failure of any teaching-learning situation.

Recently, a new form of Evaluation termed as Continuous Comprehensive Evaluation (CCE) has come into practice in the school education. Let us understand in a brief overview as to what is meant by CCE and how is it different from the conventional evaluation and its meaning.

CCE makes evaluation an inherent part and parcel of the teaching-learning process. It aims at enhancement of learning through diagnosis and remediation. The two fold objectives of CCE are continuity in evaluation and assessment of broad based learning and behavioural outcomes in a comprehensive way.

The question here may arise why do we need to maintain continuity in evaluation and why should we maintain comprehensiveness in our evaluation?

Continuity of Evaluation: By all means, we try to go through a process of evaluation to get aware of the results of the teaching-learning process, i.e., the planned changes in the behaviour of the students. The changes occurring in the cognitive, conative and affective domains of the pupil's behaviour are non-stopping and continuous. They may occur at any time well in the duration of a teaching-learning process or academic session. A teacher may notify these changes even through a simple observation or interaction with the students in the situations involving scholastic and co-scholastic aspects of students' growth and development. In case he does not take notice of these changes and neglects the needed evaluation, he will be committing a cardinal educational error. It is good from every angle to have evaluation of the concomitant changes, in the behaviour of the pupils as a result of the process of teaching and learning as early and often as possible to provide proper feedback for improving the input, process and output of the instructional and educational systems well in tune with the philosophy of "system approach" adopted in Educational Technology (ET). It is necessary, therefore, on the part of a teacher to maintain proper continuity in the use of evaluation device for keeping the teaching-learning process on a proper track for the realization of the set teaching-learning objectives, diagnosing the learning gaps, difficulties and weaknesses of the learners and teaching-learning system and then introduce timely remedies in the overall welfare of the students.

Comprehensiveness of Evaluation: Evaluation of the learning outcomes of the pupils is chiefly carried out to pass value judgement over the nature of the changes occurring in the behaviour of the students through curricular and co-curricular experiences provided to the learners. Since changes in behaviour are brought out in all the aspects of one's behaviour-cognitive, conative and affective resulting in one's overall growth and development in all the dimensions of his/her personality, it makes a strong plea to take all of them in consideration while making assessment or evaluating of the outcome of a teaching-learning process. It calls for making the process of evaluation not only continuous but also comprehensive in its coverage as well employment of evaluation tools. In bringing comprehensiveness in his evaluation, a teacher may thus be supposed to employ a number of various tools for carrying out evaluation of the students in relation to:

(*a*) Changes in their cognitive, conative and affective domains of the behaviour.

(*b*) Growth and development in all the aspects and dimensions of their personality.

(*c*) Assessment of their existing abilities, capacities, interests, attitudes and aptitudes in respect to their potential to adjust and progress in life.

The necessity of making the task of evaluation as a continuous and comprehensive process has been responsible for introducing considerable changes in the methods, techniques and overall approach adopted in measuring and evaluating the learning outcomes and progress of the students in the manner laid down below:

(*i*) In place of age old annual examination system or seasonal/half yearly examinations, the trend is now for adopting ways and means for carrying out continuous and comprehensive evaluation of outcome of the learning and achievements of the learners in the various domains of their behaviour and personality. It involves the use of multiple and comprehensive testing and non-testing tools and devices.

(*ii*) A formal scheme of CCE, asks for the use of two types of evaluation known as formative evaluation and summative evaluation helpful in carrying out the evaluation in its needed continuity and comprehensiveness.

Formative evaluation is formative and constructive in nature. It is carried out well in the duration of the teaching-learning process for knowing about its outcomes in relation to the realization of the set teaching-learning objectives. It provides useful information to both the teachers and students about the strengths and weaknesses of their teaching and learning. In the light of this information, they may plan and engage for the mid-course corrections in their teaching and learning tasks.

Summative evaluation is carried out at the end of a piece of instruction of a lesson or unit. Actually it represents a final test or measure of the student's progress or gains made by him as a result of a course of learning.

In carrying out both of these evaluations-formative as well as summative, both formal as well as informal techniques like below are in general being used by the teachers in the name of evaluating the learning/ behavioural outcomes of their students.

- The nature and quality of the responses of the students to the questions asked by the teacher in the class.
- The observation record of the behaviour of the students in the class, laboratories, workshops and other places of curricular or co-curricular activities.
- The performance of the students in the drill and practice work given to the students in the class.
- Performance of the students in the practical and project work done in the school.
- The quality of the work done by the students in relation to given assignments and home tasks.
- Performance of the students in interviews or viva voice examination.
- Performance of the students in the periodically tests and examinations such as weekly and monthly tests and quarterly, half yearly or annual examinations.
- The responses received through the assessment tools like questionnaires, rating scales, check lists, attitude scales, interest inventories, adjustment inventories and personality measures.
- Performance in the standardized diagnostic as well as achievement tests available in the areas and units of different school subjects.

IMPLICATIONS OF CCE TO FACILITATE INCLUSION

In an inclusive setup of the school, we have the presence of diverse learners differing and differentiating from each other in terms of the possession of unique abilities or capacities, social, economic and cultural backgrounds learning interest and styles as well as developmental goals set or expectations made from them. It is why we have to bring a lot of flexibility, accommodation and adaptation with regard to curriculum, methods and strategies of teaching-learning, learning or work environment and goals or objectives of school instruction in dealing with all such diversities found in the inclusive education setup. The same is also true with the planning and organization of assessment or evaluation of their learning or behavioural outcomes. Here we need to introduce necessary changes and modifications in our existing system or pattern of examination dominated uptil now by summative type evaluation governed by the philosophy of "one exam-fits-all" principle. It needs to be replaced by a scheme or system of examination or evaluation that may help in bringing needed flexibility to meet the assessment needs of the varying learning or performance outputs of the diverse learners of the inclusive education setup. Surely and certainly the adoption of CCE as a system or mode of students' evaluation or assessment can help in bringing required adaptation and flexibility for meeting the challenges faced in the assessment of the learning or behavioural outcomes of the diverse learners of the inclusive setup. Let us see how.

(*i*) We need a lot of continuity for assessing the learning or behavioural outcome of the diverse learners. Many of the differently abled students may be found to have a quite slow pace for their learning and may be found struggling in their learning. They may need persistent and continuous efforts supported by a good feedback mechanism for bringing improvement in their behaviour or performance. Step by step evaluation of their progress, thus may be a major demand for them and it can be properly availed through the adoption of CCE scheme.

(*ii*) The differently abled and diverse learners of an inclusive setting are found to be imbibed with diverse abilities, capacity, potential, and styles of learning and ways of performing in cognitive, conative and affective domains. Naturally then there arises a greater need of adopting flexibility and diversity in the assessment of their learning or behavioural outcomes belonging to all the three domain of their behaviour. The adoption of CCE scheme for the evolution or assessment offers a most viable alternative as it is found to be equipped with the use of a variety of assessment tools and techniques helpful in assessing behavioural outcome of all the domains in the form of achievement and psychological tests, oral, written and practical examination, use of observation, rating scales, checklists, questionnaire interview, portfolio assessment, seminar presentation, project reports, profile analyses, case studies and socio-metric techniques.

(*iii*) Many of the differently abled, creative and the marginalized children may be found to be quite skilled and efficient in one or the other specific areas of their interest and ability. While some of the students belonging to inclusive class may be found to be good in the scholastic areas or a particular domain of their behaviour, the others may have potential to excel in the areas of their interest lying in non-scholastic field or non cognitive domain of behaviour. A comprehensive mode of evaluation carried out in CCE scheme covering scholastic and non-scholastic areas and all the three domains of behaviour may thus prove quite helpful in making needed assessment of the learning or performance outcomes of the diverse learners of the inclusive setup. It can help us to assess and evaluate the holistic development of the learners in tune with their individual capacities, interests, motivation and goals of life.

In this way, the adoption of CCE scheme for the assessment or evaluation of the learning and behavioural outcomes of the diverse learners may serve its purpose well for realizing the objectives of inclusive education in a quite appropriate way.

PROVISION FOR FACILITATING DIFFERENTLY ABLED IN EXAMINATIONS

(As Available in CBSE and ICSE)

Differently abled students have their own specific problems and difficulties of one or the other nature for being assessed through examination particularly the public examinations conducted by the central or state boards of school education. In these examinations a number of specific exemptions/concessions are extended to differently abled students such as spastic, visually impaired, physically handicapped, dyslexic, dyscalculia, autistic and candidates with disabilities as defined in the persons with disabilities Act, 1995. We may summarize them as below:

1. For facilitating easy access, a few selected schools are made examination centres for the differently abled especially suffering from locomotor, hearing and visual impairments. They are allowed to choose any one of them according to their convenience and nature of disability.

2. They are allowed compensatory time as prescribed in their examination rules. For example. CBSE has prescribed such compensation as shown below.

For paper of 3 hours duration	– 60 minutes
For paper of 2½ hours duration	– 50 minutes
For paper of 2 hours duration	– 40 minutes
For paper of 1½ hours duration	– 30 minutes

3. They are permitted to use the services of a scribe, writer or as adult prompter depending upon the nature of their disability.

4. Suitable room is arranged for the disabled examinee for whom a scribe (free of cost) is allowed and a separate Assistant Superintendent is appointed by the center superintendent to supervise his/her examination.

5. The candidates feeling difficulty is conducting practicals are permitted to compensate for the same by being examined additional through theory examination. They are required to appear and respond to a question paper containing multiple choice questions based on the practical component in lieu of appearing in the practical examination related to the subjects like physics, chemistry, biology, home science, etc.

6. They may be permitted to opt for the practical subject like music, painting and handicraft suiting to the nature of their impairment or disability.

7. They can be provided with special arrangements to take their

examination from a hospital in case it is needed in the case of emergency.

8. Students are allowed to type out their answer on a computer. The differently abled candidates are also allowed other needed concession as per requirement of the difficulties faced on account of their impairments. For example, the visually impaired are permitted use of screen reading software (like JAWS-Job Access with speech) with prior approval of the Board. Moreover students are also allowed to use calculators for mathematics and Accountancy in case of some disabilities.

9. The question paper is read out, without being explained in any way, to candidates who have defective eye sight or a certified reading disability.

10. The differently abled as defined in the person with disabilities Act, 1995 are exempted from examination in the third language besides considering physiotherapy exercises as equivalent to Physical and Health Education of the Board.

References

Advani, Lai and Anupriya Chadda (2003), *You and Your Special Child,* New Delhi: UBS Publications.

Agrawal, Rita (1994), "Emerging Special Education in India", in Kasper Mazurek and Margret, A., Winzer (Eds.), *Comparative Studies in Special Education,* Washington DC: Gallaudet University Press.

American Association on Mental Deficiency (1973) as cited by Kisker, George W., *The Disorganised Personality,* (International Student Edition III), New York: McGraw Hill.

Bandura, A. (1977), *Social Learning Theory,* Englewood Cliffs, N.J.: Prentice Hall.

Biggie, M.L., (1967), *Leaning Theory of Teachers,* (Indian Reprint), Delhi: Universal Book Stall.

Bowen, B.B. (1847), Blindman's offering (4th ed.), New York: Author.

British Mental Deficiency Act, (1929), cited by Shanmugam, T.E., Abnormal Psychology, New Delhi: Tata McGraw-Hill, 1981.

Bromberg, W. (1975), *From Shaman to Psychotherapist: A History of the Treatment of Mental Illness,* Chicago: Henry Regnery.

Conway R. (2008), 'Encouraging Positive Integration', in Forman (ed.), *Inclusive in Action,* pp.128-249, Australia: Thomson.

Dash, M (2001), "Classroom for All", in Julka A. (eds), *Inclusive Education: Orientation Package for Teacher Educators,* Unpublished manuscript, *NCERT*

Deschenes C., Ebeling D., and Sprague J. (1994), *Adopting curriculum and Instruction in Inclusive Classrooms: A Teachers Desk Reference,* ISDDCSCI Publication.

Durant, W. (1944), *Caesar and Christ,* New York: Simon and Schuster.

French, St. Jeorge, M. (1932), *From Homer to Helen Keller: A school and Educational Study of the Blinds,* New York: American Foundations for the Blind.

Giangreco, M, Cloninger, C., and Salce Iverson, V. (1998), *Choosing outcomes and accommodations for children* (2nd ed.), Baltimore: Paul H. Brooks.

Giangreco, M.F. (1997), *Quick-guides to Inclusion: Ideas for Educating Students with Disabilities,* Baltimore, M.D.: Brookes.

Government of India (1995), Persons with Disabilities (Equal opportunities, Protection of Rights and Full Participation), New Delhi: Ministry of Law, Justice and Company Affairs.

Individual with Disabilities Education Act (IDEA), (1990), Federal Law of USA, 20, USC, Washington, D.C.

Kanner, L. (1964), A History of the Care and Study of the Mentally Retarded, Spring field, III: Thomas.

Kauffman, J.M. and Hallahan, D.P., (eds.) (1995), *The Illusion of Full Inclusion,* A comprehensive critique of a current special education, Band wagon, Austin, TX: Pro-Ed.

Kirk, S.A. and Kirk, W.D. (1971), Psycholinguistic Learning Disabilities: Diagnosis and Remediation, Urbana II: University of Illinois Press.

Manivannam, M. (2001), "Inclusive Education for Disabled Children", http://www.dinf.ne.Jp/doc/english/asia/resource.retrieved on 23/9/2015.

Ministry of Social Justice and Empowerment (2012), The Draft Rights of Persons with Disabilities Bill, 2012, Government of India, http://www.socialjustice.nic.in/pdf/draftpwed 12.pdf retrieved on 20/05/2016.

National Curriculum Framework, (NCF) (2005), New Delhi: NCERT.

National Institute of Health (1993), '"Research Plan for the National Center for Medical Rehabilitation Research," (NIH Publication No. 93-3509), Berthesda, MD. Author.

National Policy for Persons with Disabilities (2006), New Delhi: Ministry of Social Justice and Empowerment, Government of India.

National Policy on Education (1986), New Delhi: Ministry of Human Resource Development, Government of India.

National Policy on Education, (1968), New Delhi: Ministry of Education and Culture, Government of India.

NCERT (2007), *Meeting Special Needs in School – A Manual,* New Delhi: NCERT Publication Department.

NCERT, (2014), *Including children with Special Needs-Primary Stage* New Delhi: Department of Education of Groups with Special Needs.

Organization for Economic Cooperation and Development (OECD) (1999), "Inclusive Education at Work: Students with Disabilities in Mainstream Schools – A Report," htpp//www.inclusionuive; ac.UK/inclusion week/articles/worldwide retrieved on 30/8/2006."

Page, James D. (1976), *Abnormal Psychology,* New Delhi: Tata McGraw Hill.

Programme of Action (1992), New Delhi: Ministry of Human Resource Development, Government of India.

Rane, (1985), in Hifzur Rehman (2005), *History of Special Education in India,* New Delhi: SANJAY Prakashan.

Rehabilitation Council of India Act (1992), New Delhi: Ministry of Social Justice and Empowerment, Government of India.

Safford, Phillip, L. and Safford Elizabeth (1996) *A History of the Childhood and Disability,* New York: Teachers College Press, Columbia University.

Stainback, S. and W. Stainback (1992), *Teaching in the Inclusive Classrooms: Curriculum Design, Adaptation and Delivery,* Baltimore: Brookes.

Striker, Henri Jacques (1982), *A History of Disability,* translated by William Savers, (1999), Michigan: The University of Michigan Press.

UNESCO, 1994, *The Salamanca Statement and Framework for Action on Special Needs Education,* Paris: UNESCO.

Uppal, Jagmohan and Harinder Dey (2001), "Inclusive Education: Essential Aids and Appliances for Children with Disabilities", *Employment News,* Dec. 3.

Webster's, 7th New Collegiate Dictionary (1970), Spring field, Massachusetts, USA: G&C. Merriam company.

Winzer, Margret A. (1993), *The History of Special Education: From Isolation to Integration,* Washington DC: Gallaudet University Press.

World Health Organization (WHO), (1980), *International Classification of Impairments, Disabilities and Handicap,* Geneva, Switzerland: Author.

Review Questions

CHAPTER 1

A. Essay Type Questions

1. What is exclusion? Throw light on the types of exclusion suffered by the children in their community and school settings.
2. Discuss in detail the nature and consequences of one of the following types of exclusion suffered by the children
   (*a*) Exclusion with respect to Gender (*b*) Exclusion with respect to caste (*c*) Exclusion with respect to locale (*d*) Exclusion with respect to disability (*e*) Exclusion with respect to socio-economic status (*f*) Exclusion with respect to language
3. What do you understand by the type of exclusion with respect to gender of the children in their community and school? Discuss in detail.
4. What type of exclusion is suffered on the part of the migrant children in the community and school belonging to other states and regions of the country? Discuss in detail with their consequences.
5. Throw light on the nature of the exclusion suffered by the disabled children in their community and school settings. Why do the parents favour the exclusion of the disabled children instead of advocating for the adoption of inclusion in the schools? Discuss.
6. What type of exclusion is suffered on the part of the student on account of their socio-economic status? Discuss in detail with its consequence.
7. Discuss the types of exclusion being suffered by the student on account of his/her language different from the language of the mainstream.

B. Short Answer Type Questions

1. Define the term exclusion.
2. Name the different types of exclusion suffered by the children in the community and school setup.
3. What do you understand by the exclusion of children with respect to gender/with respect to caste/with respect to locale/with respect to disability?
4. Tell about two things regarding the exclusion of the children with respect to one of the following types of their exclusion.
   (*a*) Exclusion with respect to gender, (*b*) Exclusion with respect to caste, (*c*) Exclusion with respect to locale, (*d*) Exclusion with respect to disability, (*e*) Exclusion with respect to language, (*f*) Exclusion with respect to socio-economic status.

CHAPTER 2

A. Essay Type Questions

1. What may be the different provisions for the placement and education of the differently or disabled children? Discuss their functionability or applicability in brief.

2. Discuss in detail the transition from segregation to inclusion.
3. Why the placement option of segregation is discarded or condemned?
4. What is integration? Discuss its applicability or functionability in brief.
5. What is inclusion? Discuss its concept along with its viability for the proper placement and education of the exceptional children.
6. Differentiate inclusive education from special education involving, segregation and integrated education involving integration.
7. "Inclusion is the only alternative to meet the needs of exceptional children for our country in the present scenario." Throw light on this statement.
8. Discuss in detail the meaning, need and scope of inclusive education.
9. What is inclusive education? Discuss its concept in the light of various definitions given by different scholars.
10. Define the term inclusive education and throw light on its benefits and advantages.
11. Throw light on the philosophical and sociological bases of inclusive education.

B. Short Answer Type Questions

1. Name the different approaches or provisions for the placement and education of the exceptional children.
2. What is segregation/integration/inclusion?
3. Why segregation is not considered an in appropriate provision for the placement and education of the exceptional children?
4. Why integration is not considered a good alternative for the placement and education of the exceptional children.
5. Differentiate between special education and integrated education.
6. Differentiate between integrated and inclusive education.
7. Provide a suitable definition of the term inclusive education.
8. Point out two needs of inclusive education in our schools.
9. Point out two advantages of inclusive education provided in the schools.
10. Point out two things related to philosophical and social basis of inclusive education.

CHAPTER 3

A. Essay Type Questions

1. Throw light on the historical development of care and education for the children with diverse needs or disabled in relation to a global scenario.
2. Throw light on the historical development of care and education for the children with diverse needs or disabled in relation to the Indian Scenario.
3. Throw light on the type of care and treatment provisions made available to the CWSN or disabled children in the form of institutionalization, special schools, special classes and inclusive schools during the different ages.

B. Short Answer Type Questions

1. How disabled children were treated by Greeks/Romans/other civilization of the world in the era of exclusion in the form of extermination and abandonment?
2. How disabled children were treated in the Era of Acceptance as a subject of amusement and fun by people?
3. How disabled children/people were implicated in the name of witchcraft in the olden days?
4. What is institutionalization/segregation/integration/inclusion? How such treatment has been available to CWSN or disabled children?

CHAPTER 4

A. Essay Type Questions

1. Throw light on the meaning and concept of the term 'disabilities' in detail by distinguishing it from the terms impairment and handicap.
2. Name the various types of disabilities usually encountered or faced on the part of the children in an inclusive setup and discuss any one of them in detail regarding its meaning, characteristics and types.
3. Discuss in detail the meaning, characteristics and types of any one of the following types of disabilities visible among the students of an inclusive setup.
   (*a*) Visual disability, (*b*) Hearing disability, (*c*) Locomotor disability, (*d*) Cerebral palsy or disability associated with neurological disorders, (*e*) Mental retardation (*f*) Learning disability
4. What types of special needs are in general, felt by the children with disabilities. Discuss them in brief.
5. Throw light on the nature of special educational needs and problems felt by the following types of disabled children in terms of their learning and adjustment in an inclusive setup.
   (*a*) Hearing impaired (categorized as deaf and hard of learning), (*b*) Visually impaired (Blind and partially blind), (*c*) Orthopaedically impaired or locomotor disabled, (*d*) Dyslexic and Dyscalculic children, (*e*) Mentally retarded (educable and trainable)

B. Short Answer Type Questions

1. What is impairment/disability/handicap?
2. Name six types of disabilities that may be visible among population of the students belonging to an inclusive setup.
4. Name any three special characteristic of any one of the following types of children with special needs or disabled.
   (*a*) Children with hearing impairment, (*b*) Children with visual impairment, (*c*) Children with locomotor impairment, (*d*) Children suffering from learning impairment, (*e*) Children suffering from mental retardation.
5. Name any three educational needs and learning problems of any one of the following types of disabled children,
   (*a*) Children with locomotor impairment, (*b*) Children with mental retardation, (*c*) Children with hearing impairment, (*d*) Children with visual impairment, (*e*) Children suffering from dyslexia, (*f*) Children suffering from dyscalculia
6. Name the special needs in general felt by the children with disabilities in an inclusive setup.
7. Name the special learning needs of deaf/hard of hearing/blind/partially blind/ locomotor disabled/Dyslexic/Dyscalculic/educable mentally retarded.

CHAPTER 5

A. Essay Type Questions

1. What do you mean by Assistive technology used for providing inclusive education to the students? Mention the purposes and objectives of making use of such technology for inclusive education.
2. What are the assistive and adaptive technologies used for providing inclusive education? Make a clear distinction between these technologies.
3. What types of assistive and adaptive technology can be used for the adjustment and education of the disabled children in an inclusive setup? Answer in detail by

keeping in view of the special needs of these inclusive children.

4. Discuss about the assistive and adaptive technologies used for the adjustment and education of the following types of disabled or differently abled children in an inclusive setup.
   (*a*) Orthopedically impaired children, (*b*) Visually impaired children, (*c*) Speech and communication impaired children, (*d*) Learning disabled children, (*e*) Autistic children.

B. Short Answer Type Questions

1. What is inclusive setup?
2. What do you mean by assistive technology used for providing inclusive education?
3. Point out the difference between the assistive and adaptive technologies.
4. Name any five equipments/devices or means of assistive and adaptive technology used for inclusive education.
5. Mention any four means/ devices used for the adjustment and education of any one of the following types of disabled children:
   (*a*) Orthopedically impaired children, (*b*) Visually impaired children, (*c*) Hearing impaired children, (*d*) Learning disabled children, (*e*) Autistic children.

CHAPTER 6

A. Essay Type Questions

1. Discuss the need of bringing adaptations and accommodation in the instructional objectives, curriculum and co-curricular activities for providing needed learning experiences to the disabled children in an inclusive setup.
2. What do you mean by adaptation and accommodation? Discuss the need as well as the nature of adaptations to be carried out for diverse learners of an inclusive school.
3. What is curriculum adaptation and accommodation? Discuss the need, and ways and means of carrying out such adaptation for the diverse learners belonging to an inclusive setup.
4. What types of curriculum adaptations and accommodation can be made for meeting the needs of various types of diverse learners belonging to an inclusive class? Discuss in detail.
5. What is curriculum adaptation and accommodation? Discuss two types of curriculum adaptations namely (*i*) curriculum adaptation allowing multi-level curriculum instructions, and (*ii*) curriculum adaptation allowing curriculum overlapping with examples.
6. What is adaptation and accommodation in co-curricular activities? Discuss its need and essentials for bringing out such adaptation for the benefit of diverse learners of an inclusive setup.
7. What is the need of bringing adaptations and accommodation in co-curricular activities organization? Mention the things to be kept in mind while making such adaptations for the benefit of the disabled children of an inclusive setup.

B. Short Answer Type Questions

1. What is adaptation and accommodation? Why it is needed in the system of inclusive education for the benefit of diverse learners?
2. What do you understand by the term adaptation and accommodation in instructional objectives/adaptations in curriculum/adaptations in co-curricular activities?
3. Tell two means and ways of bringing modifications or adaptations

and accommodation in instructional objectives/curriculum/co-curricular activities.

4. Tell about the nature of adaptations and accommodation needed in the instructional objectives/curriculum/co-curricular activities in brief.

CHAPTER 7

A. Essay Type Questions

1. Provide an account of what has been emphasized and stated in the international document and declaration "The Salamanca Statement and Framework of Action (1994)" in terms of the principles, policy and practice in Special Needs Education.
2. Describe the things emphasized in "Salamanca Statement and Framework of Action (1994)" as Framework for Action for the education of the CWSN including disabled.
3. Provide an account of what has been emphasized in the 'Preamble' of the proceedings of the UN Convention on the Rights of Persons with Disabilities (UNCRPD), 2006.
4. What type of educational provisions has been emphasized for the disabled in the proceeding of the UN Convention on the Rights of Persons with Disabilities (UNCRPD), 2006?

B. Short Answer Type Questions

1. What is Salamanca Statement and Framework of Action, 1994?
2. What is the document related to UN Convention on the Rights of Persons with Disabilities (UNCRPD) 2006?
3. What has been urged in "Salamanca Framework of Action" for CWSN? Point out two important measures in this concern.
4. What has been urged to do on the part of UNESCO in the field of special needs education? Point out any two important measures.
5. Point out any two things emphasized in the Framework of Action brought out in the proceeding of Salamanca Statement and Framework of Action, 1994 in any one of the following areas as a guide lines for action at the National level:
   (*a*) Policy and organization, (*b*) School factors, (*c*) Recruiting and training of educational personnel.
6. What has been emphasized as the purpose of the convention in the Article I of the proceeding of the UNCRPD, 2006?
7. Tell two important recommendation made about the education of the disabled in the proceedings of the UNCRPD, 2006.

CHAPTER 8

A. Essay Type Questions

1. Discuss any one of the following in laying downs measures and provisions for the education of the children with disabilities.
   (*a*) PoA (1992), (*b*) PWD Act, (1995), (*c*) RCI Act (1992), and (*d*) National Policy for Persons with Disabilities (2006).
2. What has been recommended in the National Educational policies, 1968 and 1986 about the education of the disabled?
3. What is PWD Act, 1995? What has been prescribed in this act about (*i*) Prevention and early detection of disabilities, (*ii*) Education of the disabled?
4. What is RCI Act, 1992? Give an account of the function of the Rehabilitation Council of India in the interest and welfare of the disabled.
5. What is RTE Act, 2009? Mention what has been provided in the various clauses of this act for the education and welfare of the children including disabled.

6. What is National Policy for Persons with Disabilities, 2006? Mention what has been laid down in this policy for the education of the disabled.

B. Short Answer Type Questions

1. Mention what has been recommended in NPE, 1968 for the education of the disabled.
2. Mention three main things emphasized in NPE, 1986 about the education of the disabled/handicapped.
3. Mention any three important things emphasized in POA, 1992 about the education of the disabled/handicapped.
4. What is the responsibility of appropriate government/local authority towards the education of the disabled laid down in PWD Act, 1995?
5. What are the two main functions of Rehabilitation Council of India?
6. What was the objective of bringing out RCI Act, 1992?
7. What does RTE Act, 2009 say about Right of child to free and compulsory education/Right of transfer to other school/Duty of parents and guardians.
8. Mention three important things laid down for the education of persons with Disabilities in the National Policy for Persons with Disabilities, 2006.

CHAPTER 9

A. Essay Type Questions

1. Discuss in detail the concept of an inclusive school.
2. Throw light on the essentials and measures of the organisation and management of an inclusive school with special reference to
   (*a*) Proper-infrastructures and accessibility
   (*b*) Awareness and positive attitude towards disability.
   (*c*) Proper human resources.
   (*d*) Appropriate materials resources
3. What do you mean by the term adoption of whole school approach for the organization and management of an inclusive school? Discuss in detail.
4. How can you work towards addressing inequality and diversity in the classrooms through pedagogical and curriculum means? Discuss
5. What attempts can be made of address inequality related to gender in the school? Discuss.

B. Short Answer Type Questions

1. What is an inclusive school?
2. What type of infrastructure and accessibility is required in an inclusive school?
3. What type of human resources are needed for running an inclusive school?
4. What do you mean by positive attitude towards disability?
5. What is whole school approach towards inclusive education?
6. What type of material resources and required for running an inclusive school?
7. Name two pedagogical/curriculum means for addressing inequality and diversity in the classroom.
8. Name two means for addressing inequality related to gender in the school.

CHAPTER 10

A. Essay Type Questions

1. What type of support services can be secured for the running of an inclusive school? How will you initiate to secure them in your school? Discuss.
2. Discuss the features and securing of the following types of support services for the

effective running of inclusive setup in the school.
(*a*) Support services provided by professionals and experts
(*b*) Support services available through external specialized agencies
(*c*) Support services available through parental cooperation and community involvement.

3. Discuss in detail the role of any two from the following professional and experts providing their services to inclusive school.
(*a*) Special education teacher, (*b*) Guidance and counselling personnel, (*c*) Audiologist cum speech therapist, (*d*) Physiotherapist, (*e*) Occupation therapist

B. Short Answer Type Questions

1. Name a few professional and experts needed to provide support services to inclusive setup of a school.
2. Name any five external specialized agency helpful in providing support services to inclusive setup of a school.
3. What type of support services can be provided by the parents/community personnel for the proper running of an inclusive setup of a school.
4. Tell in brief about the role played by audiologist cum speech therapist/ physiotherapist/occupational therapist for providing support to an inclusive school.

CHAPTER 11

A. Essay Type Questions

1. How does the responding to special needs help in making learning more meaningful to the differently abled? Discuss.
2. How the strategy named as differentiating content proves helpful in responding to the special needs of the differently abled and making learning more meaningful to them? Discuss.
3. How the strategy named as curricular adaptation proves helpful in making learning more meaningful to the differently abled by meeting their special needs? Discuss.
4. How the efforts made by the teacher in the planning of the lesson make the learning more meaningful to the differently abled by meeting their special needs? Discuss.
5. Discuss the use of appropriate teaching-learning material (TLM) for making learning more meaningful by focussing on the satisfaction of their specific learning needs of the disabled students.

B. Short Answer Type Questions

1. Give an example of the strategy differentiating content/curricular adaptation/ proper lesson planning/use of appropriate teaching-learning material for making learning more meaningful to them.
2. Name a few teaching-learning material helpful for making the learning meaningful to visually impaired/hearing impaired/locomotor disabled/ mentally retarded students of an inclusive class.

CHAPTER 12

A. Essay Type Questions

1. What are Pedagogical or teaching strategies? Name a few strategies employed in the teaching-learning of an inclusive education setup and describe any one of them in detail.
2. What is peer tutoring? Discuss the use and utility of this strategy for the teaching-learning in the inclusive education setup.

3. What is cooperative learning? Discuss the use of cooperative learning strategy in the context of inclusive setup in its various forms and modes.
4. What is social learning? As a teaching strategy, how it can be employed in the inclusive education setup? Discuss.
5. What do you understand by the term buddy system? What is its role in the teaching-learning carried out in an inclusive education setup? Point out the essentials for successful employment of buddy system for the adjustment and education of the learners in an inclusive setup.
6. What is reflective teaching? How does it differ from memory and understanding levels teaching? Discuss the employment of reflective teaching strategy in the inclusive education setup.
7. What is multisensory teaching? Discuss the use and significance of multisensory teaching strategy for the learners belonging to inclusive education setup.

B. Short Answer Type Questions

1. What are pedagogical or teaching strategies?
2. Name any four pedagogical or teaching strategies used for the teaching-learning of the students belonging to inclusive education setup.
3. What is peer tutoring/cooperative learning/social learning/reflective teaching/ multisensory teaching in context of its use in inclusive education setup?
4. What is buddy system?
5. Mention about the two uses/benefits of making use of any one of the following pedagogical or teaching strategy for the teaching-learning in an inclusive setup. (*a*) Peer tutoring, (*b*) Cooperative learning, (*c*) Social learning, (*d*) Buddy system, (*e*) Reflective teaching, (*f*) Multisensory teaching.

CHAPTER 13

A. Essay Type Questions

1. What is Continuous and Comprehensive Evaluation or CCE? Discuss in detail by highlighting the concepts of continuity, comprehensiveness of evaluation and ways and means used for carrying out such evaluation.
2. Discuss the need and implication of CCE to facilitate inclusion of the diverse learners in the schools.
3. Discuss the main provisions laid down by the boards of school examination for the differently abled candidates in their public examinations.

B. Short Answer Type Questions

1. What we mean by continuity in the assessment or evaluation of the learning outcomes of the students?
2. What is comprehensiveness of an evaluation or assessment of learning outcomes of the students?
3. Mention in brief the need of maintaining continuity/comprehensiveness of evaluation?
4. Tell three things related to the implication of CCE to facilitate inclusion of the diverse learners in the school.
5. Tell any three important concessions/exemptions provided to the differently abled in the public examination conducted by board of school examination.